Epigraphic Evidence

Inscriptions are a rich source of information about ancient Greek and Roman culture. Yet the constantly increasing mass of available material and the specialized conventions of epigraphic editing and publication can make the study of these crucial sources intimidating for the non-specialist.

This readable and fully illustrated study demystifies epigraphic evidence. It offers a wide-ranging exploration of the significance of inscribed texts for understanding the ancient world, and points out the hazards and limits of their use as historical sources.

Individual chapters address:

- the significance of inscribed writing in the ancient world
- the linguistic and inscriptional diversity that resulted when the epigraphic cultures of Greece and Rome encountered native traditions
- the contribution of epigraphy to our knowledge of personal names and individual identities (onomastics and prosopography), the family and society, and civic and religious life
- the relevance of inscribed implements for daily use (*instrumentum domesticum*) for ancient economic history

A useful appendix guides the reader around the arrangement of the major epigraphic corpora and serial publications.

John Bodel is Professor of Classics at Rutgers University and Director of the US Epigraphy Project.

Approaching the Ancient World
Series editor: Richard Stoneman

Epigraphic Evidence

Ancient history from inscriptions

Edited by John Bodel

London and New York

First published 2001
by Routledge
11 New Fetter Lane, London EC4P 4EE

Simultaneously published in the USA and Canada
by Routledge
29 West 35th Street, New York, NY 10001

Routledge is an imprint of the Taylor & Francis Group

© 2001 selection and editorial matter, John Bodel; individual
chapters, the contributors

Typeset in Baskerville by The Running Head Limited, Cambridge
Printed and bound in Great Britain by TJ International Ltd, Padstow, Cornwall

British Library Cataloguing in Publication Data
A catalogue record for this book is available
from the British Library

Library of Congress Cataloging in Publication Data
A catalog record for this book has been requested

ISBN 0–415–11623–6 (hbk)
ISBN 0–415–11624–4 (pbk)

Mary Gibney Bodel
matri optimae

Contents

Figures

---

* Inscriptions in the USA are identified by their US Epigraphy numbers, for which see
  J. Bodel and S. Tracy, *Greek and Latin Inscriptions in the USA, A Checklist* (New York and
  Rome, 1997) xiii–xv or http://usepigraphy.rutgers.edu

Contributors

John Bodel is Professor of Classics at Rutgers University and Director of the US Epigraphy Project. His most recent book, co-authored with Stephen Tracy, is *Greek and Latin Inscriptions in the USA, A Checklist* (New York and Rome 1997).

Maryline Parca is Associate Professor of the Classics at the University of Illinois at Urbana-Champaign and Director of the American Center of the International Photographic Archive of Papyri. She is the author of *The Franchetti Collection in Rome, Inscriptions and Sculptural Fragments* (Opuscula Epigraphica 6, Rome 1995).

Giuseppe Pucci is Professor of Archaeology and History of Greek and Roman Art in the University of Siena. He is a fellow of many learned societies and has been Visiting Professor in France and the United States. Besides specializing in ancient material culture and economic history, he is interested in the history of archaeology and the idea of antiquity in modern culture.

James B. Rives is Associate Professor in the Division of Humanities at York University in Toronto. He has published a number of articles on aspects of religious life in the Roman empire, as well as *Religion and Authority in Roman Carthage from Augustus to Constantine* (Oxford 1995).

Richard Saller is Professor of History and Classics at the University of Chicago. His research has centered on Roman social and economic history. His most recent book is *Patriarchy, Property, and Death in the Roman Family* (Cambridge 1994).

Olli Salomies is Professor of Latin at Helsinki University and former Director of the Finnish Institute at Athens for the three-year period 1997–2000. He is the author of a number of books on onomastics and epigraphy.

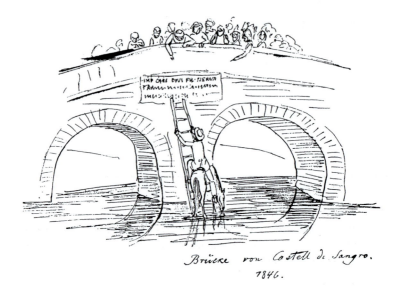

Brücke von Castell di Sangro.
1846.

Frontispiece Sketch of Theodor Mommsen inspecting an inscription on a bridge at Castel di Sangro (ancient Aufidena) in Samnium, Italy, in September, 1846, drawn by his friend and travelling companion Julius Friedländer. The text, of which the first line seems to record the imperial nomenclature of the emperor Trajan, corresponds to none of the known inscriptions from Castel di Sangro (cf. *Suppl. Ital.* n.s. 8 [1991] 47–69: Buonocore). That on the Ponte della Maddalena transcribed by Mommsen in 1846 is an epitaph with a very different text (*CIL* IX 2816; cf. *Suppl. Ital.* n.s. 8: 55–6). (Reproduced from L. Wickert, *Theodor Mommsen: Eine Biographie* vol. 2 [Frankfurt am Main: Vittorio Klostermann 1964] Taf. 8, above the caption "The epigrapher at work.")

Preface

"Epigraphy is a subject in which it is unwise merely to dabble," warns the author of one recent and valuable introduction to the study of Greek inscriptions, in words more likely to deter than to encourage the sort of reader for whom this book is intended (Woodhead 1992: xvi). Not every student of classical antiquity who wishes to learn what inscriptions have to say has the time or inclination to undergo the technical training required of those who would call themselves epigraphists. This book is intended to prevent a little knowledge of the subject from becoming a dangerous thing by introducing non-specialist readers to some of the ways in which inscriptions contribute to the study of ancient history and by pointing out some of the hazards of their use as evidence. It is not a manual of epigraphy, nor is it a systematic introduction to the reading and interpretation of ancient Greek and Latin inscriptions: good books in both categories exist (see the Appendix, page 157). Very little is said about the many instances in which inscriptional texts uniquely preserve direct information concerning events of political significance. These cases are unquestionably important, but when an inscription records the name of an Athenian archon or the titles of a Roman emperor, the significance of these facts normally emerges only when they are set into a broader historical context. While this is true to a certain extent of every inscriptional text, in the following pages attention is focused on cases in which the inscribing of a document—the fact that its text is written on a durable surface, usually (but not always) for public display in a particular place —is itself historically significant, and on categories of information for which inscriptions constitute an especially important source of evidence.

Chapter 1 provides a basic orientation to the subject and considers the place of Greek and Latin inscriptions more generally in the ancient world. Understanding why the peoples of classical antiquity inscribed what they did where they did and when they did is fundamentally important to our use of Greek and Latin inscriptions as historical evidence, and yet the nature of the Greco-Roman epigraphic habit remains in many respects enigmatic and obscure. Detailed investigation of this problem is beyond the scope of an introductory essay, but some of its more obvious manifestations and implications are briefly explored. Chapter 2 examines some of the ways in which inscriptions provide a glimpse of the linguistic and cultural interaction that resulted when the epigraphic cultures of Greece and Rome came into contact with native traditions. In Chapter 3 the relevance of epigraphy to the study of personal names (onomastics) is linked with the investigation of individual identities (prosopography), two areas of study in which inscriptions play a leading role. The next two chapters address large topics—the family and society (Chapter 4) and civic and religious life (Chapter 5)—for which inscriptions provide only part, but an important and in certain respects uniquely informative part, of our ancient evidence. Chapter 6 (translated by the editor from the original Italian) considers the significance of inscribed implements of daily use for ancient economic history, an area in which inscriptions raise as many questions as they answer but which we could scarcely begin to investigate without epigraphy. Throughout the emphasis is on historical issues rather than categorization of texts, on broad questions of interpretation and significance rather than on particular problems of transcription or translation.

Restrictions of space have necessitated selectivity and, regrettably, omissions. Little is said about ancient inscriptions in languages other than Greek and Latin, although epigraphy in many cases provides our best evidence for the variety of cultures that constituted the richly diverse world of classical antiquity. Chapter 2 redresses the balance somewhat, but in no sense can the book be said to provide a representative overview of the epigraphy of the ancient world. The inscriptional patrimony of the Near East is especially rich—more than half of the 6,000 ancient inscriptions known from the Sinai and the Judaean desert are written in Nabatean (Stone 1992: 1.255–8, 2.227–30; cf. *CIS*)—but an accurate epigraphic profile of even such a central and "classical" area as the Italian peninsula would have to take account of a substantial number of inscriptions in Etruscan (*CIE*) and the Italic dialects (Vetter 1953, *REI*), which continue to come to light (the longest bronze Etruscan inscription known was recently unearthed near Cortona). Almost nothing is said about the important contribution to our understanding of late antiquity made by Christian epigraphy—virtually a field unto itself (more than 50,000 relevant inscriptions survive: see Marucchi 1912; *ILCV*, see below)—nothing at all about the traditions of Jewish epigraphy from which it sprung (*CIJ*; Horbury–Noy 1992; Noy 1993, 1995). In general, the focus is on the central period of classical Greco-Roman history, from the late fifth century BCE to the early third century CE. Beyond those limits greater attention is devoted to the early development of Greek epigraphy down through the sixth century BCE than to the fourth century CE and beyond—not because the Greek archaic age is considered more important or more interesting than the period of the Roman empire after Constantine but because historians may be presumed to have a natural interest in origins and because in many respects the epigraphy of late antiquity—both Greek and Latin—belongs as much to the world of the middle ages as to the classical period.

Everyone who knows the fields of Greek or Latin epigraphy will notice something missing, or not given sufficient weight. The book could easily have been twice as long and not have adequately covered the territory. For there are few, if any, areas of ancient Greco-Roman culture that inscriptions do not somehow illuminate; and if there are many questions of historical interest that inscriptions cannot help us answer, there are many others that we would not think to ask were it not for their testimony. If the readers for whom the book is primarily intended—students of ancient history, general classicists, and any others interested in learning what kind of historical evidence Greek and Latin inscriptions provide—find in these pages incentive to explore the field of Greek and Latin epigraphy beyond them, the book will have fulfilled its purpose.

Among many who have responded to my requests for help by reading parts of the manuscript, by supplying information, or by offering much-needed advice, I wish to thank especially Géza Alföldy, Charles Crowther, Joan Gómez Pallarès, Silvio Panciera, Denis Rousset, and Stephen V. Tracy. The usual disclaimer about responsibility for error is in this case especially justified, since none of these advisors has been given the opportunity to read the whole work: the book would be better had I made greater impositions on their generosity. I am grateful also to Richard Stoneman, an editor of unfailing tact and Penelopean patience, and to the contributors whose good efforts have been withheld from the public longer than they had reason to expect. To them my apologies as well as my thanks.

JB

Abbreviations

The following list of modern epigraphic corpora and standard reference tools is highly selective and covers mainly those works cited in the text. More complete lists of abbreviated titles of epigraphic works can be found in the *Guide*[2/3] (see below) and Horsley–Lee (1994) (Greek only). Entries followed by an asterisk are described more fully in the Appendix.

For the abbreviated words found in ancient Greek and (especially) Latin inscriptions, consult any of the epigraphy manuals. The best still, for this purpose, are the great French compilations of Reinach (1885) and Cagnat (1914); see also Guarducci 1967–78: 1.391–407 and, for numerals, Guarducci 1967–78: 1.417–28 (Greek) and Gordon–Gordon 1957: 166–70 (Roman).

AE*	*L'Année épigraphique* (Paris 1888–)
ATL	B. D. Merritt, H. T. Wade-Gery, and M. F. McGregor, *Athenian Tribute Lists* (Princeton 1939–53)
BE* or *Bull. ép.**	*Bulletin épigraphique*, published annually in *Revue des études grecques* (Paris 1888–)
BES	*Bulletin d'épigraphie semitique*, published annually by J. Teixidor in *Syria*
Bruns[7]	C. G. Bruns and O. Gradenwitz, *Fontes Iuris Romani Antiqui*, 7th ed. (Leipzig 1909–12)
CEG	P. A. Hansen, *Carmina Epigraphica Graeca saeculorum VIII–V a. Chr. n.* (Berlin 1983)
CIE	*Corpus Inscriptionum Etruscarum* (Leipzig and Florence 1893–)
CIG	*Corpus Inscriptionum Graecarum*, A. Boeckh et al. (Berlin 1828–77)

CIJ	J. B. Frey, *Corpus Inscriptionum Iudaicarum* (Rome 1936–52)
CIL*	*Corpus Inscriptionum Latinarum*, Theodor Mommsen et al. (Berlin 1863–)
CIS	*Corpus Inscriptionum Semiticarum* (1881–)
CLE	F. Bücheler, *Carmina Latina Epigraphica*, vols 1–2 (Berlin 1895–7); E. Lommatzsch, vol. 3 (Berlin 1926)
Dar. Sag.	C. Daremberg and E. Saglio, *Dictionnaire des antiquités grecques et romaines d'après les textes et les monuments* (Paris 1877–1919)
Diz. epigr.	E. De Ruggiero et al., *Dizionario epigrafico di antichità romane* (Rome 1886–) (complete through "Magnentius")
EphEp	*Ephemeris Epigraphica (Corporis Inscriptionum Latinarum Supplementum)* (Berlin 1872–9, 1903–13)
FGrH	F. Jacoby, *Die Fragmente der griechischen Historiker* (Berlin 1923–)
FIRA	*Fontes Iuris Romani Anteiustiniani* (Florence 1940–3), vol. 1 *Leges*, ed. S. Riccobono, 2nd ed. (1941); vol. 3 *Negotia*, ed. V. Arangio Ruiz (1943)
GHI*	M. N. Tod, *A Selection of Greek Historical Inscriptions*, vol. 1, down to 403 BCE, 2nd ed. (Oxford 1951); vol. 2, down to the death of Alexander (1948) and R. Meiggs and D. Lewis, *A Selection of Greek Historical Inscriptions* (Oxford 1969, 2nd ed. 1988) (see Meiggs–Lewis)
*Guide*²ᐟ³	F. Bérard, D. Feissel, P. Petitmengin et al., *Guide de l'épigraphiste, Bibliographie des épigraphies antiques et médiévales*, 2nd ed. (Paris 1989, with supplements in 1990), 3rd ed. (Paris 2000)
GVI	W. Peek, *Griechische Vers-Inschriften, I. Die Grabepigramme* (Berlin 1955)
ICret	M. Guarducci, *Inscriptiones Creticae* (Rome 1935–50)
ICUR (n.s.)	G. B. De Rossi et al., *Inscriptiones Christianae Urbis Romae septimo saeculo antiquiores*, vols. 1–2.1, ed. De Rossi (Rome 1857–88); suppl., ed. G. Gatti (1915); A. Silvagni and A. Ferrua, *Inscriptiones Christianae Urbis Romae*, Nova Series (Rome 1922–)

IDelos	F. Durrbach, P. Roussel, M. Launey et al., *Inscriptions de Délos*, 7 vols (Paris 1926–72)
IEphesos	R. Merkelbach et al., *Die Inschriften von Ephesos*, 8 vols (Bonn 1979–84)
IG*	*Inscriptiones Graecae* (Berlin 1903–)
IGLS	*Inscriptions grecques et latines de la Syrie* (Paris 1929–)
IGRR*	R. Cagnat et al., *Inscriptiones Graecae ad Res Romanas Pertinentes* (Paris 1906–27), vols 1, 3, 4 (vol. 2 was never published)
IGUR	L. Moretti, *Inscriptiones Graecae Urbis Romae* (Rome 1968–79)
IK	*Inschriften griechischer Städte aus Kleinasien* (Bonn 1972–)
ILCV*	E. Diehl, *Inscriptiones Latinae Christianae Veteres*, vols 1–3 (Berlin, Dublin, Zürich 1925–31); vol. 4: Supplement, J. Moreau and H. I. Marrou (cf. A. Ferrua, *Nuove correzioni alla Silloge del Diehl*, Vatican City 1981)
ILLRP*	A. Degrassi, *Inscriptiones Latinae Liberae Rei Publicae* (Florence, vol. 1, 2nd ed. 1965, vol. 2 1963)
ILS*	H. Dessau, *Inscriptiones Latinae Selectae* (Berlin 1892–1916)
ILTun.	A. Merlin, *Inscriptions latines de la Tunisie* (Paris 1944)
Imagines	A. Degrassi, *Inscriptiones Latinae Liberae Rei Publicae, Imagines* (Rome 1965)
IMagn.	O. Kern, *Die Inschriften von Magnesia am Maeander* (Berlin 1900)
InscrIt	*Inscriptiones Italiae* (Rome 1931–) (vol. XIII = A. Degrassi, 1. *Fasti Consulares et Triumphales*, 1947; 2. *Fasti anni Numani et Iuliani*, 1963; 3. *Elogia*, 1937)
IPhilae	A. Bernand, *Les inscriptions grecques de Philae* vol. 1. *Époque ptolémaïque*; E. Bernand, *Les inscriptions grecques et latines de Philae* vol. 2. *Haut et Bas Empire* (Paris 1969)
IRT	J. M. Reynolds and J. B. Ward-Perkins, *The Inscriptions of Roman Tripolitania* (Rome 1952)
Kaibel	G. Kaibel, *Epigrammata Graeca ex lapidibus conlecta* (Berlin 1878)

LSAG	L. H. Jeffery, *The Local Scripts of Archaic Greece: A Study of the Origin of the Greek Alphabet and its Development from the Eighth to the Fifth Centuries* BC, revised edition with a supplement by A. W. Johnston (Oxford 1990)
LSAM	F. Sokolowski, *Lois sacrées de l'Asie Mineure* (Paris 1955)
LSCG	F. Sokolowski, *Lois sacrées des cités grecques*, 2nd ed. (Paris 1969)
LSS	F. Sokolowski, *Lois sacrées des cités grecques, Supplément* (Paris 1962)
MAMA	*Monumenta Asiae Minoris Antiqua* (Manchester 1928–)
Meiggs–Lewis	R. Meiggs and D. Lewis, *A Selection of Greek Historical Inscriptions* (Oxford 1969, 2nd ed. 1988) (see *GHI*)
Moretti	L. Moretti, *Iscrizioni storiche ellenistiche*, 2 vols (Rome 1967, 1976)
*OGIS**	W. Dittenberger, *Orientis Graeci Inscriptiones Selectae* (Leipzig 1903–5)
PA	J. Kirchner, *Prosopographia Attica* (Berlin 1901–3)
PIR	*Prosopographia Imperii Romani*, 1st ed., E. Klebs, H. Dessau and P. von Rohden (Berlin 1897–8); 2nd ed. (now complete through "P"), E. Groag, A. Stein, L. Petersen et al. (Berlin 1933–). A searchable index of entries is available at the *PIR* website, http://www.bbaw.de/vh/pir/suche.html
P. Oxy.	B. P. Grenfell, A. S. Hunt et al., *The Oxyrhynchus Papyri* (London 1898–)
RDGE	R. K. Sherk, *Roman Documents from the Greek East, Senatus Consulta and Epistulae to the Age of Augustus* (Baltimore 1969)
RE	A. Pauly, G. Wissowa, W. Kroll, K. Mittelhaus, K. Ziegler (eds), *Paulys Realencyclopädie der classischen Altertumswissenschaft* (Stuttgart 1894–1980)
REI	*Rivista di epigrafia italica*, annually in *Studi Etruschi*, beginning in 1973; see *SE*
RÉS	*Répertoire d'épigraphie sémitique* (Paris 1900–68)
RIB	R. G. Collingwood et al., *Roman Inscriptions of Britain* (Oxford 1965–)

RMD	M. M. Roxan, *Roman Military Diplomas* 1 (1954–1977), 2 (1978–1984), 3 (1985–1993) (University of London, Institute of Archaeology, Occasional Publications, 2, 9, 14), London, 1978, 1985, 1994
RS	M. H. Crawford, ed., *Roman Statutes*, volume I: *Epigraphically Attested Leges* (Bulletin of the Institute of Classical Studies Supplement 64) (London 1996)
SCPP	W. Eck, A. Caballos and F. Fernández, *Das Senatus Consultum de Cn. Pisone Patre* (Vestigia 48) (Munich 1996)
SDHI	*Studia et documenta historiae et iuris* (1936–)
SE	*Studi Etruschi*, since 1927; containing *REI*
*SEG**	*Supplementum Epigraphicum Graecum*, vols 1–25 (Leiden 1923–71), vols 26– (Amsterdam 1979–)
SGDI	H. Collitz and F. Bechtel, *Sammlung der griechischen Dialekt-Inschriften* (Göttingen 1884–1915)
Suppl. Ital.	E. Pais, *Corporis Inscriptionum Latinarum Supplementa Italica*, I *Additamenta ad vol. V Galliae Cisalpinae* (Rome 1888)
Suppl. Ital. (n.s.)	*Supplementa Italica*, Nuova serie (Rome 1981–)
*Syll.*³* or *SIG**	W. Dittenberger, *Sylloge Inscriptionum Graecarum*, 3rd ed.; vol. 4, index, by F. Hiller von Gaertringen (Leipzig 1915–24)
Tab. Vindol.	*Tabulae Vindolandenses*, A. K. Bowman and J. D. Thomas, *Vindolanda: the Latin Writing-Tablets* (Britannia Monograph Series 4) (Gloucester 1983) [= *Tab. Vindol.* 1]; A. K. Bowman and J. D. Thomas, *The Vindolanda Writing-Tablets* (London 1994) [= *Tab. Vindol.* 2]
TAM	*Tituli Asiae Minoris* (Vienna 1901–)
TLE	M. Pallottino, *Testimonia Linguae Etruscae*, 2nd ed. (Florence 1968)
Vetter	E. Vetter, *Handbuch der italischen Dialekte* (Heidelberg 1953); Supplement: P. Poccetti, *Nuovi documenti italici a complemento del Manuale di E. Vetter* (Pisa 1979)

Editing conventions

Listed below are some of the editorial conventions commonly employed by editors of ancient Greek and Latin inscriptions (and adopted by current editors of *CIL* and *IG*). For further details, see Krummrey–Panciera 1980 and Panciera 1991b. The so-called "Leiden system" developed in 1931 by papyrologists at the Eighteenth International Congress of Orientalists at Leiden, though now somewhat out of date, has formed the basis for most subsequent systems and is still widely used: see Dow 1969 and Woodhead 1981: 6–11.

ạ	The letter is fragmentary and the reading uncertain.
+	The letter is so badly damaged that it cannot be restored.
ABC	The letters are clear but their significance is uncertain.
a̲b̲c̲	Letters seen by a previous editor but no longer visible.
a͡b or âb	The letters appear in ligature (a circumflex over a letter indicates that it is joined to the next letter).
[abc]	Letters missing because of damage to the writing surface and supplied by the editor.
(abc)	An abbreviation expanded by the editor.

((abc))	Any letters or symbols represented differently on the stone, e.g. inverted or backwards letters, numerals ((*decem milia*)), symbols ((*centurio*)), ((*mulieris*)).
⌐abc⌐	Text corrected by the editor.
{abc}	Text included by mistake and removed by the editor.
<abc>	Text omitted by mistake and supplied by the editor.
⟦abc⟧	Letters erased in antiquity.
«abc»	Letters inscribed in an erasure.
`abc´	Letters added in antiquity in order to correct or supplement the text.
[- c.5 -]	Approximately five letters of text are missing.
(vac. c.5)	The surface is left blank for a space of approximately five letters.

Chapter 1

Epigraphy and the ancient historian

John Bodel

> The province of Epigraphy is, in one respect, wider than that of Palaeo-
> graphy, for, while Palaeography confines itself to the study of the forms
> of writing found in ancient manuscripts, Epigraphy not only deals with
> the lettering, but is even apt to concern itself with the subject-matter
> of ancient inscriptions, thus unduly encroaching on the provinces of
> History, and of Public and Private Antiquities.
>
> J. E. Sandys, *Latin Epigraphy* (Cambridge 1918: 1)

Few ancient historians nowadays would agree with Sir John Edwin Sandys
that the relationship between epigraphy and history is one of undue
encroachment of the former upon the latter. Most would concede that
the history of classical antiquity could not be written without epigraphy,
and many would assert that the proper business of the epigraphist is
not only to edit inscribed texts but to set inscriptions into their cultural
contexts and thus to demonstrate their contribution to history. And yet
epigraphists have often been viewed as narrow technicians whose con-
ceptual myopia prevents them from seeing beyond the edges of their
stones. The father of modern historiography, Barthold Georg Niebuhr,
did not see things this way. Already in 1815, in his proposal before the
Berlin Academy to create a *Corpus Inscriptionum* of all the languages of
Roman antiquity, Niebuhr recognized that inscriptions were to the
study of antiquity what documents were to modern history: essential
primary sources (Niebuhr 1815). But a disparaging perception of
epigraphists and their work has a long pedigree. Theodor Mommsen
recalled being laughed at more than once, while touring Italy as a young
man in search of material to be included in his edition of the inscriptions of the kingdom of Naples, as a "man addicted to stones" (*lapidarius
homo*) and, because so many of the inscriptions were epitaphs, a "morbid

undertaker" (*feralis designator*) (Mommsen 1852: xvi; see Frontispiece). By the end of his career Mommsen had published more ancient inscriptions than anyone before or since, and yet most today would not regard him primarily as an epigraphist but as a Roman historian. In fact, most of those specializing in the study of Greek and Latin inscriptions since Mommsen's day have interpreted their role as differing in particulars but not essentials from that of ancient historians exploiting other types of evidence.

Definition and scope

What, then, is an epigraphist, or epigrapher—even the name, in English, is variable (compare German *Epigraphiker*, French *épigraphiste*, Italian *epigrafista*)? The question of definition, famously posed nearly half a century ago by the great French epigraphist, Louis Robert (1953: 8, "qui sommes-nous?"), is deceptively simple. "Epigraphy," according to the *Oxford English Dictionary*, is "the science concerned with the classification and interpretation of inscriptions"; epigraphists, then, are those who practice this science. But if the first procedure—classification—is technical and specific and to that extent "scientific," the second—interpretation —requires as much art as science and covers a good deal of uncertain ground. Nor is the meaning of "inscription" unproblematic: as the word is used in this book, "inscription" refers to a piece of writing or lettering engraved, etched, incised, traced, stamped, or otherwise imprinted into or onto a durable surface. In fact, certain types of ancient writing squarely included in this definition—the legends on coins or engraved gems, for example—long ago developed their own special disciplines (numismatics, gemology) and are no longer generally considered to fall within the epigraphist's realm. Others not so obviously pertinent, such as words spelled out in mosaic tiles (Gómez Pallarès 1997) or painted on plaster walls (Franklin 1980) or impressed into carbonized loaves of bread (Manacorda 1993: 45), have found a place in epigraphy. The study of Greek and Latin inscriptions inevitably impinges on other areas in the study of ancient writing, notably papyrology and palaeography, and the boundaries between the fields have never been precisely drawn. Some general guidelines may nonetheless help to delimit the field.

Palaeography, focused on letter-forms, embraces both epigraphy and papyrology but excludes much of what the latter concern, notably, as Sandys observed, consideration of the contents of the texts.[1] The territory covered by the other two can generally be divided according to the permanence of the writings each treats; but many documents transcribed on papyri were no more transitory in intent—and have proved no more ephemeral in fact—than the scribblings painted or scratched onto pottery fragments at Athens (Lang 1975) or onto tombs at Pompeii (Sabbatini Tumolesi 1980). Geography has conventionally provided one useful criterion of discrimination: inscribed bone or ivory tags (*tesserae*) found in Egypt have traditionally belonged to papyrologists, whereas those discovered elsewhere in the Roman world are cataloged by epigraphists (e.g. in *ILS* 6118–20; cf. Dar. Sag., s.v., 1912). But the ongoing recovery of inked wooden writing leaves from Roman forts at Chesterholm (Vindolanda) (Bowman–Thomas 1994) and Carlisle (Tomlin 1998) in northern Britain and of various normally perishable documents from throughout the Near East (Cotton–Cockle–Millar 1995) has challenged this arbitrary division by place of discovery and has expanded the papyrologist's territorial range. The inscribed waxed tablets unearthed at Vindolanda are naturally being studied by the same scholars who are editing the wooden writing leaves with which they have been found (Bowman–Thomas 1994), whereas those from Pompeii and Dacia known in the nineteenth century were included in the *Corpus Inscriptionum Latinarum*, and examples found subsequently in the same regions have continued to be handled by epigraphists (e.g. Camodeca 1999).

If neither place of discovery nor vehicle of transmission (the type of object that "supports" the text) provides a clear means of distinguishing the papyrologist's territory from that of the epigraphist, neither does the medium of writing nor the material of the writing surface. The painted signatures and labels that formed part of the original decoration of fine ceramics have traditionally been the preserve of vase specialists and art historians (Immerwahr 1990), whereas words painted on large clay vessels subsequent to their manufacture are studied by epigraphists (see below), and texts written in ink on fragments of broken pottery (*ostraka*) are generally handled by papyrologists—unless they come from an area rich in other types of inscriptions, such as the agora at Athens, in which case epigraphists claim their due (Lang 1990). There is no logical reason, much less necessity, for this fragmentation, and although the development of specialized skills within the subdisciplines of palaeography, papyrology, epigraphy, and numismatics is natural and inevitable, everyone who works in any of these fields sooner or later feels the need to know something about the others, and anyone who wishes to understand the place of writing in the ancient world must try to keep in mind the variety of media in which it was recorded and the range of purposes it served (Harris 1989: 26–9).

Even with parts of the territory parceled off to related disciplines, the temporal and geographical range of the material traditionally included within the field of Greek and Latin epigraphy is wide. To try to describe definitively the body of inscribed writing in Greek and Latin—to say nothing of the dozen or so other ancient languages attested epigraphically throughout the Mediterranean world (Harris 1989: 175–90)—would be an impossible task and would serve no useful purpose. Of the 600,000 or so surviving Greek and Latin inscriptions, produced over a millennium and a half (c. 800 BCE–700 CE), our sample runs from a metrical graffito scratched onto a cup ("of Nestor") deposited in a grave on Pithecusae toward the end of the eighth century BCE (*CEG* 454 = *LSAG* 239 no. 1); to an archaic dedication to Mars on a stone base at Satricum, south of Rome, by the companions (*suodales*) of a P. Valerius, probably the "Publicola" who was consul in the first year of the Roman Republic (the so-called *lapis Satricanus*, *CIL* I² 2832a; Versnel 1997); to a bilingual edict, in Greek and Aramaic, of the Buddhist Indian king Asoka (c. 250 BCE) from Kandahar in eastern Afghanistan (Pugliese Carratelli–Garbini 1964; cf. Millar 1983: 87–9); to the record of personal accomplishments (*res gestae*) composed by the emperor Augustus shortly before his death and originally displayed in front of his mausoleum at Rome (Suet. *Aug.* 101)—probably the most widely studied document of antiquity (e.g. Gagé 1977; Ramage 1987); to a bronze military diploma recording the award of citizenship rights to a Roman soldier serving on the northern frontier in Britain in 146 CE (*RIB* 2041.9 = *RMD* 2.97); to a fulsome honorific dedication by Smaragdus, exarch of Italy, to Phocas, emperor in the East, inscribed over an earlier text on a monument erected in the Roman Forum early in the seventh century (*CIL* VI 1200, 31259a); to a Christian epitaph carved on the cover of a tomb near Osuna (Urso) in Spain in February 708 CE (*CIL* II²/5 1115).[2]

No one has ever tried to control this vast assemblage of material, with good reason. As a body of data, the corpus of ancient Greek and Latin inscriptions is amorphous, heterogeneous, and inert. A category of writing so arbitrarily defined—by a quality (durability) secondary and in many cases incidental to its particular function—does not have the same underlying unity as do medieval manuscripts or coins or even papyri. The purposes for which inscriptions were composed and the types of objects on which they were inscribed are more diverse than those with which the palaeographer, the numismatist, or the papyrologist generally has to contend. Consequently, the range of historical issues they illuminate tends to be wider, and the variety of possible methods of approaching the texts greater, than they are in the related fields. There is no single correct way to exploit inscriptional evidence, any more than there is a single correct way to write ancient history. In order to yield useful information, the epigraphic corpus must be prodded into responsiveness by well-honed questions directed at appropriate points of its sprawling bulk: asking epitaphs about maritime commerce is less profitable than asking them about commemorative behavior or onomastic practices; consulting amphora stamps for patterns of office holding will provide few answers. For the most part these points are obvious, but some large classes of inscription—notably, epitaphs (see below)—have not always had the right questions asked of them. Others, such as curse tablets (Gager 1992: 3–41) or Greek manumission records (Guarducci 1967–78: 3.263–94; Hopkins 1978: 133–71) or Roman military diplomas (Eck–Wolff 1986) prompt questions about ancient mentalities and behaviors that we might not otherwise have been inclined to pose.

The challenge for the historian approaching the heterogeneous mass of Greek and Latin inscriptional writing is to choose analytical tools suitable to the particular task and to apply them with care. In many cases this means trying to combine the skills of an archaeologist with those of a philologist in order to understand the physical context in which a document was produced and the significance of the monument that carried the text as well as the message of the text itself (Marcillet-Jaubert 1960; Raubitschek 1964). In others, the expertise of a demographer or a statistician or a prosopographer may be required (e.g. Parkin 1992: 4–19; Hahn–Leunissen 1990; see Chapter 3). Even when the goal is a synthetic analysis of thousands of similar inscriptions, attention to the peculiar characteristics of individual specimens is often essential for their basic interpretation and in many cases leads to a more nuanced appreciation of the entire class of document. Conversely, understanding the significance of any particular inscription requires a broad knowledge of the group of similar texts from which it derives, so that its conventional elements and distinctive features can be recognized. In practice most investigators venturing into this vast territory at one time or another feel lost or inadequately equipped for the expedition, owing to the lack of some specialized knowledge or breadth of experience; and yet the most perplexing uncertainties often center on the most basic questions about the nature of the evidence. How were inscriptions viewed by the persons for whom they were written? What motives inspired those who wrote them? What was the place of inscribed writing in the Greco-Roman world?

The Roman epigraphic habit

Nearly twenty years ago Ramsay MacMullen, in a celebrated essay (MacMullen 1982), noted that the number of Latin inscriptions apparently grew steadily over the first and second centuries CE before falling off sharply in the third (cf. Mrozek 1973, 1988) and that throughout the western provinces, much of the Danube region, and most of North Africa, the practice of inscribing documents on stone, particularly epitaphs, seems not to have been a native tradition but was instead a custom learned from the Romans (Móesy 1966: 419–20). With these two observations MacMullen outlined the contours of an "epigraphic habit" he found to be characteristic of the Romanized peoples of the western empire, a habit that peaked around the turn of the second and third centuries CE. A few years later, he noted a similar pattern of epigraphic production in the Greek east, from which he concluded that the habit was cultural rather than linguistic, "Roman" rather than "Latin" (MacMullen 1986; cf. Roueché 1989: xix–xx). MacMullen did not attempt to interpret this phenomenon but suggested only that the rise and fall of epigraphic production was controlled by a "sense of audience" (MacMullen 1982: 246). When the custom of inscribing memorials in stone experienced a resurgence in late antiquity, beginning in the second half of the fourth century CE, it was virtually restricted to epitaphs and had a distinctly Christian cast, centered on a belief in resurrection and the afterlife (Galvao-Sobrinho 1995; cf. Shaw 1996: 101–7). The causes of the earlier growth and decline are more difficult to identify.

E. Meyer, focusing on epitaphs, has argued that Roman tombstones were a distinctive badge of Roman citizenship and that, when the latter lost its cachet following the emperor Caracalla's extension of the rights of citizens to all free inhabitants of the empire in 212 CE, the fashion for inscribed epitaphs likewise lost its appeal (Meyer 1990: 78–81). But Roman tombstones were never restricted to citizens, and the methods of dating and periodization used to chart the supposed rise and fall of their popularity are suspect (Cherry 1995: 143–50). G. Woolf has pointed out that in Roman Gaul, as the epigraphic habit spread during the second century CE, the number of Roman-style epitaphs erected by and to persons without Roman names and Roman citizenship actually increased (Woolf 1998: 103). In his view, names provide one key to understanding the phenomenon. Woolf remarks the prominence in Latin inscriptions of naming as a means of asserting identity and suggests that the epigraphic habit may be viewed as a barometer of social anxiety expressed by individuals seeking to establish their place in an increas-

ingly changing world; the diffusion of the Roman epigraphic culture during the first and second centuries is a sign of the expansion of Roman
society (Woolf 1996). This idea may help to account for the rise of the
phenomenon but seems ill suited to explaining its decline, for if the
number of epitaphs fell off sharply after the time of the Severi, in Italy,
at least, where Roman citizenship had long been a prerogative of the
freeborn, the number of honorary inscriptions, which even more than
epitaphs linked social identity to a name, not only did not decrease during the third century but may even have grown (Forbis 1996: 101). A
single explanation for such widespread changes, based on an isolated
political act or a presumed commonality of psychological responses to
the world, is perhaps unlikely.[3] More probably a variety of mundane
and interconnected forces—economic, demographic, and social, as well
as psychological and, perhaps, political—gradually shaped the prevail-
ing cultural practice in different localities, with the result that a micro-
cosmically variegated galaxy of epigraphic behaviors appears to us
deceptively regular and uniform when viewed from a distance. With greater
confidence, we may assert that the epigraphic universe of the Roman
empire began with a bang.

The explosion of epigraphic activity at the start of the period of expansion, around the end of the first century BCE, can be plausibly traced to
the first emperor, Augustus. Building inscriptions, milestones (recording
not only distances but the names of the officials responsible for constructing
the road), votive dedications on altars and statue bases, honorific texts,
boundary markers, epitaphs—all these types of inscription not only pro-
liferated in number but changed in form as a result of the influence
of the first Princeps, who effectively transformed the existing epigraphic
culture of Rome into an empire-wide vehicle of Augustan ideology
(Alföldy 1991). Whether or not Augustus purposefully set out to reshape
the epigraphic landscape, the example he set at the capital for acceptable forms of public display established a pattern and a set of standards
that quickly spread throughout Italy and the western provinces (Eck 1984;
Wallace-Hadrill 1990). Earlier in the first century BCE Roman epigraphy in two of its most characteristic forms—honorific inscriptions and
epitaphs—had already left its mark in northern Italy, parts of southern
Gaul, and much of the Iberian peninsula, where it variously transformed
and conformed to the diverse native epigraphic traditions it encountered
(Beltrán Lloris 1995). But it was not until the time of Augustus, when a
ready supply of strong, fine-grained white marble, quarried in the
Apuan Alps north of Pisa (modern Carrara) and shipped to Rome through
the port of Luni (whence its name, Luna), made possible the carving of

artistically refined lettering, with contrasting thick and thin strokes formed by a V-shaped groove ("shading": Gordon–Gordon 1957: 80–2), that the popularity of stone-cut inscriptions as verbal monuments began to spread throughout Italy, parts of western Europe, and North Africa.

Subsequently, the epigraphic revolution of Augustus swept unevenly across the western provinces, manifesting itself differently in various parts of the territory. In North Africa the wealth of surviving Latin inscriptions (more than 60,000), mainly tombstones, so dominates our view of the region that it creates a misleading picture of pervasive Romanization and threatens to obscure the persistence of native Libyan and Punic institutions (Mattingly–Hitchner 1995: 169–79). In Roman Britain, on the other hand, where stone suitable for carving is largely restricted to the highland zone to the north-west (the region occupied by Roman troops: Mann 1985), and where the largest category of surviving inscriptions is votive altars (Biró 1975: 42), funerary commemoration on tombstones was shunned by the elite but was embraced instead by those seeking to establish their place in the new order, notably auxiliary soldiers and women (Hope 1997). In the western provinces of Aquitania, Lugdunensis, and Belgica, the practice of inscribing texts in stone never caught on at all, although those areas became highly Romanized in other respects (Eck 1993: 378). Among individual regions of the empire, the discrepancies in epigraphic density (as measured by the approximate number of surviving Latin inscriptions found per 1,000 square kilometers) are striking: of all the western provinces, Africa Proconsularis ranks highest, with 127, Mauretania Tingitana lowest, with only three. Within peninsular Italy, Campania is first, with 411, Lucania last, with 19 (Harris 1989: 265–8; cf. Duncan-Jones 1982: 339, 360–2). To put these figures in perspective, excluding inscribed *instrumentum domesticum*, the city of Rome, the most densely "epigraphic" zone in the ancient world, has yielded nearly 100,000 Latin inscriptions within an area of approximately 30 square kilometers, more than half again as many as in all of North Africa, the most thickly blanketed region in the Roman West outside Italy.[4]

In general, inscriptions seem to have been concentrated in urbanized areas and militarized zones, places where distinctions of social rank, and hence, perhaps, the attraction of publicly asserting one's status, were especially acute (Woolf 1996: 36–7). Clustering at particular sites is pervasive throughout the empire, and within individual provinces the patterns of distribution frequently conform to the natural and human landscape in predictable ways. In Roman Gaul, for example, inscriptions are found predominantly along river valleys and around communities located at key points along the major Roman roads, reflecting the patterns of habitation and communication. Less easy to explain are the concentration of inscriptions in larger groups located more closely together the further east in the province one looks and the striking discrepancies in epigraphic density between individual towns: whereas more than a thousand inscriptions survive from Narbonne, a city of perhaps 10,000 to 15,000 inhabitants during the second century CE, Paris, with a population of between 5,000 and 8,000, has yielded fewer than 50 (Woolf 1998: 82–91, 98–102). A similar phenomenon, but a different pattern, of predictable and unpredictable distribution emerges from a consideration of one particular type of inscription—votive dedications—in northern Gaul: very few are found in the southwestern part of the region (a demilitarized area), whereas a great number are concentrated along the Rhine (a frontier zone); within the Rhineland, however, notable discrepancies between individual settlements are difficult to account for (Derks 1998: 81–7).

Naturally, the patterns of distribution of many types of inscription reflect the purposes of the objects that carried them: stamped amphorae are prevalent along the coasts (Peacock–Williams 1986: 64 and Figures 21, 35, 82, 88, etc.); milestones are found beside major thoroughfares (*CIL* XVII); epitaphs derive from tombs along the roads outside of towns (Hesberg–Zanker 1987); official decrees and commemorative statues are concentrated in civic centers and "the most frequented places" (e.g. *CIL* V 532, VI 31883–4; *AE* 1984, 508, IIb.26–7; *SCPP* 170–1); and so on. In individual communities, however, puzzling exceptions to the expected patterns are common enough that we must be wary of overestimating the pervasiveness of even widespread epigraphic trends. The important Roman colony of Colonia Agrippinensis (Cologne), for example, yields a number of Latin inscriptions of various sorts but, oddly, not a single honorific dedication to a Roman official (Eck 1982: 542–3). At the commercial port of Puteoli on the Bay of Naples, on the other hand, two lengthy and unique marble inscriptions recording public contracts, one detailing specifications for the construction of a wall (*CIL* I^2 698 and p. 936; see below and Figure 1.7), the other recording the terms of the funerary concession let to the local undertakers (*AE* 1971, 88; cf. Bodel 1994: 72–80), point to a local custom of carving in stone certain administrative documents that elsewhere must have been posted in more ephemeral media, such as on whitened boards, if they were publicly displayed at all. Cases such as these remind us that while certain epigraphic behaviors became prevalent throughout the Roman West, parochial traditions and conventions always exerted a powerful influence on local practices.

Sometimes it is the surprising diversity of the Romans' "sense of audience" that raises questions about the nature of the Roman epigraphic habit. The discovery in a private room of a large luxury villa at Lucus Feroniae outside Rome of two honorific inscriptions detailing the public careers of two early imperial consuls (of 3 and 56 CE) from the prominent family of the Volusii Saturnini provides an unprecedented glimpse of commemorative behavior in action (*AE* 1972, 174, 175). In form and formula both inscriptions fully conform to the protocol of honorific inscriptions on statue bases and other public monuments; if we did not know their origin, we would without hesitation assign them to an official civic context. Their placement instead in a sort-of family museum, at the heart of a rural residence, is striking and leads one to wonder how many similar inscriptions from Rome and its environs, conventionally assigned because of their texts to public civic spaces, might have originated instead in private domestic settings (Eck 1992; Bodel 1997: 26–32). The case of the Augustan senator P. Paquius Scaeva (*PIR*[2] P 126) presents another surprise. A funerary inscription erected at Rome by three freedmen to the divine shades (*Dis Manibus*) of P. Paquius Scaeva (*CIL* VI 1483) would normally be taken to suggest that the man was buried there, but in fact the marble sarcophagus in which both he and his wife were laid to rest survives intact at his home town of Histonium (Vasto) in Samnium (cf. Eck 1984: 156 n. 36). On that monument a pair of epitaphs recording the joint burial of husband and wife and detailing the senatorial career of Scaeva are duly inscribed—on the inside of the sarcophagus (*CIL* IX 2845, 2846 = *ILS* 915; cf. *Suppl. Ital.* n.s. 2: 108–9). For whose eyes were these texts intended? It is difficult to say. For all its broad, clear outlines, the nature of the Roman epigraphic habit remains in many respects enigmatic and obscure.

Greek epigraphic cultures

In the Greek world, the contours of the epigraphic culture—or rather cultures, for diversity is the hallmark of Hellenic epigraphy—are even more sharply defined than in the Roman West. This has not always been apparent. Until recently, the study of Greek epigraphy was so dominated by research on the public inscriptions of Athens that it was easy to forget that in one important area—the invention and early development of the Greek alphabet—Athens was a relative late-comer (Immerwahr 1990: 175–6; Jeffery–Johnston 1990: 66–78, 431–3) and that among the earliest Greek inscriptions (those of the archaic period, c. 800–650 BCE) we have not one specimen of any of the types of public document (decrees, treaties, inventories, catalogues, building specifications) that later came to characterize the epigraphy of the *polis,* nor does our surviving sample include a single commercial text of the sort one might expect to find in an age of colonial expansion and far-ranging maritime trade. Writing in Greece seems to have emerged around the late ninth or early eighth century BCE from contacts between Phoenicians and Greek traders, probably in the northern Levant (Wachter 1989; Marek 1993), but the existence from this period of commercial inscriptions other than trademarks (Johnston 1979: 1, 27) can only be postulated, since no examples survive. The epigraphic culture of the Greek archaic age centered instead on the individual and private concerns: the ownership or authorship of portable possessions, the relationship with a god, remembrance after death (Powell 1991: 123–80; cf. *SEG* 39.1764).

In Attica the earliest inscriptions seem to have been intended to ennoble their writers by perpetuating the association of their names with the heroic past, but with the proliferation of writing in public and civic contexts during the sixth century BCE, this elevating power of inscriptions became dissipated and was lost (Várhelyi 1996; cf. Harris 1996). Elsewhere, the purposes and early development of inscribed writing varied considerably. If there was an epigraphic revolution in the Greek world, it arrived sometime in the latter half of the seventh century BCE, when the first laws were written down on stone—by Drakon at Athens (*IG* I³ 104; Stroud 1968), possibly at Tiryns (*SEG* 30.380), and (our earliest example) at Dreros in Crete (*LSAG* 315 no. 1a = Meiggs–Lewis 2). It appears to have caught on only sporadically and variously: quickly in some places, such as Attica, where the number of surviving inscriptions down to the end of the seventh century BCE (some 130, almost all graffiti and dipinti —painted texts—recording personal names) increases ten-fold over the next 120 years; much more slowly at others, such as Crete, where the total count down to the middle of the fifth century BCE comes to fewer than seventy, more than half of which are legal texts on stone or bronze, and where personal names are notably rare (Whitley 1997: 641, 651–2; cf. Stoddart–Whitley 1988: 763–6). The great growth in numbers of inscriptions in Attica (Hedrick 1999: 390–2) and throughout the Hellenic world came only in the fourth century BCE with the general expansion of the various civic organizations of the *polis* and the conquests of Alexander.

During the archaic and classical periods local variations in natural resources and political systems produced very different epigraphic profiles in different cities and regions. Classical Attica, with its ready supply of marble and its peculiar democratic institutions, such as ostracism (Lang 1990), does not look much like Corinth, where stone suitable for carving was not readily available and where government by oligarchy did not result in the same passion for the public display of documents. The distribution of inscribed pottery fragments from the same two cities, on the other hand, paints a very different picture of the commercial ambitions of the two maritime powers (Lorber 1979). On Cyprus, where monarchical rule flourished and where the distinctive syllabic system of writing remained virtually unchanged from the third millennium down to the classical age, public inscriptions are notably rare before the Ptolemaic period.[5] At Sparta, where the assembly voted by acclamation and civic life was conducted without reliance upon the written word, the total number of surviving inscribed texts down to the middle of the fifth century BCE comes to under one hundred (cf. Détienne 1988: 56–8; see Chapter 2). What is more, in contrast to Attica, where graffiti and dipinti greatly outnumber dedications on stone and where inscribed tombstones become common after the middle of the sixth century, at Sparta not a single graffito, only seven dipinti, and a solitary inscribed gravestone are known before the middle of the fifth century BCE. From Crete, down to the end of the seventh century, we know of 15 dedications (of which 13 are inscribed on armor), seven graffiti, a single tombstone, and three legal texts; subsequently, down to the middle of the fifth century, we have four more dedications (none on armor), six graffiti, four gravestones, and no fewer than 35 laws (Whitley 1997: 645–51).[6]

The discrepancies are significant: whereas in Attica both the number and the variety of inscriptions seem to have increased steadily throughout the sixth century, at Sparta during the same period only dedicatory inscriptions are at all common, and on Crete the numbers drop in every category except inscribed legal texts, which outnumber the total from Attica by an order of nearly six to one (Attica n. = 4; Crete n. = 23; Laconia n. = 0). Where the figures are small, statistical arguments are precarious, and we cannot forget that in any community significant numbers of texts may have been written on perishable materials that have not survived. Even so, the implications are arresting: contrary to a commonly held belief in the association of widespread literacy, the publication of laws, and the growth of democracy, the surge of popular epigraphic expression at Athens during the sixth century evidently did not inspire any wholesale inscribing of public texts in the civic sphere, whereas on Crete during the same period the monumentalization of law accompanied an overall decline in epigraphic production in other contexts and did not lead to any adoption of democratic reforms (Whitley 1997). Even at Athens, where publicly inscribed documents later came to be seen as a cornerstone of democracy, the practice of recording laws on stone probably in origin had more to do with religious than with civic life and was perhaps reserved for procedural matters of secondary importance, those lacking the authority of the time-honored unwritten laws (Thomas 1995). During the archaic period at Athens, as elsewhere, inscribed laws seem to have been deliberately kept at a distance from the public civic spaces they later came to occupy and were displayed instead at the temples of the gods (Hölkeskamp 1992: 99–102; 1994). In this respect, unusually, there seems to have been some consistency of practice among the archaic *poleis*. Nor can the proliferation of inscriptions in classical Athens be explained as simply a byproduct of democracy: other Greek democracies produced few epigraphic texts. The peculiar democratic ethos associated with the epigraphic habit at Athens must be sought instead in distinctive features of Attic epigraphy, such as the formulae of disclosure regularly appended to honorific inscriptions, rather than in the sheer volume of Athenian epigraphic production (Hedrick 1999).

Even after Alexander, when Greek became the common language of business throughout the eastern Mediterranean, no unifying panhellenic influence comparable to that emanating from Augustan Rome ever encouraged any uniformity of epigraphic practice across the region.[7] In some places, such as the great sanctuaries of Asclepius at Epidaurus (Pausanias 2.27.3; *IG* IV² 380–588; Peek 1969, 1972) and Pergamum (Habicht 1969), or of Apollo at Didyma (Rehm 1958), or of Isis on the island of Philae in Egypt (Bernand–Bernand 1969), the epigraphic character of the site was determined by pilgrims from elsewhere and was shaped by the nature of their quest. In others, such as the international centers of Delphi (*Fouilles de Delphes* III; cf. Daux 1936) and Delos (*IG* XI; *IDelos*; cf. Reger 1994), a welter of specialized documents, many involving foreigners and foreign relations, dominates and complicates the epigraphic profile of the site. Elsewhere, native customs and traditions produced idiosyncratic classes of inscription, such as the debt-marking boundary stones (*horoi*) of Attica (Finley 1952; Lalonde–Langdon–Walbank 1991), or the so-called confession inscriptions of Lydia (Petzl 1994; *SEG* 44.951), or the thousands of rock-cut Safaitic graffiti inscribed by nomadic tribes in the Syrian desert—an epigraphic culture geographically and linguistically on the edges of the Greek world—which reflect a range of functions peculiar to the itinerant character of the peoples who carved them (Winnett 1957).

Sometimes the epigraphic profile of an otherwise ordinary community is inexplicably prominent. The minor Hellenistic city of Oenoanda in northern Lycia, which seems to have minted only a single coin during the nearly 400 years of its existence, is home to four of the most remarkable inscriptions to survive from antiquity: the lengthy dossier of a local citizen "personally known to the emperors," C. Iulius Demosthenes, concerning the foundation of an artistic festival (*agon*) in 125 CE (with more than 2,250 words, the most complete such record we have: Wörrle 1988; Smith 1994); the philosophical dogma of a local Epicurean, Diogenes, carved for the benefit of future generations (in part, it seems, by the same stonecutter who inscribed Demosthenes' text) across several courses of a wall eighty meters long in a stoa in the center of town (more than 200 fragments survive, but most of the text remains buried: Smith 1993; Etienne–O'Meara 1996); parts of a lengthy epitaph (seven columns comprising some 225 lines of text) composed around 210 CE and tracing the genealogy of a certain Licinnia Flavilla back more than 300 years, over twelve generations, to a Spartan, Cleander, who founded the neighboring town of Cibyra (*IGRR* 3.500; cf. Hall–Milner–Coulton 1996, identifying another lengthy genealogical inscription on the opposite façade of the tomb); and a theological oracle of the late second or third century CE from Claros, carved high onto the exterior town wall so as to catch the rays of the rising sun, in which Apollo speaks as a messenger of God (Robert 1971; Lane Fox 1986: 168–77). None of these documents is typical—each, indeed, is uniquely informative about its subject—but each can be placed within a well defined category of similar inscriptions, which allow its distinctive characteristics to be recognized. Collectively, they illustrate two features of the epigraphic culture of western Asia Minor: its local variety and its dominant physical presence in the public life of the city. What we should like to know is "why Oenoanda?" The town was located on a major road joining Lycia to the north, but nothing we know about the community explains this profusion of public writing in stone.

Elsewhere, local epigraphic cultures exhibited distinctive linguistic or formal characteristics equally difficult to explain. In the Syrian trading emporium of Palmyra, unlike in all other Greek cities in the Roman Near East, the residents used the local Semitic language (a dialect of Aramaic) not only in private epitaphs but in public inscriptions (normally beside Greek and, occasionally, Latin), although Greco-Roman terms for civic institutions were regularly transliterated rather than translated, and although the epigraphic habit of inscribing texts was not native but had been acquired from the Greeks and Romans (Millar

1995: 408–19). In the upper Hermus valley in Lydia, in the region of Saittae, all the standard types of inscriptions (votive dedications, honorific decrees, above all epitaphs) are to be found, but, for reasons that remain obscure, almost half (405) of the nearly 850 surviving examples from the imperial period include a precise dating formula in the first line (*TAM* 5.1). Although certain broad trends in the production and display of inscribed documents throughout the eastern Mediterranean can and should be recognized, in many respects (to paraphrase a well-known dictum about politics), all Greek epigraphy was local. The customs of one community were not necessarily followed by neighboring communities and were, moreover, likely to change with time. In this sense, the diversity and autonomy of the various epichoric alphabets that marked the beginning of writing in Greece set a pattern for the development of independent epigraphic cultures throughout the Hellenic world.

Inscriptions, orality, and literacy

Who read inscriptions? The concept of epigraphic cultures inevitably raises the question of literacy, since inscriptions, it is generally assumed, were meant to be read. Not all inscriptions had an obvious readership—witness the epitaph of P. Paquius Scaeva at Histonium or the oracle of Apollo at Oenoanda (see above)—but the sheer number of inscribed texts surviving from the classical world has often been taken to indicate that reading was common in antiquity. W. V. Harris has argued forcefully, however, that the level of literacy in most parts of the Greco-Roman world at most periods did not rise above ten per cent: notwithstanding the impressions created by a profusion of humble graffiti at sites like Pompeii (Harris 1983: 102–11) or the mass-produced stamps on common objects of daily use (Harris 1995), the necessary preconditions for mass literacy simply did not exist in antiquity, and reading and writing skills are unlikely ever to have been acquired by more than a small segment of the population (Harris 1989: 11–12, 260–4). Debate about numbers and percentages will no doubt continue, and it is clear that more subtly articulated views of the phenomenon are needed: what level of reading and writing was practiced by what segments of what populations for what purposes? (Harris 1996: 70–4). But even if one grants more plausibility than Harris is willing to concede to the idea that many in antiquity learned to read from perusing inscriptions, without the benefit of formal schooling (a freedman in Petronius' satiric novel of Neronian Italy claims to know *lapidariae litterae*, *Sat.* 58.7), or believes that in certain periods the evidence for literacy below the elite level is far from negligible, Harris' arguments have usefully focused attention on the question of the place of writing in a culture in which only a minority of the population could read and write. On this issue inscriptions, of course, provide only part of the picture, but since their texts were by and large more publicly accessible than most others in the ancient world, their position in the debate is central.

One obvious question concerns the interrelation of orality and literacy (Thomas 1992: 15–28). At the most basic level, certain inscribed texts simply put into writing words that were originally and primarily enacted orally. Inscriptions of public laws and decrees generally fall into this category and were in fact frequently preceded by oral publication: the text of the statute was read out loud by a herald in a prescribed location, so that all concerned might learn its contents (Mommsen 1887: 391, 418; Crawford 1996: 9, 33; Rhodes–Lewis 1997: 6). The prescripts of Roman statutes bearing the names of witnesses to the oral passage of laws and decrees were normally inscribed in larger letters because it was the witnesses' authority that sanctioned the documents (Williamson 1995). The ratifying act was not the inscribing of names but the oral expression of intent—*censuerunt* in senatorial decrees, *velitis*, *iubeatis*, in *rogationes* to the people (cf. Crawford 1996: 10, 14–15). Even some official communiqués composed for written publication, such as the edicts and epistles of Hellenistic kings and Roman emperors to their subjects (Figure 1.1), normally represented spoken responses to petitions that were originally submitted orally (Welles 1934: xxxix–xl; Oliver 1989: 18–21). In these cases, the inscribed texts were corroborative but not constitutive of the official acts they recorded; they merely commemorated an oral performance.

In other cases, inscriptions engendered speech. Epitaphs, for example, implicitly—and sometimes explicitly—addressed themselves to an audience as well as a readership. The gravestone set up for an Aeginetan, Mnesitheos, at Eretria in Euboea sometime during the first half of the fifth century BCE urged a passerby to "read out" (ἀνάνεμαι) the name of the man buried there and declared that "someone" (i.e. the reader) would tell passersby that the monument had been set up by Mnesitheos' mother (*GVI* 1210 with Svenbro 1993: 44–56). Some 700 years later, a Pannonian foreigner (*barbarus*) erected at Sulmo in central Italy a long verse epitaph in which he wished well to "whoever read, or listened to one reading, the inscription" (*titulumque quicumque legerit, aut lege*[*ntem*] *ausculta*(*ve*)*rit*) (*Suppl. Ital.* n.s. 4: 78–84 no. 58, vv. 42–3; cf. *AE* 1989, 247). In a world in which reading out loud was normal (Hendrickson 1929)—a fact not refuted by recognition that the ancients

Figure 1.1 Letter of the Roman emperor Hadrian to the Macedonian *Koinon*, from Chalkidike (?). Marble stele (75.2 × 48.3 × 3.1 cm), 137 CE (*SEG* 37.593). Hadrian confirms a request from the *Koinon* that officials intending to nominate successors to their positions inform the potential nominees thirty days in advance. The heading and first paragraph are distinguished by oversized letters protruding beyond the left margin; sentences are concluded with decorative ivy leaves (*hederae*), except in line 17, where space did not allow (lines 7, 13, 18); the date (deducible from the titles in the heading) is formally recorded at the end (Museum of Art, Rhode Island School of Design; Mary B. Jackson Fund. 1988.060; photographed by Cathy Carver. RI.Prov.RISD.MA.G.1988.060).

could and often did read silently (Burnyeat 1997; Gavrilov 1997)—any inscription potentially motivated a voiced communication. That fundamental reality imparted to ancient inscriptions a dynamic quality not naturally felt by modern readers accustomed to a more passive reception of the written word. Thus epitaphs sometimes invoked a contrast between the silence of the gravestone and the "voice" given to their inscribed words, whether activated or merely imagined by the reader (e.g. *CIL* I² 1210 = *CLE* 53; cf. Theognis 568–9; Häusle 1980: 41–63; Svenbro 1993: 56–63). Tombstones that urged passersby to pause and read their texts often invited not only contemplation but conversation (cf. Lattimore 1942: 230–4, 256–8). In the most elaborate cases, they engaged the reader in actual dialogue, represented in amoebean form of question or command and response: "Who died?" "Herois." "How and when?" "Being pregnant she died in labor . . ." (*GVI* 1842 = *SEG* 8.802; cf. *GVI* 1831–87); "Hail, traveler, come here and rest a little. You refuse and say no? You'll have to come back here anyway" (*CIL* XI 4010 = *CLE* 120; cf. *CLE* 513, 1097, 1212; see also Figure 1.2).

The location of the "voice" in this last inscription is ambiguous, for if the marker in the salutation points to the monument itself ("come here"), the one in the response to the presumed refusal ("come back here") suggests a more general provenance of the grave or the underworld. A whole class of inscribed texts of various types—labels declaring ownership or authorship, *ex-voto* dedications, honorific inscriptions, as well as epitaphs —gave voice to inarticulate objects by imprinting upon them words imagined as originating from the objects themselves (Burzachechi 1962; Agostiniani 1982; Colonna 1983). The so-called "speaking inscriptions" not only enabled objects to "speak" for themselves, as, for example, with the message painted around the mouth of an Athenian amphora of the mid-sixth century BCE, "Kleimachos made me and I belong to him" (Guarducci 1967–78: 3.482), but also for persons associated with them but unable or unwilling to speak, as with a silver sheet from an archaic tomb at Poseidonia, which declares, on behalf of the deceased, "I belong to the goddess Kore (Persephone)" (*LSAG* 260 no. 4; cf. Agostiniani 1982: 23), or the Roman slave collar from Velitrae, which advises "hold on to me, because I have run away" (*CIL* XV 7172 = *ILS* 8727; cf. *ILS* 8726–33, Bellen 1971: 27–9). It is not, of course, the silver sheet that belongs to Persephone or the tin collar that demands to be held but rather the persons found with them. This sort of metonymic transference of a verbal capacity represents a feature of ancient writing peculiar to inscribed texts. Whether or not their words were pronounced out loud is irrelevant to their purpose; indeed, in the case of the Poseidonian inscription, the participation of any earthly reader may be doubted. Conceptually they belong to a world in which inscribed writing enacted the function of speech by imparting to inanimate objects an independent identity and a mode of discourse normally conveyed by the spoken rather than the written word.

In the earliest inscriptions the perspective seems always to have been that of the first-person—the object "speaks" as "I"—as already, probably, with the archaic cup from Pithecusae that proclaimed its ownership by Nestor (*CEG* 454 = *LSAG* 239 no. 1, a piece of erotic magic, it seems, rather than a sophisticated joke: West 1994, Faraone 1996). Subsequently, beginning around the middle of the sixth century BCE, the use of a demonstrative adjective signifying the object introduced ambiguity into these egocentric texts, an ambiguity that was articulated by the flexibility of Greek syntax, which allowed such expressions as "I am this tomb of Gleukitas" (Pfohl 1967: no. 152). This linguistic ambivalence was not simply the manifestation of a primitive animism (Burzachechi 1962: 53) but rather an emphatic assertion of the physical presence of the object that bore the text (Svenbro 1993: 26–43). The physicality of ancient inscriptions, the fact that their writing was inextricably linked with the surfaces on which it appeared, lent itself to a potential expansion of their significance beyond a straightforward verbal communication of their texts. The ambiguous epitaph quoted above, with its dual perspective from monument and grave, is one manifestation of this semiotic flexibility. In other cases, the meaning of an inscription seems to have had very little at all to do with the verbal message of its text.

Symbolic epigraphy

The term "symbolic" has been aptly invoked to describe an aspect of ancient epigraphy that defies precise definition but that broadly pertains to the extra-textual meaning inscriptions always, to some extent, conveyed and that sometimes constituted their primary purpose (Beard 1985: 115, 139–41; 1991: 38). In certain religious contexts, for example, texts seem to have been inscribed not in order to be read but to represent through their writing that particular acts had been duly performed. The inscribed temple inventories at Delos, which belong to a period between around 430 BCE and around 130 BCE, record the annual rendering of accounts by boards of administrators turning over the treasure to their successors. Carved in small letters half a centimeter tall in long lines (of more than 100 letters, in many cases) of continuous narrative disposed in tall columns, often of more than 200 lines, across expanses of stone nearly a meter wide and two meters tall, these texts would have been difficult to read in the best of circumstances and were certainly not designed to facilitate consultation. More plausibly they were inscribed as symbolic monuments to pious duties duly discharged, the records themselves perhaps being offered as tribute to the gods whose property they protected, just as, for instance, the so-called Athenian tribute lists (*ATL*) are records, not of the total amount of tribute collected from Athens' allies, but of the one-sixtieth portion of it dedicated to Athena (Linders 1992). Similarly, at Rome during the first three centuries CE, the Arval Brethren every year at their headquarters at the grove of the Dea Dia just outside the city inscribed on marble tablets and, when space constraints intervened, on the sides of the stone furniture within their precinct, a detailed and, with time, increasingly expansive record of their cult activities—not in order to guide subsequent generations of priests in the performance of the same tasks but as a formal part of their own ritual; the monumentalizing of a written record was itself, it seems, an act of cult (Beard 1985).

Private religion and magic, too, made use of inscriptions in non-utilitarian, symbolic ways. It is difficult to understand precisely the function of an Orphic prayer engraved on a small gold sheet sometime in the latter half of the fourth century BCE found folded up in a bronze cinerary urn in a grave in Thessaly, but the text was designed to help the deceased gain access to the underworld, and the material on which it was inscribed and the way in which it was deposited were evidently instrumental to this purpose (Breslin 1977, *SEG* 27.226 *bis*; Figure 1.2). There is no mistaking the general intent of the authors (or commissioners) of the numerous inscribed curse tablets (*defixiones*, κατάδεσμοι) found throughout the Mediterranean world (Audollent 1904; Jordan 1985), though often the precise sense of their imprecations remains obscure. Figure 1.3 reproduces a drawing of one side of an opisthographic lead curse tablet (that is, one inscribed on both sides) deposited along with fifty-six others in a small terracotta sarcophagus in a tomb beside the Via Appia outside the Porta San Sebastiano at Rome sometime around 400 CE.[8] Alternating lines of text are written upside down and backwards with respect to one another, evidently because the tablet was turned around, top to bottom, after each line was inscribed, probably in order to twist the intended target (a certain Cardelus, son of Fulgentia) homeopathically by the process of writing. The text includes a number of cryptic incantations (*voces mysticae*) and signs (*charakteres*) and, beneath the left arm of the horse-headed figure, a vowel series (the seven Greek vowels,

Figure 1.2 Orphic prayer from a grave in Thessaly (?). Gold sheet (2.2 × 3.7 cm), c. 350–300 BCE (*SEG* 27.226 *bis*; cf. Breslin 1977). Probably inscribed as a reminder for the deceased of the formula needed to gain salvation in the underworld, the text presents a dialogue (in dactylic meter) between the dead man's soul and a stream springing from the lake of Mnemosyne (Memory): "Parched with thirst I am, and dying." "Then drink of me, an ever-flowing stream; on the right is a white cypress. Who are you? Where are you (from)?" "I am the son of Earth and of starry Heaven, but my race is from Heaven." (The J. Paul Getty Museum, Malibu, California, unknown artist, *lamella Orphica*. CA.Malibu.JPGM.G.75.AM.19.)

repeated in order, here with eta represented in both upper and lower case)—all designed to enhance the efficacy of the spell (cf. Dornseiff 1925: 35–60; Gager 1992: 7–11).[9]

The purpose of this sort of inscribed writing was not to preserve or to convey information but to effect an action through its physical presence; its function was not descriptive or commemorative but, in the useful formulation of the anthropologist Stanley Tambiah, persuasive and performative: the ritual of inscribing was meant to encourage the result it described (Tambiah 1968, 1973). Sometimes words were of secondary importance to the delivery of the objects that carried them. The imprecations imprinted on lead sling bullets (*glandes*) hurled at their enemies by combatants at the siege of Asculum in the Social War between Rome

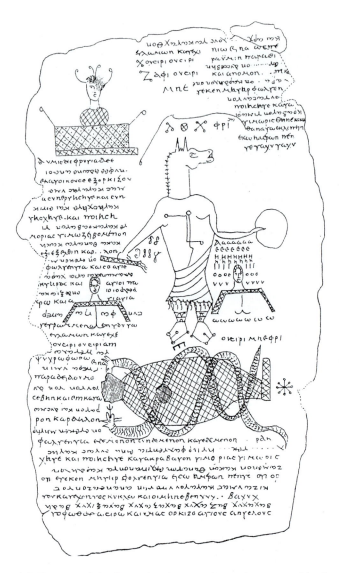

Figure 1.3 Drawing of the first side of an opisthographic curse tablet from a tomb beside the Via Appia, Rome. Lead (13 × 21 cm), c. 400 CE (Audollent 1904: no. 155). The horse-headed figure probably represents a horse-spirit (*daimon*) from the circus; the figures to left and right are "assistants" (*paredroi*). The mummified figure entwined by two biting snakes below represents the target of the spell, duly killed and buried. At the upper left, Osiris emerges from his coffin (Preisendanz 1972: 17–18). For the writing and other symbols, see pp. 20–1 (after Wünsch 1898: 16).

and her rebellious allies in 90 and 89 BCE suggest a variety of purposes: threats such as "You're dead, runaways!" (*CIL* I² 861 = IX 6086, xiii) were evidently designed to demoralize the rebels, whereas the exhortation "Strike Pompeius" (*CIL* I² 857 = IX 6086, ix) seems to have been intended to guide the missile itself to its target, the Roman commander Cn. Pompeius Strabo (cf. Plut. *Marc.* 8). Half a century later, the sexual insults hurled in both directions on sling bullets at the siege of Perugia in 41/40 BCE aimed to humiliate as well as to intimidate the opposing leaders, Octavian and his enemies Fulvia and L. Antonius (*EphEp* 6.52–78; cf. *CIL* XI 6721, Hallett 1977; for Greek *glandes* see Guarducci 1967–78: 2.516–24).

Performative writing operated in reverse as well, when the cancellation of an inscribed text signaled the negation of its contents. The practice of erasing a condemned person's name from public monuments, particularly common during the Roman empire, symbolically represented the abolition of the memory of his or her existence (*damnatio memoriae*) (cf. Kajava 1995b). Since the chiseling out of carved lettering normally left a visible scar on the face of the stone (see Figure 1.6), the obliteration of the name did not in fact achieve its purported objective but instead demonstrated graphically the punishment it was designed to effect. The condemned was conspicuously eliminated, removed but not forgotten.

Other extra-textual, metaphorical elements often reinforced this kind of symbolic writing. The material on which the text was inscribed, the location of the inscription itself, and the way in which it was presented were variously significant. Curse tablets were normally of lead, not only because lead was cheap and easy to inscribe but because its density and pallor conveyed negative associations appropriately directed at the target: "Just as this lead is cold and useless, so let them [my enemies] be cold and useless" (*IG* III, 3 105–7; cf. Gager 1992: 3–4; Graf 1997: 132–4). Orphic prayers were engraved on gold, because the words they carried were valuable and the world to which they promised access was golden (cf. Giangiulio 1994). Roman statutes were inscribed in bronze, because bronze was thought to impart an inviolability and permanence not conferred by other materials (*CIL* VIII 17896; Pliny, *NH* 34.99; Williamson 1987). Greek treaties and decrees were carved in stone partly, it has been suggested, because in archaic Greece rocks had served as monuments and mnemonic aids (Thomas 1992: 87–8).

Location too was important. Curse tablets were deposited in graves, particularly of those who died before their time, so that the written spells would be close to the restless spirits who could put them into effect (Faraone 1991: 9–10; Gager 1992: 18–20); often, graves located near the customary haunts of their intended targets, such as race courses, were preferred (Heintz 1998). At Rome the Capitoline hill around the Temple of Jupiter Optimus Maximus was sheathed in bronze documents—statutes, treaties, honorific decrees and, especially, military diplomas (some 3,000 were reportedly destroyed by fire in 69 CE: Suet., *Vesp.* 8.5)—which derived authority from being displayed near the religious center of the state (Williamson 1987: 165–6, 179–80). With the military diplomas, prestige accrued also from their proximity to the military treasury and to monuments associated with victorious battles (Dušanić 1984). The oracle of Apollo at Oenoanda was carved high on the outside of the town wall, facing east, so that it would catch the first light of the rising sun (see above, page 14). For the same reason, pilgrims to the "speaking" colossus of Memnon in the Valley of the Kings (Bernand–Bernand 1960) and to the temple of Mandulis at Talmis in upper Egypt carved or scratched or painted their testaments to the manifest power of the sun on the eastern faces of those monuments (Lane Fox 1986: 166–7).

Presentation mattered. Curse tablets were folded and pierced with nails, because the transfixing of the object was thought to reinforce the binding power of its textual spell (Piccaluga 1983). In the example from the Via Appia described above (Figure 1.3), holes were punched in the lead at the places where the head and heart of the intended victim were represented, to pinpoint the location of the target. Orphic leaves were placed in the mouths of corpses, so that the words of their prayers would be ready on the tongue and thus easy to deliver (Guarducci 1974: 15–17). Votive dedications were carved on miniature altars, so that the inscription would not only verbally attest but could physically represent the fulfillment of the vow (Veyne 1983: 286–8). Similar thinking no doubt inspired the fashioning into the cylindrical shape of Roman milestones of four silver cups dedicated at the thermal springs of Vicarello on the shores of Lake Bracciano north of Rome sometime during the third century BCE, which record a complete itinerary of the land route from Gades to Rome, with the names of more than 100 towns and stopping points and the distances between them (from five to 32 miles) engraved in parallel vertical columns around the circumference (*CIL* XI 3281–4).

Examples could be multiplied. The point to note, in all these cases, is that the material on which the text was inscribed or the place in which the object was located or the way in which the inscription was displayed had nothing to do with its legibility but was dictated instead by some extra-textual function it was meant to serve.

Visible words[10]

Other than their power to activate speech or to represent writing symbolically, inscriptions conveyed their meaning visually, in a variety of ways. As integral elements of the monuments they accompanied, inscribed texts from an early date contributed to a complex semiological message of which their contents constituted only a part. The funerary statue of a Greek girl buried in the Attic deme of Myrrhinous around the middle of the sixth century BCE holds in its hand a closed lotus flower, a symbol of the domestic hearth and hence of the source of her reputation, and thus engages in iconographic dialogue with the "speaking" text of the accompanying epigram (*IG* I² 1014 = *GVI* 68), which declares itself to be the monument (σῆμα) of the maiden Phrasikleia, whose name means "she who draws (or pays) attention to her fame" (Svenbro 1993: 8–25). Seven hundred years later, toward the end of the second century CE, someone at Ostia erected to a certain M. Modius Maxximus, a chief priest (*archigallus*) in the precinct of the Magna Mater, a curious monument consisting of a stone cylinder in the shape of a Roman corn-measure (*modius*) crowned by a cock (*gallus*) whose tail turns into ears of corn (bounty of Cybele, for the *modius*?); on the side of the cylinder are inscribed Maxximus' name and office, with the anomalous double Xs of the *cognomen* slightly outsized and centrally disposed, and with the words of his title divided by a sculpted representation of Pan-pipes (a distinctive instrument of the cult); around the inscription are depicted scenes from the life of Attis, beginning with his abandonment as a baby on the banks of the river Gallus (*CIL* XIV 385 = *ILS* 4162). Each of the artistic elements of Maxximus' monument responds verbally or visually to some aspect of his life, his name, or his position as a priest of Cybele (Beard 1998: 83–8). During the classical and Hellenistic periods of Greece and especially under the Roman empire, beginning with the age of Augustus, grave monuments of this sort presenting visual puns in the form of artistic representations of objects or ideas associated with the name of the deceased—and, occasionally, as with Phrasikleia, suggesting an essential character trait—enjoyed a notable vogue (Ritti 1974–5, 1977). The inscriptions of Maxximus and Phrasikleia are unusual only in going beyond mere word play: not only the verbal content but the graphic presentation (MaXXimus) and acoustic vocalization (Svenbro 1993: 17–18) of the texts support the iconographic imagery of the monuments in representing the lives of their subjects.

The lettering of epitaphs inscribed on Roman gravestones and tombs regularly worked with other visible features of the monuments to entice passersby to approach and learn the identity of the deceased: lines of writing defined vertical and horizontal spaces and articulated architectural forms; names written large beneath sculpted busts labeled portraits and established identities; funerary epigrams in smaller letters explained figured scenes or described familial relationships or enumerated personal qualities of the deceased (Sanders 1970; Koortbojian 1996). How the letters were laid out and marked on the stone determined how they were read and understood. Beginning in the second century BCE in Greek epitaphs (*GVI* 662 seems to be the earliest example) and from the second century CE in Latin texts, acrostichs (sometimes telestichs, rarely mesostichs) spelled out the name of the deceased or, less often, that of the dedicator or some other message (Barbieri 1975: 364–71; 1977: 339–42; Sanders 1979). When a name was inscribed both vertically and horizontally, with the first letter serving as the pivot (as, e.g. in *CLE* 301, 514; *AE* 1967, 113), the narrative and visual elements of the inscription coincided. Reading and viewing were in these instances inextricably combined.

Inscribed palindromes (e.g. *CIL* IV 2400a, ἤδη μοι Διὸς ἆρ᾽ ἀπάτα παρά σοι Διομήδη), word patterns keyed to a central letter (Bua 1971; cf. *SEG* 8.464) and magic word squares (Guarducci 1965) took this synthesis of reading and viewing to an extreme. Letter games that seemed to embody mystical qualities of harmony and balance were eventually coopted by religious sects (notably Christianity), which imputed to them a symbolic significance, but they originated in the pagan world as epigraphic *jeux d'esprit* (Guarducci 1978).[11] One type of inscribed gameboard popular in Rome for the game of "Twelve Writings" exploited a widely perceived relationship between letters and numbers (Dornseiff 1925: 11–14) by employing a standardized grid of letters arranged in six groups of six to spell out various banal exhortations designed to attract players (Purcell 1995: 18–19, 28–37).

Funerary and gaming texts were not the only types of inscriptions that conveyed their messages through their visible form. The names and formulae stamped or scratched onto small portable objects (*instrumentum domesticum*) were often repeated, as if to reinforce their texts in compensation for the object's mobility and consequent instability. Large bronze letters inset into pavements were designed to be read by walking across their epigraphic fields: their fixed stability imposed mobility on the viewer (cf. Susini 1987–8). Certain inscriptions depended upon the interplay of light and shadow to activate their texts. The vast sundial laid out by

Augustus in the Campus Martius in Rome in 10 BCE presents a striking example of the last two types (Buchner 1996). Inlaid on either side of a meridian line stretching across a travertine pavement some 160 meters wide and 75 meters long, large bronze Greek letters, twenty-five centimeters tall, set one to one-and-a-half meters apart, spelled out the signs of the zodiac. In order to read the sundial, the viewer had to walk across the face of the monument where the shadow fell and thus to experience the relationship between the Greek text, the Egyptian obelisk (the first in Rome) that served as the gnomon, with its hieroglyphics commemorating Psammetichus II, the pedestal from which it rose, recording in Latin that "Augustus gave it as a gift to the Sun, Egypt having been brought under the sway of the Roman people," (*CIL* VI 702 = *ILS* 91), and the Roman Ara Pacis axially aligned to the east, which celebrated the peace that united Greece and Egypt under the benevolent light of the new Roman sun god, Apollo. Monument and inscriptional text, or rather texts—in Greek, Latin, and pictographic Egyptian—here combined to express the triumph of the Augustan peace.

Sometimes visual aesthetics compromised comprehensibility. The earliest inscribed writing generally followed the contours of the objects it adorned and eventually, when words came to be inscribed in their own right on flat surfaces, replicated the pattern of an ox plowing, first in one direction then in the other, turning at the end of each furrow (*boustrophedon*), so that the reader's eye never had to leave the text. The fashion that developed in Attica during the classical period, however, of inscribing texts, particularly decrees, in a checkerboard pattern (*stoichedon*) made reading difficult, since the treatment of individual letters as figures in a geometric design obscured word-division and broke words irregularly at the ends of lines (Woodhead 1981: 24–34). Clarity and beauty, as measured by balance and symmetry and the precise carving of individual letters, were in these cases paramount, and legibility was not a primary concern (Austin 1938; see Figures 1.4, 1.5).[12] By contrast the Roman penchant during the early Empire for scaling and framing produced texts that were not only laid out logically in accordance with their contents (Sartori 1995) but were designed to be read from the perspectives from which they were viewed—by readers moving along a road or gazing upward at a monumental facade (Susini 1988; 1992; see Figure 3.2). Aesthetic considerations in these instances served the interest of functionality.

Human figures in paintings and mosaics were regularly identified by labels, and captions of other sorts accompanied figured scenes in both media. The so-called *tabulae Iliacae*—stone plaques depicting episodes from

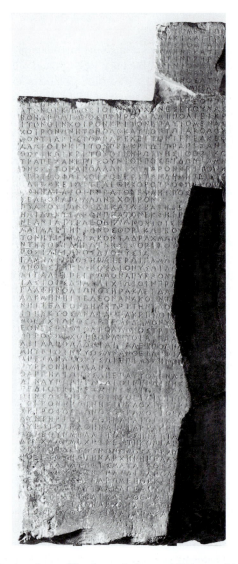

Figure 1.4 Calendar from Thorikos, Attica, exhibiting *stoichedon* writing. Pentelic marble (132 × 56 × 18–19 cm), c. 385–370 BCE? (*IG* I³ 256 *bis* [addenda]; cf. Daux 1983; *SEG* 33, 147; *Bull. ép.* 1984, 190). The text, written continuously, records the sacrifices due each month, beginning with Hecatombeion (July–August), which is named at the end of line 1 and the beginning of line 2. Traces of the horizontal guidelines used to align the letters are visible along the left side of the stone. (The J. Paul Getty Museum, Malibu, California, unknown artist, religious calendar of Thorikos, 440–430 BCE? CA.Malibu.JPGM.G.79.AA.113.)

Figure 1.5 Calendar from Thorikos, Attica. Detail of Figure 1.4 showing the beginning of lines 32–44 (the left side of the stone, about half way down). Despite the quality of the lettering, the text is replete with carver's errors, and its checkerboard layout, with no spaces between words, does little to facilitate reading of the monthly record (The J. Paul Getty Museum, Malibu, California).

the Trojan cycle (and other legends) sculpted in low relief and surrounded by inscribed summaries, commentary, quotation and a miscellany of obscure and often faulty erudition—present an interesting case, inasmuch as the carved letters are so small and the texts, which are not always related to the images they accompany, are so full of mistakes that the writing seems designed to decorate rather than to explicate the figured scenes (Sadurska 1964; Horsfall 1979, 1983b). In other media inscriptions were incorporated into pictorial representations as part of the image itself. Written texts insinuated themselves into the pictorial field as ornamental parts of the design, and recognizable types of inscribed monument—funerary stelae, building dedications, portable placards, and the like—appeared as realistic or symbolic elements in pictorial compositions (Lissarague 1988; Corbier 1995).

Sometimes inscribed writing bridged the gap between figural and verbal representation. The funerary altar erected at Rome for a boy, Q. Sulpicius Maximus, dead at the age of 11, commemorates his success in the Capitoline poetic competition of 94 CE with a Latin epitaph dedicated by his parents, a full-figure sculpted portrait of the boy clad in a toga, and three Greek poems: two ten-verse funerary epigrams about the boy and the 43 extempore hexameters for which he won acclaim, of which the last three verses (completing a text carved mainly along the left side of the front face of the altar) are inscribed on an open book roll held in the boy's left hand (*IG* XIV 2012 = *CIL* VI 33976; cf. Gordon 1983: no. 52). Here the conventional vocabularies of the standard vehicles of commemoration in Greek and Roman funerary monuments—a portrait of the deceased and an inscribed epitaph—have been transposed and blended into a synthetic whole: the verbal text not only describes but represents, in the Roman *tria nomina* and the Greek hexameters, the boy's virtues as Roman citizen and poet; at the same time the words themselves lead physically into a visual portrayal of the boy that conveys, in the sculpted toga and the book roll (symbolically rather than factually, inasmuch as he had not yet reached the age for assuming the *toga virilis* and his performance at the Capitoline contest had been oral and extempore), the sources of his well deserved fame. The interplay between visual and verbal representation is in this instance unusually rich, but many less elaborate monuments similarly drew upon the physical visibility of inscribed writing to effect a unifying and integrative relationship between image and text.

Epitaphs

Epitaphs account for perhaps two-thirds of all surviving Greek and Latin inscriptions and provide our most informative epigraphic evidence—indeed, overall our best ancient evidence—for the lives of persons below the upper levels of society.[13] They are instructive in a variety of ways, some of which have been suggested in the preceding paragraphs and several of which are discussed below in Chapter 3, on onomastics and prosopography, and Chapter 4, on the family and social status. Here it will be enough to indicate briefly two fundamentally different ways in which they can be of use to the ancient historian by providing both a macroscopic and a microscopic view of the ancient world.

Epitaphs are helpful for two apparently contradictory reasons: because they tend to exhibit recognizable formal and rhetorical conventions and survive in sufficient quantities to permit meaningful statistical

analysis and because, in individual instances, they depart from the predictable patterns and offer unexpected glimpses of particular lives. They
are usefully studied, in other words, both in bulk, where they can illuminate broad historical trends, and individually, as unique documents,
where they add flesh to the skeletal structures of ancient society. Often
the same inscription can serve both purposes, although it is normally
difficult to consider a text from both perspectives simultaneously. In fact
epitaphs are most beneficial for statistical arguments when the constituent
elements of their texts are isolated and registered singly, and for individual study when they are considered in their entirety, both as verbal
documents and as physical artifacts; in practice, the two approaches
cannot—and should not—be divorced from each other: each benefits
the other. A gravestone set up at Puteoli sometime in the late first or
early second century CE by a certain L. Herennius Epaphroditus may
illustrate the point (Figure 1.6).

The text, as printed in *L'Année épigraphique*, reads as follows:

> Dis Manibus. / L. Herennius Epaphroditus / sibi et Herenniae Clade
> et He/renniae Marcellae patronabus /[5] et Herennio Fideli et
> Herennio / Crescenti et Herenniae Tyche con/iugi suae et libertis
> meis liber/tabusque posterisque eorum et / Volussio Lamyro
> nepoti et Herennio Synergo /[10] et Herennio Africano et Hereniae
> Meniadi.
>
> (*AE* 1974, 251)[14]

From this typical epitaph a number of discrete "facts" can be extracted
and marshaled as evidence for the geographical distribution and interrelation of Latin *nomina gentilicia* (Herennius and Volusius) or of Latin
(Marcella, Fidelis, Crescens, Africanus) and Greek (Epaphroditus,
Clade, Tyche, Lamyrus, Synergus, Menias) *cognomina*; for the workings
of Roman patronage (the freedman Epaphroditus provides space in his
monument for his two patronesses and for his own freedmen and
freedwomen and their descendants); for family structures (both a wife,
coniunx, and a *nepos*—whether nephew or grandson is uncertain—are
explicitly mentioned); and so on. Each of these items of information can
usefully be compiled and compared with similarly acquired data to yield
a broad picture of the particular socio-historical questions they concern
(see further below, Chapters 3 and 4).

The same epitaph, considered as a whole, suggests a different set of
questions. An initial examination of the stone prompts several observations. In contrast to the generous fullness of the text (except for the *praenomen*

Figure 1.6 Gravestone of L. Herennius Epaphroditus from Puteoli (Pozzuoli), Italy. Marble (63.5 × 53.5 × 0.6 cm), c. 75–125 CE? (*AE* 1974, 251 = D'Arms 1973: 156–7, pl. 29, Fig. 5). The text records an epitaph erected by a freedman for himself, his two patronesses, two other Herennii, his wife, and his own freedmen and their descendants. The last two lines, inscribed in a different hand, record the subsequent addition of four other persons to the monument. Line 7 shows an erasure and the word *meis*, evidently intended for the space occupied by the cancelled text, written above the line (Kelsey Museum of Archaeology, Ann Arbor: MI.AA.UM.KM.L.1053).

of the dedicant, no words are abbreviated), the letters are unevenly aligned and irregularly cut, and the slab itself, oblong rather than rectangular, has been roughly chiseled away along the lower edge (possibly in modern times): this is not a first-rate piece of workmanship. In line 7, five or six letters have been erased after the word *libertis* and the word *meis* is carved above the line just before the cancelled text; closer inspection reveals traces of a vertical stroke at the start of the erased spaces. It is plausible to suppose that the carver began to inscribe the word *libertabus*, realized his omission of *meis*, chiseled out the mistaken letters, and supplied the omitted word where it could be fit in. Finally, the last two lines were evidently added after the initial text was carved, by a different hand (note the more "rustic" shapes of the letters, particularly M and N, and the use of medial interpuncts between words).

Of what use are these observations? First, the initial omission of *meis*: why? Stone carvers made mistakes for a variety of reasons (Solin 1995), among the most common of which was force of habit. Comparison of thousands of Roman epitaphs in which the owners of tombs made provision for the inclusion within their monuments of freedmen and their descendants (that is, resort to the methods of studying inscriptions in bulk) reveals that the formulaic phrase *libertis libertabusque posterisque eorum* is extremely common and that the intrusion into this formula of a restrictive adjective is rare. The carver's slip in this instance calls our attention to the restriction of occupancy of Epaphroditus' tomb to his own freedmen and the exclusion of those of his wife. A freedman who both explicitly provides a place in his tomb for his own two patrons and excludes the freedmen of his wife is considerably more interesting for the history of Roman patron–freedman relations and the construction of the Roman *familia* than one who conforms to more conventional practices. Second, recognizing that the last two lines of Epaphroditus' epitaph were not part of its original composition—a fact obscured by a simple transcription of its text—casts their testimony about the configuration of the Roman family in a new light: the apparent inclusion of a *nepos* in Epaphroditus' tomb cannot, without qualification, here be taken as evidence in favor of the theory that familial relationships were organized along lines of agnatic descent rather than around the nuclear family, since we cannot assume that Epaphroditus himself intended to include the *nepos* in his monument (cf. below, pages 100–2). The addition of the last two lines may indeed reflect Epaphroditus' own subsequent revision of his plans for his monument, but the provision within the tomb of burial space for the four persons named may equally well have been made without Epaphroditus' consent, or even against his wishes, after his death. We do not know.

Consideration of the sequence of persons mentioned in the text raises further questions not likely to emerge from an examination of the names and social relationships individually. It is reasonable to surmise, from their "respectable" Latin *cognomina* and the recording of their names between those of Epaphroditus' two patrons and his wife, that Fidelis and Crescens were the freeborn sons of Epaphroditus and Tyche; but, if so, why was their freeborn status (normally an object of pride among the descendants of ex-slaves) not indicated by "filiation" (see below) in the normal fashion (D'Arms 1973: 156–7)? Perhaps they were Junian Latins, a juridical status held by many informally manumitted slaves and their offspring during the early imperial period, of which we could scarcely guess the importance without epigraphy (Weaver 1990, 1991). And what, if anything, may we conclude about relative positions of honor or prestige—or rather, about the conventions of representing those positions in funerary commemoration—from the fact that Epaphroditus names himself first, then his patrons, then his sons (let us assume), and only then his wife? There are various possible answers to these questions, and a variety of extenuating circumstances might shape our interpretation of their significance. We need not here enter into details; it is enough to recognize that the questions would not arise if we did not consider the epitaph comprehensively as a coherent document with its own internal organization and structure.

The sorts of questions posed in the last paragraph raise an issue of fundamental importance for the interpretation of any epitaph—or indeed of any inscription—that of epigraphic bias. With this phrase I mean to describe the distortion introduced into any set of data derived from inscriptions by the fact that inscriptions are the source of the information in question. The selection of what to inscribe and in what form to write it was never determined solely by what one wished to communicate or to record but by what was considered appropriate to communicate or to record in inscribed writing on a particular object in a particular place at a particular time. When Trimalchio, the fictional freedman hero of Petronius' novel, rehearses the text of his epitaph to his dinner guests and asks the stonemason commissioned to inscribe the stone whether it seems suitable enough (71.12), the answer almost certainly is "no," but not because the claims it makes are wholly out of line with the social realities of Neronian Italy. Rather the humor derives from Trimalchio's subtle distortion of a narrowly circumscribed and readily recognizable set of epitaphic conventions (D'Arms 1981: 108–16; Beard 1998: 95–8). In the real world manifestations of this epigraphic bias can often be readily identified. When Roman grave markers from Spain proclaim with unusual frequency the piety of the persons they commemorate (Curchin 1982: 180–1), or when the epithet προσφιλής is found almost exclusively on gravestones from Thasos (Tod 1951: 184, 187), the inference to be drawn is not that Spaniards were exceptionally pious or that Thasians enjoyed a monopoly in kindliness but that the local customs of funerary commemoration favored recognition of those qualities in inscribed epitaphs. No one would conclude from the relative paucity of tombstones erected to parents at Rome that mothers and fathers were unimportant in the Roman family (Nielsen 1997: 172–3), since too much literary, legal, and artistic evidence points to the opposite conclusion. But when inscriptions constitute a principal source of direct information on issues on which our other sources are silent, their testimony has not always been treated with the caution it deserves, and the consequences of this form of epigraphic bias have not always been adequately recognized.

Epitaphs in bulk

Perhaps the most notorious case of a quantity of epigraphic evidence seducing the unwary into believing that its testimony, because explicit and abundant, is also accurate and representative centers on the question of life expectancy. Roman tombstones from throughout the western Mediterranean and ranging over half a dozen centuries of imperial rule provide tens of thousands of detailed records of ages at death. The data have been compiled, tabulated, categorized, and averaged to produce impressive looking statistics (Szilagyi 1961–7) which have in turn formed the basis for broad generalizations about Roman mortality. Their value as evidence for this purpose, however, is severely compromised by a number of inherent biases, most of which cannot be corrected (Hopkins 1966, 1987). Compared with the majority of Romans, those commemorated with inscribed epitaphs were not a representative cross-section of the population but were, for example, more wealthy (tombstones were not expensive, but not everyone could afford one) and more likely to have lived, or at least to have been buried, near cities and towns than in the countryside. Furthermore, those whose epitaphs recorded an age at death tended to have survived infancy and early childhood, whereas a great many Romans—perhaps as many as a third—died before reaching their fifth birthday. On the other hand, a disproportionate number of those whose ages are specified seem to have died either young or (especially in Africa) improbably old (cf. Shaw 1984: 473–81; 1991: 75–6). A suspiciously high percentage of those who lived neither very long nor only into adolescence is reported to have died at ages precisely divisible by five, which suggests that age-rounding (a common phenomenon in societies where accurate birth-records are not kept systematically), as well as age-exaggeration and a widespread propensity to remark the ages of those who died before their time, probably further distorts the picture and raises the possibility that even those recorded ages that are not multiples of five may not be based on accurate information (Duncan-Jones 1990: 79–92, 101–3). Geographical and chronological variation and an imbalance in the sex-ratio represented (roughly three males are commemorated for every two females) further vitiate the sample, so that it is almost impossible to extrapolate any meaningful conclusions about mortality rates from the surviving epitaphs (Parkin 1992: 5–19).

What the data reflect are not demographic realities but commemorative practices, and these, unlike biological necessities, might vary considerably for cultural reasons independent of the more easily identifiable variables of time and place and economic status. A single example may suffice to illustrate the point. From the city of Rome, during the early imperial period, a sizable sample of some 9,980 recorded ages at death yields an average life-expectancy at birth of under 23 years—a plausible number. If, however, one considers from this sample only the epitaphs written in Greek (822 in number), the figure for average life-expectancy rises to 51, a number not matched in modern western European society until well into the nineteenth century (Éry 1969: 60). That Greek-speakers residing alongside other Romans in a mixed population lived more than twice as long as their Latin-speaking neighbors is inherently unlikely; more plausibly the discrepancy is to be accounted for by a difference in behavior—in this case, in the recording of ages at death on tombstones—between the two groups.

Recognizing that epitaphs attest commemorative habits rather than demographic realities does not diminish their value as evidence but merely reorients our attention to a different set of questions, of which the most basic are: who commemorated whom, and why? In a groundbreaking article in which a large sample of some 12,000–13,000 tombstones from the western provinces was surveyed, R. Saller and B. Shaw found that close-family relationships (father–mother–child) were commemorated much more frequently than any other type and argued from this evidence that Roman kinship relations were mainly organized around the nuclear rather than the extended family (Saller–Shaw 1984; cf. Shaw 1984). Their methodology has been criticized on the grounds that counting individual relationships rather than groups of relationships as attested in individual inscriptions—a potential hazard of the standard technique of studying epitaphs in bulk rather than independently as self-contained documents—prejudices the results in favor of the nuclear family and underrepresents the evidence for other arrangements. Examination of some 1,160 epitaphs from seven cities and regions of Roman Asia Minor (those collected in *TAM*) suggests the prominence there of a Roman household characterized by extended kinship relationships (D. B. Martin 1996). But familial organization and household configuration are not the same thing (the arguments of

Saller and Shaw leave open the question of how Roman households were constituted), and the survey of epitaphs from Asia Minor arbitrarily centers on one of several different types (the inclusive style of Olympus in Lycia) to the exclusion of others (Rawson 1997). What emerges most suggestively from the critique of Saller's and Shaw's arguments are the multiplicity of familial relationships manifested in the epitaphs of Asia Minor and the possibility of a broad difference in commemorative practices between the inhabitants of the eastern and western parts of the Roman empire. A more fundamental question concerns the relationship between commemorative behavior and social organization, to what extent, that is, the conventions of inscribed epitaphs meaningfully reflect either familial structures or household configuration.

Consideration of the patterns of personal relationships attested in Roman epitaphs has led others to different conclusions. In attempting to explain MacMullen's profile of the rise and fall of an epigraphic habit, E. Meyer (1990) concluded not only that Roman epitaphs represent social assertions of the privileged status of citizen (see above, page 6) but that in most cases (those in which both the deceased and the commemorator are named, around 80 per cent in the western provinces) heirship rather than kinship was the principal reason for setting up a grave monument. The link between inheritance and commissioning an epitaph to the deceased, however, is tenuous and indirect, and several prominent categories of commemorative relationship (e.g. of father to child or of husband to wife) argue against the idea that heirship was the principal motivation for Roman funerary commemoration (Saller 1994: 98–9; Cherry 1995: 150–6; see below, page 102).

The second part of Meyer's thesis associating the erection of an epitaph with a claim to membership in a privileged body of citizens she further developed in a subsequent article and extended to classical Athens, where she detected a similarly striking peak in the numbers of inscribed funerary monuments erected in Attica during the fourth century BCE, precisely the period when citizenship in the Athenian *polis* was most highly valued (Meyer 1993). This apparent burst of commemorative activity following a significant change in the political and social value of citizenship (triggered, perhaps, by the overthrow of the oligarchs in 403 BCE: Meyer 1993: 117–19), conformed nicely with the picture of the Roman evidence elaborated earlier, where the so-called *constitutio Antoniniana* of the emperor Caracalla extending Roman citizenship to all free inhabitants of the empire in 212 CE had seemed to explain the sudden drop in Roman commemorations during the third century (Meyer 1990: 89–90). As with the Roman epitaphs, however (see above), establishing the chronological parameters of the phenomenon is problematic. The lumping together of dated and undated material into temporal blocks defined by 25-year intervals, the arbitrary assignation of much of the undated material (e.g. epitaphs labeled "first–second century CE" are divided, equally it seems, between the periods 75–100 CE and 100–125 CE), and the uncertain foundations—and, in many cases, spurious precision—of much of the dated evidence render the conclusions suspect. What are in effect being charted by chronological analyses of this sort are not—or, at any rate, not necessarily—historical changes but modern dating methods, in this case those of J. Kirchner in *IG* II and III² (cf. Cherry 1995: 147). To the argument that Kirchner's dates are stable, in the sense that they have not, by and large, been overturned by subsequent scholarship (Meyer 1993: 121), it may be observed that neither have they been confirmed or rendered more precise. However attractive in appearance the results, attributing broad shifts in funerary commemorative practice to specific political events, no matter how consequential, requires sharply focused investigation of the historical circumstances surrounding the presumed watershed, and for this purpose the very general and often tentative datings assigned by modern scholars to inscribed epitaphs provide an exceedingly blunt instrument.

More reliably, epitaphs, in bulk, can be compared with other types of inscription, in bulk, to demonstrate broad chronological or demographic developments. For example, although Athenian gravestones do not in themselves provide an accurate indicator of the size of the citizen population, when considered beside lists of *prytaneis* and ephebes, they indicate that the demes of Attica fluctuated in size from the fourth century BCE through the Roman period, whereas the population as a whole declined in Hellenistic times and rose sharply again under Roman imperial rule (Hansen et al., 1990; cf. Hedrick 1999: 393–5). Comparison of the profiles of pagan and Christian epigraphy in late antiquity reveals that while the number of non-funerary inscriptions steadily declined after the middle of the third century CE, a resurgence of epitaphs beginning in the second half of the fourth century marked the spread of Christianity to the lower classes and the rise of a specifically Christian "epitaphic habit" (Galvao-Sobrinho 1995; cf. Shaw 1996: 105–7). By measuring the production of epitaphs against the production of other types of inscription within a well-defined, epigraphically self-contained, geographical area (Attica) or with the aim of identifying a phenomenon that, though varying from region to region, is fundamentally independent of regional variation (being a Christian, which is more absolute and easily defined than, for example, being a

Roman), and by attempting to chart changes only broadly, over centuries rather than decades, studies such as these avoid some of the risks that any analysis of inscriptions in bulk is bound to entail.

Individual biographies

When studied singly, epitaphs usefully illuminate aspects of ancient life rarely seen in other sources (papyri are a notable exception) by opening windows onto individual lives. Biographical themes in Greek and Latin epitaphs cover a wide variety of human experience but tend to fall into several basic categories—causes of death, reversals of fortune, the accomplishments of the deceased—with Roman gravestones (both Greek and Latin) generally providing greater detail and wider variety of circumstance than their classical Greek counterparts (Lattimore 1942: 266–300). The most informative examples are funerary poems (*carmina funeraria*), which tend to combine greater freedom of expression with a propensity to articulate not only personal vicissitudes but individual attitudes and values, aspirations and regrets. Three examples may suffice to suggest the sort of detailed perspectives these miniature biographies can offer on three areas of Roman life commonly studied by analysis of inscriptions in bulk: the cultural "Romanization" (an inadequate but convenient term) of native populations in the provinces; marital arrangements and the configuration of Roman households; and civic identity and political life in Roman towns.

Sometime around the middle of the second century CE, T. Flavius Secundus, the patriarch of a leading family of the Roman colony of Cillium in the province of Africa Proconsularis (just south of modern Kasserine, Tunisia) erected for his father and namesake, and for himself, a three-storey tower-mausoleum on which he eventually had carved two inscriptions, a dedicatory register naming the family members buried inside (*CIL* VIII 211) and an extensive Latin verse epitaph (the longest known), in two parts: 90 hexameters, in which the elder Secundus converses with his heir, declaring his pride in the filial piety manifested by the construction of such a magnificent monument and epitaph, and a 20-line coda in elegiac couplets (not coincidentally bringing the total number of verses to 110, precisely the number of years the elder Secundus is said to have lived—another instance of symbolic epigraphy), in which the younger Secundus professes to have forgotten to mention in the earlier poem a weather-vane in the form of a cock in flight that crowns the structure (*CIL* VIII 212–13 = *CLE* 1552 = Courtney 1995: no. 199A–B). The elder Secundus, the first Roman citizen of the family, won his citizenship after 33 years of service as an auxiliary soldier in the Roman army and achieved wealth and status in his community by becoming the first in the region to grow vines—specifically, that is, by applying native African techniques of irrigation to the cultivation of a characteristically Roman crop (A 51–3). Throughout the first poem, reflections on the elder Secundus' afterlife and the journey of his soul through the underworld are linked with the permanency of his monument as a guarantee of his immortality—a typically Greco-Roman sentiment expressed through the typically Greco-Roman medium of an inscribed funerary poem. The second poem, focusing on the weather-cock at the summit of the mausoleum (B 11–16), introduces a distinctive symbol of Libyo-Punic mortuary expression. Like the tower-mausoleum structure, an African architectural form, which is explicitly set into a Greco-Roman context by hyperbolic comparison with the lighthouse at Alexandria, the colossus of Nero, and the obelisk of the Circus Maximus at Rome (A 79–85), Secundus' inscribed verse epitaph represents a fusion of Greco-Roman and native Libyan concepts and modes of expression (*Les Flavii de Cillium* 1993; Hitchner 1995).

Allia Potestas of Perugia was an exemplary freedwoman, as the verse epitaph erected at Rome by her patron sometime in the late second or third century CE amply attests (*CIL* VI 37965 = *CLE* 1988 = Gordon 1983: no. 65). Funerary epigraphy provides our best and most abundant evidence for women—or the ideal of women—in the ancient Roman world (see below, pages 103–4, on "Turia" and Murdia), but even against this background Allia stands out (Horsfall 1985). Among other more traditional virtues, she was first to rise for work and last to retire at night (12–13); she was not unduly pleased with herself and never imagined herself a free(born) woman (16). That her hands were hard merely showed how hard she worked (24–5). In describing her beauty, Allius departs from convention to describe in rare (and idiosyncratic) erotic detail the shape of the breasts on her snow-white chest, the position of her legs, like those of Atalanta on the comic stage, and the generous way she shared her lovely body (20–3). Now that she is gone, Allius bears her name engraved in gold on his arm (40–1) and reveres a likeness of her with garlands (44–5). Most strikingly, Allia managed two young lovers, who lived together (with her?) under one roof, like Pylades and Orestes; since her death they have grown apart and grown old (28–31; Horsfall 1985: 265–7). It seems easiest to imagine that Allius himself is one of the two lovers, but even so, the sort of arrangement that made the freedwoman Allia the nucleus of a triangular relationship involving her patron and another male lover who lived together as friends casts unexpected light on the complexity of patron–freed relations and on the manifold variety of configurations possible in the Roman household.

Municipal benefaction was the engine that drove the Roman civic enterprise, and honorary inscriptions of the first two centuries CE generally give the impression of a smoothly running machine. The epitaph, now fragmentary, erected near Ausugum in the Italian Alps by a wife for her husband sometime in the second half of the first century CE presents a different picture (*CIL* V 5049 = *CLE* 417 = *Suppl. Ital.* n.s. 12: 162–5 = Courtney 1995: no. 108). The man had produced a wonderful gladiatorial spectacle and at personal expense had subsidized the purchase of grain on three occasions, in return for which some grateful men honored him as patron with a gilded statue (1–7). But this aroused the envy of the local citizenry who, swarming like locusts, tried to drive him out (8–15). Here the inscription breaks off, and we do not know the end of the story. But the tantalizing glimpse the narrative provides of popular politics in a Roman municipality, with its suggestion of rivalries among the local aristocracy, enriches our understanding of the vibrant civic life of early imperial Rome, which emerges as less placid and more dynamic than the stately parade of contemporary honorific inscriptions would otherwise make it seem (see Wistrand 1981, who, following Mommsen, believes the text to be a votive, rather than a sepulchral, inscription; F. Martin 1996).

The standard corpora of Greek and Latin inscriptions contain thousands of stories such as these. Individually engaging, occasionally curious, collectively they add detail and color to the social history of the ancient world.

Inscriptions and literature

The relationships between epigraphy and literature are numerous and various. Since 1959 the *Bulletin épigraphique* each year has registered under the heading "Rapports avec la littérature" various contributions pertaining to the Greek world, and there is a helpful (if now somewhat out-of-date) synthetic overview of the subject for Roman authors and Latin texts (Chevallier 1972). Ancient authors, especially historians, cite and quote inscriptions, and beginning in the fourth century BCE some Greek antiquarians, notably Craterus of Macedon (*FGrH* 342), systematically sought out and published collections of epigraphic documents (Stein 1931; Higbie 1999). Certain Greek inscriptions record historiographical narratives of a sort more normally associated with literary works (Chaniotis 1988), and some extensive epigraphic texts, such as the Epicurean treatise of Diogenes of Oenoanda (see above, page 14) or the funerary praises of the Roman matron known as "Turia" (see below, pages 103–4), present carefully written compositions of a non-historiographical nature that deserve to be analyzed as works of literature in their own right (cf. Millar 1983: 98–110). Even shorter, more formulaic, inscriptions exhibit their own stylistic conventions and artistic modeling, so that one can properly speak of a distinctly epigraphical form of rhetoric (Judge 1997). Inscribed poetry, in particular, has profitably been subjected to stylistic and thematic analysis of the sort regularly applied to literary texts (e.g. Galletier 1922; Robert 1940–65: vol. 4; Cugusi 1985), and the influence of individual authors on *carmina epigraphica* and of epigraphic poems on literary compositions has been productively explored. Here it will be enough to mention a pair of exemplary studies, on Vergil (Hoogma 1969) and on the Neronian epigrammatist Lucillius (Robert 1968), and to note that new texts of literary interest come to light all the time: recently a 60-line poem of elegiac couplets in praise of Halicarnassus, datable to the second century BCE, was discovered *in situ* on the remains of an ancient wall at the promontory of Salmakis in Caria (Isager 1998). Even graffiti have yielded insights into the world of letters in antiquity, for example by evoking the literary culture of Pompeii (Gigante 1979).

The particular relevance of this theme to the ancient historian, however, concerns those cases in which inscriptions and literary sources document the same historical events or institutions and usefully illuminate one another, not only by exposing, through mutual comparison, the omissions and biases in each, but also by establishing the broader historiographical or epigraphic context into which each must be set. To cite a simple example, Thucydides reports that Pisistratus, the son of Hippias and grandson of the famous Pisistratus, during his archonship at Athens dedicated an altar in the precinct of Pythian Apollo with an inscription "in faint letters" (ἀμυδροῖς γράμμασι) that could still be read in Thucydides' day and which he quotes (6.54.6–7). In 1877 five fragments of a sculpted marble cornice bearing most of the inscription reported by Thucydides were discovered near the Ilissos (*IG* I^2 761 = *GHI* 11; cf. Guarducci 1967–78: 1.139–40). From Thucydides' narrative we learn the ancient site of the dedication and (indirectly) the date of the younger Pisistratus' archonship (probably in 522/1 BCE, certainly not later than 512/11 BCE), which allows us to place and date the inscription. From the inscribed text we observe the ἀκρίβεια of the historian and deduce that the adjective ἀμυδρός must in this context mean "faint" rather than "obscure," possibly because the painted reddening had faded, since the carved letters are clear and distinctly legible to this day. More importantly, since the letter-forms are of a style and elegance generally associated with a slightly later period, in the early fifth century BCE, the early dating of this inscription establishes an important bench-mark for measuring the development of classical Attic lettering (cf. *GHI* 11; Higbie 1999: 60–1). In this instance, the inscribing of the dedica-tion constitutes part of the historical episode Thucydides records, and he adduces the inscription in his narrative as evidence of the event. In other cases, an historical narrative is independent of an inscription docu-menting the same event and allows a more penetrating comparison of the two.

The suppression by the Roman senate of the cult of Bacchus in 186 BCE is reported at length by Livy (39.8–19) and is recorded in a decree of the senate inscribed (it seems) *in agro Teurano* on a bronze tablet dis-covered in southern Italy in 1646 and preserved, since 1727, in the Kunsthistorisches Museum in Vienna (*CIL* I² 581 = X 104 = *ILS* 18 = *ILLRP* 511; cf. Gordon 1983: 83–5 no. 8). Livy's dramatic narrative, centering on a tale of familial blackmail and intrigue, fabricates a sud-den discovery by the consul of a secret plot by a cadre of worshippers of Bacchus previously unrecognized in the heart of Rome. The sena-torial decree, which refers to both Roman and Latin worshippers and is addressed to the allied communities (lines 2–3, 8–9), confirms what other archaeological and literary evidence suggests, that the cult of Bacchus was widespread and had long been tolerated in Italy before the senate decided to suppress it in 186 BCE. Why the senate moved to exert its religious authority in this area at this time cannot be surely known, but the inscription provides a more precise indication of the target of sen-atorial concern than does Livy's account in making it clear, as Livy's narrative does not, that it was not the worship of Bacchus *per se* that was to be curbed (though it was to be reduced to a smaller scale) but the highly structured internal organization of the individual Bacchic cells (lines 10–14). The control exercised by Bacchic leaders over their fol-lowers must have posed a threat to the traditional Roman organization of familial authority vested in the *pater familias*, an aspect of contempor-ary anxieties well brought out by Livy's narrative of familial tensions but scarcely hinted at in the senatorial decree (North 1979; cf. Pailler 1988; Gruen 1990: 34–78).

Occasionally both an inscription and an historical narrative purport to represent a text they independently document. Perhaps the most famous example concerns the speech that the emperor Claudius delivered in the Roman senate in 48 CE advocating the admission of leading citizens of

Gaul into that body. The circumstances of the speech are reported and an abridged and adapted version of it is recorded by Tacitus in his *Annals* (11.23–4), and the oration itself is beautifully engraved and largely preserved on a large bronze tablet (more than 200 kilograms in weight) found at Lyons (ancient Lugdunum), where it was originally displayed (*CIL* XIII 1668 = *ILS* 212; cf. Gordon 1983: 117–18 no. 42). The two versions of the speech have been repeatedly discussed and analyzed, usually for the light they shed on Tacitus' historiographical methods, but comparison of the two also reveals fundamental differences in historical perspective between the emperor and the historian (Griffin 1982). Other well-worked examples might be invoked, but it may help to illustrate the vitality of this type of study to mention briefly two recently discovered inscriptions that bear on our understanding of Greco-Roman literature which, though hardly obscure, have not yet been fully explicated.

The first shows that it is not only historians whose writings epigraphy can illuminate. In 1981 a lead tablet preserving a *lex sacra* inscribed in the local alphabet of Selinous in Sicily was presented to the J. Paul Getty Museum. Returned to Italy in 1992, the inscription (our longest Greek inscription on lead) received its *editio princeps* a year later (Jameson–Jordan–Kotansky 1993) and has been the subject of intense discussion ever since (e.g. *SEG* 43.630). Many aspects of this remarkable document remain obscure, but its date, around the middle of the fifth century BCE, and its references to Zeus Eumenes, the Eumenides, and vengeful spirits similar to Erinyes (here called ἐλάστεροι: cf. Eurip. *IT* 970–1), make it obviously relevant to the central themes of Aeschylus' *Oresteia* (Clinton 1996: 165–70). Two independent columns of text written upside down with respect to one another concern pollution, hostile demons, and rites designed, it seems, to mark a transition of the latter from dangerous polluting entities to spirits worthy of worship. The first column, a list of rituals to named deities, is addressed to some group or community; the second is addressed to individuals harassed by wrathful ἐλάστεροι. It is probable, though not absolutely certain (North 1996: 295–9), that the pollution arises from murder and bloodshed, in which case the network of associations involving individual and community, impure and pure (and the rituals which effect a transformation from the former to the latter), murder and atonement, and ancestral spirits (*Tritopatores*) of two sorts—chthonic/heroic and pure/godlike (cf. Jameson–Jordan–Kotansky 1993: 107–14)—renders the text, if as yet imperfectly understood, of central interest not only to the history of Greek religion but to much of Greek tragedy of the fifth century.

The second text is widely known and well understood, but the questions it raises have only begun to be explored. In the late 1980s several bronze tablets (six or seven, one almost complete), recording a decree of the Roman senate passed on 10 December 20 CE posthumously condemning Cn. Calpurnius Piso for the murder of Tiberius' adopted son Germanicus and other political crimes, came to light in Andalusia (the Roman province of Baetica) in southern Spain. Together with the *tabula Siarensis*—two large fragments of a bronze tablet unearthed in the same region in 1982 and preserving senatorial decrees of December 19 CE conferring honors on Germanicus following his death in October of that year (*RS* no. 37; *AE* 1991, 20–2)—the *s(enatus) c(onsultum) de Cn. Pisone patre*, as the heading in the most complete surviving copy describes it (*SCPP*), provides an unprecedentedly detailed view of the workings of the Roman senate during one of the most significant crises in the history of the early Empire (Caballos–Eck–Fernández 1996, on the archaeological context and physical characteristics of the inscriptions; Eck–Caballos–Fernández 1996, for the historical significance of the document). It further invites comparison with the detailed account of the episode in Tacitus' *Annals* (2.41–3.19). Far more than in the case of Claudius' oration and the Lyons tablet (see above), the possibility here exists not only of analyzing the historian's reworking of his source material but of assessing the accuracy of his historical vision. What emerges clearly is the tendentiousness of both narratives, with the obsequious senate heaping blame on its isolated victim and praising the beneficent equanimity of the Princeps, and with the historian sowing seeds of doubt about Tiberius' motives and Germanicus' virtue. Significant discrepancies between the two versions center on questions of chronology, not only of Tacitus' narrative, in which an ovation celebrated by Drusus on 28 May 20 CE immediately follows the account of the trial (*Ann.* 3.19), but of the publication of the text preserved in Baetica, which refers, first, to *haec senatus consulta* (plural), to be inscribed on bronze and published wherever the emperor sees fit (*SCPP* 169), and then to *hoc senatus consultum* (the one passed on 10 December), to be published in similar fashion in the provinces and at the winter quarters of the legions (*SCPP* 170–2). Resolution of these issues, which have excited considerable debate (see, e.g. the views surveyed in Damon–Takács 1999, *passim*), will necessarily involve consideration not only of questions of historiography but of epigraphical publication, a subject on which the new document provides important textual and material evidence (Eck–Caballos–Fernández 1996: 279–87; cf. Crawford 1996: 25–34).

Pitfalls

Epigraphic bias

The most pervasive difficulty encountered by those who look to inscriptions for historical evidence is the problem of epigraphic bias discussed above in the section on epitaphs. Inscriptions seldom respond directly to the questions we want to ask of them, and the information they provide is invariably filtered through the medium by which it is transmitted. With epitaphs, the problem is essentially one of distinguishing commemorative practices from demographic and social realities; even if the bias cannot be corrected, it can be recognized and can itself become a useful object of study. The same holds with other types of inscription, although in many cases the orientation of the bias is not easy to discern. Sometimes the information inscriptions provide not only is distorted but fundamentally misrepresents the historical reality it purports to describe. Roman building inscriptions provide a case in point.

Perhaps the most widely read inscription of antiquity is the simple statement spelled out in massive bronze letters across the frieze of the façade of the Pantheon in Rome declaring that Agrippa built the structure in 27 BCE: *M. Agrippa L.f. cos tertium fecit*. In modern times it was not until the late nineteenth century that scholars recognized traces of a secondary inscription carved on the architrave giving the imperial titles of the emperors Septimius Severus and Caracalla in 202 CE and declaring that "they restored the Pantheon, deteriorated by age, with all its decoration" (*CIL* VI 896 = 31196 = *ILS* 129). In fact, stamped bricks subsequently found throughout the structure show that the monument we see was largely constructed during the early years of Hadrian's reign and that the Severan restoration was restricted to three minor areas (Bloch 1947: 102–17). Neither of the principal building inscriptions adorning the façade accurately represents the surviving structure. Claims of restoration and rebuilding such as that asserted by Septimius Severus and Caracalla are especially problematic and often bear little correspondence to the architectural realities. It is not simply a matter of exaggerating the work done, as with the alleged Severan re-building of the Pantheon "with all its decoration": temporal concepts such as "old age" (*vetustas*), the most frequently invoked reason for rebuilding, were variable; perceptions of decay were relative. Some-times entirely new buildings were represented as mere restorations in order to justify their construction (Thomas–Witschel 1992). As with epitaphs, what Roman rebuilding inscriptions attest are not historical realities but Roman attitudes toward those realities, in this case public buildings and architecture.

Sometimes, inscriptions were reused in ways that concealed their original purpose; occasionally we can recover the original texts sufficiently well to reconstruct the history of their use and reuse. One famous example is the duplex inscription carved into opposite sides of the shaft of the red-granite obelisk brought by the emperor Caligula to Rome and set up in the Vatican circus (Pliny, *NH* 16.201; *CIL* VI 882). Now partially erased on both sides, the inscription records a joint dedication to the deified Augustus and to the emperor Tiberius, that is, uniquely, as Mommsen recognized, to both a deified and a living emperor. Despite appearances, it cannot have been inscribed when the obelisk was brought to Rome by Caligula but must belong to an earlier phase of its life in Egypt, when Tiberius ruled; indeed, it was no doubt Caligula who was responsible for the partial erasure of the text carved under Tiberius (Iverson 1965). What is more, in 1962 F. Magi discovered under the surviving inscribed text traces of an earlier duplex inscription formed by individually attached bronze letters, of which only the bottoms of the holes used to hold the letters survive. According to the original text, which Magi was able to reconstruct by connecting the holes, the obelisk was originally set up at the bidding of Octavian by C. Cornelius Gallus, as *praefectus fabrum*, to celebrate the building of a Forum Iulium, evidently at Alexandria. The original letters were presumably removed following Gallus' condemnation and suicide in 26 BCE (Magi 1963; *AE* 1964, 255; cf. Alföldy 1990 and, briefly, Gordon 1983: no. 35).

More recently G. Alföldy has employed the same technique of decipherment to uncover a hidden history of the Flavian amphitheater at Rome. Beneath an inscription on the architrave of the Colosseum recording a restoration sometime in the second quarter of the fifth century CE (*CIL* VI 32089 = *ILS* 5633) Alföldy found holes for the bronze letters of the original dedication which, when connected, revealed that the structure was built by *I*[*mp.*] *T. Caes(ar) Vespas[ianus Aug(ustus)]* . . . *ex manubis* (*CIL* VI 40454a; Alföldy 1995a). To judge from the spacing of the letters, the *praenomen* "T." was squeezed in between *I*[*mp.*] and *Caes(ar)*, which suggests that Titus usurped his father Vespasian's prerogative by dedicating the building under his own name. More striking is the reference to "spoils" (*manubiae*), which can only be those of the Jewish War, celebrated in the triumph of 71 CE. The great stone amphitheater, like the Arch of Titus erected across the valley on the lower slopes of the Palatine, *in summa sacra via*, was a triumphal monument.

Sometimes epigraphic pitfalls emerge as windfalls. More often, they deceive the unwary into believing things that are not so.

Fakes

Already in antiquity the implicit authority attributed to inscribed texts led to the practice of falsifying inscriptions in order to lend credence to otherwise dubious assertions of antiquity or distinction. Herodotus, who knew that inscriptions could be forged (1.51.3–4), claimed to have transcribed in the sanctuary of Ismenian Apollo at Thebes texts carved in ancient "Cadmean" letters on three votive tripods declaring them to be gifts of the mythical persons Skaios, Laodamas, and Amphitryon (5.59–61: West 1985: 289–95). More than 400 years later Livy complained of the *falsi imaginum tituli* with which ambitious Romans attempted to glorify their ancestors (4.16.4, 8.40.4, 22.31.11; cf. Plut. *Numa* 1.1). Of greater concern to modern historians than these ancient deceptions are the numerous spurious inscriptions, mainly in Latin, fabricated from various motives ever since the Renaissance. A count made at the beginning of the twentieth century of those identified in *CIL* put their number at over 10,500, or roughly one for every fourteen authentic inscriptions then included in the corpus (Abbot 1908: 22; cf. Billanovich 1967).

Certain infamous antiquarians from the sixteenth to the nineteenth centuries raised the practice of forgery to an art. First among them, in audacity and productivity, was the Neapolitan Pirro Ligorio (1510–83), who succeeded Michelangelo in overseeing the construction of St Peter's basilica and who is (dis)credited with nearly 3,000 (more than three-quarters) of the spurious inscriptions registered in part five of volume six of *CIL*, devoted entirely to the *falsae* of Rome (Mandowsky–Mitchell 1963). Less notorious but more typical was Girolamo Asquini (1762–1837), count of Udine, who faithfully, if stolidly, recorded many genuine inscriptions in the tenth Augustan region of Italy (Venetia and Histria) before succumbing late in life to the allure of fame, which led him to fabricate a number of texts (Panciera 1970). Mommsen's judgment on Asquini was typically harsh, and the procedure he followed in *CIL* in dealing with Asquini's work was characteristically rigid: all texts known only from Asquini were relegated to the *falsae*, regardless of their inherent plausibility (*CIL* V, p. 81 ch. xxiv; cf. *CIL* IX or X, p. xi). Inevitably some genuine inscriptions were unjustly impugned (see Panciera 1970: 35–84 *passim*). The challenge of dealing with *falsae*, it emerges, is not only to avoid the spurious but not to discard the authentic, many of which are now branded as suspect in the standard corpora.

When the expertise of the forger is high, detection can prove difficult. For a hundred years following its supposed discovery in 1871 in a grave near Palestrina, the so-called *fibula Praenestina* was widely believed to preserve the oldest known Latin inscription—*Manios med fhefhaked Numasioi*, "Manios made me for Numasios"—and as such occupied a position of prominence in virtually every handbook and anthology of Latin inscriptions (*CIL* I² 3 = XIV 4123; *ILS* 8561; *ILLRP* 1). Branded a fake in 1981 in a lengthy exposé (Guarducci 1981; Gordon 1983: 75–6 no. 1; cf. Guarducci 1984–86), the *fibula* was equally vigorously defended in 1989 (Lehmann 1989) and now stands as a salutary reminder that no accumulated weight of scholarly opinion about any ancient inscription, no matter how authoritative, can ever be considered unshakably secure.

Nor is the modern forgery of ancient inscriptions limited to Latin texts. Spurious Greek inscriptions, more numerous than Latin *falsae* in antiquity (Guarducci 1967–78: 1.488–501), are still being produced today. Beginning in 1980 the texts of (so far) nine bronze tablets recording a series of decrees of the Sicilian city of Entella during the time of the First Punic War (254–241 BCE) have begun to be published and, despite (or perhaps because of) the mystery surrounding their origin and current whereabouts, have attracted considerable scholarly attention (see *SEG* 30.1117–23, 32.914, 34.934, 43.619, and most volumes in between). The authenticity of several of the tablets seems beyond dispute, but one (VII), manifestly modeled on another (VIII), is clearly a fake and now raises questions about the authenticity of the others, which have not yet been subjected to expert inspection and scientific analysis (Loomis 1994). The verdict for historians eager to exploit the fascinating glimpse these documents provide of the perspective of a minor player in one of the Hellenistic era's great military events must, for now, remain a frustrating *non liquet*.

Dating

Because inscriptions are frequently called upon to date the archaeological contexts in which they are found or the persons named in their texts, the methods by which they themselves are dated are important. Sometimes an inscription can be dated by reference in its text to some securely datable event, for example, the accession of a Roman emperor or the term of office of an Athenian archon; at others the circumstances

of an inscription's discovery—in a region known to have been first occupied or settled by Greeks or Romans at a particular date, for example,
or marking an undisturbed grave with a datable coin or other object
among the grave goods—provide a *terminus post quem* for its display in a
particular location; at others the material in which a text is inscribed or
the style of the monument that carries it allows it to be assigned to a
more or less well defined period (cf. Woodhead 1981: 52–62; Gordon
1983: 40–2). But when such indications are lacking and an undated inscription is used to date other objects or events, caution is necessary, for two
related reasons: (1) many dates assigned to individual inscriptions, especially those for which the grounds are not specified, are more approximate and uncertain than they are sometimes made to seem (cf. Badian
1968: 243–4); (2) the frequently invoked and apparently fixed chronological *termini* on which many such tentative dates are (often tacitly) based
are themselves less secure than their apparent precision suggests.

Nowhere are these hazards more treacherous than with dates established by letter-forms. The use of the three-barred sigma in Attic
inscriptions of the fifth century BCE provides a case in point. From the
early 1960s a widespread orthodoxy held that the three-barred form went
out of use abruptly around 446 BCE and that inscriptions exhibiting that
type of sigma must therefore belong to an earlier period; recently,
however, the date has been lowered by 20 or 25 years, and the whole
question must now again be considered open.[15] Furthermore, just as
epigraphic cultures developed independently, so professional stone-
cutters in individual communities employed distinctive styles of lettering. Even after the diffusion throughout the Greek world of a single
Athenian-Milesian alphabet following its official adoption at Athens
during the archonship of Eukleides in 403/2 BCE (Guarducci 1967–78:
1.85–8), stylistic developments emerged locally. Consequently, datings
based on Attic letter-forms are applicable only to texts actually carved
in Attica. More generally, any attempt to date an inscription by the style
of its lettering except according to purely local criteria must be considered suspect (Tracy 1994: 151–2; cf. Woodhead 1981: 62–6).

The same caution holds for Latin lettering and the Roman world.
In the 1950s and 1960s A. E. and J. S. Gordon examined thousands of
inscriptions on stone from the vicinity of Rome with a view to analyzing
the characteristic features of Roman letter-forms of the imperial period
(Gordon–Gordon 1958, 1964, 1965).[16] In summarizing the results of their
research, the Gordons conclude a succinct overview of particular features of lettering (shading, module, individual letter-forms, punctuation,
etc.) with the warning that their painstakingly established guidelines should

be relied upon only to suggest approximate *termini* for tentative dates for inscriptions originating from the region of Rome (Gordon–Gordon 1957: 208–17; 1958: 3). Despite the caution enjoined by those who know the material best, others have not always resisted the temptation to place more weight on palaeographical features to date inscriptions than they can effectively bear.

As all epigraphists agree, reading inscribed texts and examining their letter-forms for clues to dating is always best done by autopsy. In practice, this is often not possible, in which case consulting visual aids—squeezes, photographs, facsimiles, drawings, tracings, and the like—is the best resort. But drawings, tracings, and facsimiles are only as reliable as the draftsmen and technicians who create them (see Figures 1.8, 1.9); paper squeezes are often imperfectly executed due to the difficulty of reaching inscriptions *in situ*; liquid latex squeezes can only be made when an inscription can be laid flat on its back; and photographs of squeezes and of actual inscriptions can mislead because of the vagaries of lighting. There is little the investigator can do to obviate these hazards except to be aware of them and to avoid expressing conviction where confidence is out of place.

More reliable for dating than letter-forms are linguistic formulae and onomastic conventions, of which various useful examples have been identified (for Greek texts, see Guarducci 1967–78: 2.380–410, Woodhead 1981: 60–2; for Latin, Thylander 1952: 50–3, Calabi Limentani 1974: 175–8, Duncan-Jones 1982: 362–3). In general, these indications are most helpful when they are based upon wide usage and a high number of attestations and when they can be applied in combination. A Latin epitaph preceded by the formula *D(is) M(anibus)* (first attested in the two-letter abbreviated form around the middle of the first century CE) and naming a man with the *praenomen* and *gentilicium* "M. Ulpius" is very likely to belong to the second century CE, after the accession of the emperor Trajan and before the recording of the *praenomen* in inscribed texts largely fell out of use in the third century. An Athenian decree that refers to *proedroi* in its preamble probably belongs to the fourth century BCE, possibly (but not certainly) to the middle half of it (c. 375–325 BCE), after the office of *epistates* was replaced by a board of *proedroi* following the democratic reforms of 403 BCE and before the mention of *symproedroi* became common around 330 BCE (Henry 1977: 39–41).

Good epigraphic practice in editing inscriptions nowadays calls for an explicit indication of the grounds upon which even a tentative dating is based, but this has not always been so, and most inscriptions published in the standard corpora (*IG*, *CIL*) are not provided with even an approximate date. The better able the investigator is to identify and control the various specific "internal" criteria relevant to dating the type of inscription under consideration, the more confidence can be placed in its use as evidence.

History from square brackets

The phrase "history from square brackets" was coined by E. Badian to describe the most pernicious of epigraphic dangers for the historian, that of building argument from speculation disguised as fact (Badian 1989). The phrase refers to the standard epigraphic editing convention of including within square brackets conjectural restorations of text presumed originally to have been part of an inscription but now missing because of breakage or accidental damage to the writing surface (see "Editing conventions", page xxv). Because of the formulaic character of many Greek and Latin inscriptions, many of these supplements are uncontroversial and virtually inevitable (cf. Woodhead 1981: 72–4). With epitaphic formulae, they are also often historically inconsequential. With more complicated texts, however, conjecture sometimes embeds itself in the scholarly discussion so deeply that it assumes the appearance of fact and can only be dislodged by a thorough reassessment of the entire epigraphic and historical context. A recent, comprehensive reconsideration of the Athenian Standards Decree provides a case in point (Figueira 1998: 319–423).

Sometimes architectural features of the object on which the text is inscribed dictate the size of lacunae with a degree of certainty that narrows considerably the range of plausible supplements that can be considered (Meritt 1940); at others, conjectural restoration of a predictable text, such as the titles of a Roman emperor or the offices of a magistrate whose career is otherwise well attested, can help to establish the physical dimensions of the monument on which the inscription was displayed (e.g. Alföldy 1992: 113–23). In many instances, however, an editor wishing to make sense of an incomplete text is tempted to propose supplements (often avowedly *exempli gratia*) that are, at best, merely possible and, at worst, no more than wishful thinking. Regrettably, there exist no generally accepted criteria for distinguishing restorations that can be agreed to be reasonably certain from those that fall in the latter category, and in any case standards of reasonableness are bound to differ (cf. Badian 1993: 134–9). At the same time, it would certainly be counterproductive to demand that the editors of inscriptions—the

Figure 1.7 Contract for constructing a wall and doorway (*lex parieti faciendo*) from Puteoli (Pozzuoli), Italy. Marble (48 × 132 cm), 105 BCE? (*CIL* I² 698 and p. 936 = X 1781 = *ILS* 5317 = *ILLRP* 518 = Calabi Limentani 1974 no. 128). Carved in three columns on a single slab of (Luna?) marble, the text is dated to 105 BCE by the names of the local *duoviri* and of the Roman consuls and by the number of the year since the founding of the Roman colony (in 194 BCE), but the surviving inscription is thought to date from the early imperial period because of the letter-forms and the use of Luna marble (cf. *CIL* I² p. 936) (National Archaeological Museum, Naples). (For a larger reproduction, refer to page 176.)

very ones most likely to have devoted serious effort and thought to the restoration of the texts they are editing—refrain from suggesting all but the most secure supplements to their fragmentary texts. The most that can be expected is that the distinction between preserved text and conjectural supplement be clearly marked and that those who rely on epigraphic editions for historical evidence judge the reliability, as well as the intrinsic appeal, of any restoration individually on its own merits (see the sensible remarks of Woodhead 1981: 67–8, 74–5).

As noted above, reading inscriptions is always best done by autopsy; when that is not possible, resort to visual aids such as photographs and drawings provides only an imperfect guide to the letter-forms of the original. Sometimes it is not only the shapes of the letters but the letters themselves that a reproduction fails to replicate faithfully. The temptation to rely upon facsimiles of well-known inscriptions, clear and neat and often with inconvenient flaws in the original object discreetly removed, is understandable, but legibility is no substitute for accuracy, and for any serious study of inscriptions the temptation must be firmly resisted.

Figure 1.7 reproduces a photograph of a famous inscription from Puteoli (modern Pozzuoli), now on display in the epigraphic wing of

Figure 1.8 Lithograph facsimile reproduction of the *lex parieti faciendo* from Puteoli (Figure 1.7) as printed in F. Ritschl, *Priscae Latinitatis Monumenta Epigraphica* (1862), Tab. LXVI. Compared with the original marble slab (Figure 1.7) the drawing reproduced by Ritschl shows letter-forms similar but not identical to those on the stone. (For a larger reproduction, refer to page 177.)

the National Archaeological Museum in Naples (*CIL* I² 698 and p. 936 = X 1781 = *ILS* 5317 = *ILLRP* 518 = Calabi Limentani 1974 no. 128). The text—a building contract for constructing a wall and monumental doorway between two private houses across the street from a temple of Serapis—is without parallel in ancient epigraphy, and the date of the inscription depends largely upon its physical qualities: the arrangement of the text in three columns, the shapes of the letters, and the use of a single slab of Luna marble to display the document. The text is accurately transcribed in the standard editions (although none remarks all its notable palaeographic features), but when one looks for published images of the stone, one finds, in Ritschl's classic volume of lithograph plates, *Priscae Latinitatis Monumenta Epigraphica* (1862), a facsimile of a drawing of the text (Figure 1.8; the first column is reproduced by Calabi-Limentani 1974: 385) and, in the volume of plates published to accompany the latest fascicle of *CIL* I², a photograph—not of the inscription but of a plaster of Paris copy of it made for the Museum of Roman Civilization in Rome (Figure 1.9). Ritschl's facsimile shows the correct text and faithfully represents various imperfections in the stone (notably a break through the middle), but the letter-forms are subtly different from those on the stone. The photograph in *CIL* not only exhibits letter-forms unlike those of the original and of Ritschl's facsimile but shows no sign of the damage to the stone and introduces an orthographical error into the *nomen gentilicium* at the beginning of the second line in the spelling FVDIDIO for FVFIDIO. It is difficult to attribute the mistake

Figure 1.9 Reproduction of the *lex parieti faciendo* from Puteoli (Figure 1.7) in the Museo della Civiltà Romana, Rome. Plaster (48 × 132 cm?), c. 1937 CE (*CIL* I², pars II, fasciculus IV, addenda tertia, 2. *Tabulae*, Tab. 25, Fig. 1). Compared with the original marble slab (Figure 1.7) the reproduction appears similar in layout but exhibits markedly different letter-forms and outright error in the second line of the heading, where the plaster shows FVDIDIO instead of FVFIDIO (Museum of Roman Civilization, Rome). (For a larger reproduction, refer to page 178.)

to anything other than inadvertence, since the letters on the stone are clear. In this instance the historical consequences are slight (the *nomen* Fudidius is unattested but can be deduced from the *cognomen* Fudidianus: Schulze 1904: 238), but the reproduction of a faulty copy in the standard corpus is bound to mislead. Nor, regrettably, is this an isolated case. In Degrassi's excellent *auctarium* to the first volume of *CIL*, concerned with Latin inscriptions down to the end of the Republic (*Imagines*), plate no. 151 (= *CIL* I² 2662 = *ILLRP* 342) reproduces another plaster copy from the Museum of Roman Civilization, in this case of a poem set up at Corinth sometime in the first years of the first century BCE by M. Antonius the orator (grandfather of the triumvir), in which several readings not preserved on the stone but restored by modern editors are presented no differently from the surviving text (see Badian 1968: 242; cf. Gordon 1983: 90–1 no. 14). Relying on this "evidence," only the truly vigilant will avoid writing history from square brackets.

For all the potential pitfalls into which the unwary may stumble, the vast, rich territory constituted by the wealth of surviving Greek and Latin inscriptions contains many more deposits of valuable information than nuggets of fool's gold. The thrill of discovery, the sense of immediacy, the excitement of dealing directly with the ancient world—these rewards of the study of inscriptions can scarcely be conveyed at second hand. Readers who venture beyond the following pages to experience them directly will better understand the joys of the epigraphist and will sooner come to recognize the special contributions, as well as the limitations, of epigraphic evidence.

Chapter 2

Local languages and native cultures

Maryline Parca

The cultural cohesion which Herodotus claimed for Greece in the second half of the fifth century (8.144.2) and the universal political sway attributed to Rome by Augustus in the preamble to his *Res Gestae* (*CIL* III, 2, 769–99; Wigtil 1982a and 1982b), telling abstractions through which Greek and Roman self-definitions were articulated, provide helpful guides to an investigation of the linguistic and cultural diversity of classical antiquity. However dissociated from practical considerations, the construct that omits a mosaic of political institutions to embrace a fiction of genetic homogeneity, and the one in which political unity overrides considerations of race, language, religion, and customs are both lucid expressions of the exigencies of ideology. These representations have each had a full measure of success and have been practically unchallenged until recently. The broadened conception of the classical world currently being sketched is one advocating that due attention be paid to the interaction of Greece and Rome with Egypt, the Near East, and North Africa. Albeit surrounded by academic polemic, this critical démarche lends particular authority to the studies which historians of literacy (Harris 1989: 175–90) and scholars of cultural identities (Millar 1968: 126–34; 1987: 143–62; 1993: 225–35) have devoted to the nature, extent, and significance of the written evidence left by the distinctive cultures which Hellenistic Greece and imperial Rome came to encompass.[1]

Because Greek and Roman mentalities stand in such stark contrast to one another—Greek distinction being defined through exclusion and Roman self-definition being premised on inclusion—and since the political landscape of classical Greece has so little in common with that made possible by Alexander and compares even less with that of Rome during the Principate, the overview which this chapter intends to provide of the ways in which, and extent to which, inscriptions afford a picture of "multiculturalism" in the ancient Greco-Roman world will naturally proceed chronologically and selectively.[2]

Documenting the cultural diversity of Hellas prior to the territorial and administrative expansion of Alexander implies looking at a mosaic of independent polities with publicly acknowledged differences in ideology, social organization, economic structure, religious practices, cultural mores, and linguistic features, a landscape whose complexities Herodotus had omitted for the sake of ideological abstraction. It is my intention to consider the dialectal diversity of pre-Hellenistic Greece both as a reality to be reconciled with the linguistic uniformity central to Greek (subjective) ethnic identity, and as an indicator of cultural variety (of the kind acknowledged in Aristophanic comedy). Turning to inscriptional evidence proper, the abundant epigraphic documentation preserved from Athens, Delphi, or Delos will be bypassed in favor of the scant inscriptions recovered at Sparta, a community whose rejection of the extensive recourse to written public communication espoused by Athens is thus clearly stated but whose remains nonetheless reveal an informed private practice (Thomas 1992: 136). Moving next to the Hellenistic period, the Greek inscriptions from Egypt will provide the object of a reflection on texts in Greek conceived alongside a voluminous epigraphic corpus in hieroglyphics, and, because native elements may be expected to surface in small provincial settings rather than in large urban centers, some attention will be paid to recent work on the "epigraphy of villages."

The scrutiny to which the linguistic landscape of the Roman world has been (and continues to be) subjected has helped refine our understanding of the extent to which the epigraphic texts document the continuing existence, evolving forms, and select uses of secondary languages in the face of the hegemony of Latin and Greek.[3] In the introduction to his engaging discussion of the spoken and written languages in the Roman empire, Harris (1989: 175–7) reminds the reader that much of the population of the empire spoke neither Greek nor Latin, that about a dozen other languages were sometimes used in written form within the empire, and that an unknown number of others were spoken but not written. While encouraging alertness to the linguistic heterogeneity of Rome, he warns that some spoken languages left no epigraphic trace (such is the fate of Getic), and while recognizing that epigraphic evidence helps us evaluate the extent of the use of a language in written form, he cautions that inscriptions at times fail to reveal the scope of the written use of a tongue (as in the case of Gallic) and naturally omit to document the range of purposes which a language served in texts written on other materials (demotic Egyptian, for example, is relatively scarce in inscriptions but extensively documented on papyrus). Our selection in this field of linguistic plenty will be guided by recent research on British Latin in light of the letters from Vindolanda and the curse tablets recovered at Bath, on the bits of Gaulish vernacular read on kiln dockets from La Graufesenque, on the interaction of Latin and Punic in the Bu Njem *ostraka*, and on the trilingual inscriptions from Palmyra, in which Latin, Greek and Palmyrene coexist in formal texts as they did in the society from which they stem.

Greek dialects

Given their geographical dispersal, it is not surprising that the Greeks privileged language in their ethnic self-determination, even if their linguistic sameness was only a convenient fiction.[4] How, from what sources, and where the Greek dialects were formed is still debated.[5] By 750 BCE the four traditional dialect groups "commonly known, by a mixture of ethnic and geographical terminology, as West Greek (of which Doric is a subdivision), Aeolic, Arcado–Cypriot, and Attic–Ionic" (Hainsworth 1982: 858) had emerged. Down to c. 400 BCE the linguistic map naturally continued to change, as it was shaped by the progressive fragmentation of dialects into ever smaller areas (Doric thus became subdivided into Laconian, Corinthian, etc.) and their acquisition of new features through interaction with neighboring dialects. No dialect is fully represented epigraphically before the fifth century BCE; few are documented before the fourth; some never are; and of those known from inscriptions, only Attic is extensively documented in the several phases of its history (Horrocks 1997: 6–15).

Early epigraphic texts represent vernacular languages and as such document different alphabets and variable orthographies. Between the seventh and fourth centuries BCE, however, Ionic usages spread throughout Greece and the Ionic alphabet eventually superseded the various local ("epichoric") alphabets (Jeffery–Johnston 1990). In Athens the change was decreed for official documents in 403/2, after which all such texts were cut in Ionic letters (Woodhead 1981: 18). From the mid-fourth century onwards, long public inscriptions in dialect but in the Ionic alphabet are found in most areas, and a uniform prose style takes hold; these developments coincide with the spread of a modified form of Attic called *koinè*, the idiom destined to become the universal language of the Greek East in the Hellenistic period (Horrocks 1997: 24–37, 61–3).

Tolerance of local forms of speech is revealing of the Greeks' keen sense of civic independence, and although members of one community may have found the manner of speech of another funny (as is often the case in the comedies of Aristophanes) or ugly to the ear, dialectal difference seems never to have prevented communication. Intelligibility or its perceived absence are to a large extent subjective: the degree of intelligibility between any one pair of dialects naturally varied according to the intensity of their contacts and is not necessarily an index of the structural similarities between them.[6] Inscriptional remains aside, the available ancient sources on Greek dialectal diversity are the literary texts and the works of the grammarians, the latter being mostly concerned with literary dialects, glosses, and accentuation systems.

Literature sheds only partial light on dialect history both because it is largely defined by the constraints of genre, each with its conventional themes and artificial norms of expression (the poetry of Hesiod, for example, in spite of the poet's Boeotian origin, subscribes largely to Homeric norms, the principal constituent of which is archaic Ionic), and because it reaches us transformed through the efforts of Hellenistic editors and the fortunes of transmission. Attic comedy admitted dialectal forms throughout its history and employed them as a proven source of humor. Besides vernacular Attic, Aristophanic comedy provides a wealth of information on Boeotian and Megarian (in *Acharnians*) and on Laconian (in *Lysistrata* and *Knights*).[7] While the evidence which Aristophanes provides for Attic can be evaluated against the bulk of Athenian literature, and while inscriptions in Boeotian and Megarian provide a fair amount of confirmatory data for Aristophanes' reproductions, the question of his trustworthiness arises in connection with those dialects for which his linguistic parodies constitute much of the extant evidence.

It is generally agreed that in the speech of non-Athenians in his plays Aristophanes primarily sought to give the Athenian audience a comic impression of alien speakers (Elliott 1914: 207–40). In *Acharnians*, for example, when the Athenian farmer Dicaeopolis meets a trader from Thebes, he mostly resorts to specifically Boeotian words and has the alien swear in his native style: ἴττω Ἡρακλῆς, "be Heracles my witness" (line 860) and νεὶ τὸν Ἰόλαον, "by Iolaus" (867).[8] Similarly, in *Lysistrata* the invocation to the Dioscuri, ναὶ τὼ σιώ, "by the Two Gods" (81) readily identifies the speaker as Spartan. Such forms, whose soundness is confirmed from other sources, coexist with incorrect dialectal forms which reflect lapses into Atticisms.

Sparta

The dearth of material evidence thwarts categorical statements about the extent of Spartan literacy.[9] The earliest known Laconian writing can be read on a bronze vessel from the Menelaion at Sparta, apparently dedicated to "Helen, wife of Menelaos" and dated to the middle of the seventh century BCE (*LSAG* 446, no. 3a), of which the sureness of execution suggests that the alphabetic system of writing reached Laconia not too long after its arrival in Greece around 775 BCE. Despite the fact that Athenian authors present Spartans as illiterate, the favor enjoyed at Sparta by the poets Tyrtaios and Alcman in the archaic period, the city's famed constitutional reform, and the political success of its governing elite in the classical period challenge the charge of complete illiteracy. It is nevertheless true that most of the extant inscriptional evidence fails decisively to prove the Athenians wrong. First, there is an almost total absence of official state documents on stone, except for a fifth-century treaty of alliance with the Aetolians (Cartledge 1976: 87–92) and a list of contributions to a war fund by several individuals and states (Cartledge 1978: 35). Second, "all known private Spartan inscriptions have accrued from formal, religious contexts" (Cartledge 1978: 31): mostly comprised of *ex-votos*, the private texts also include a large number of victory dedications and a few inscribed tombstones—all unlikely to reveal spontaneity of thought or idiosyncrasy of form. Lastly, the widespread belief among the ancients that no full Spartan citizen ever engaged in manual labor raises doubts about whether a professionally executed inscription was ever produced by a Spartiate.[10] However, sweeping suspicion should probably be relaxed in the case of dedications painted on fired pottery from the Spartan acropolis, inscribed flute bones from the sanctuary of Artemis Orthia, and masons' names incised in informal cursive script on architectural fragments, which provide evidence suggesting that some Spartans could read and write.[11]

Egypt

The local contexts from which inscriptions arise, each with its own institutional, religious, and economic particularities, necessarily color the nature of their epigraphic corpora, but despite their individual differences, each site reveals constant features in the use of epigraphical expression (Bingen 1989: 16). The Greek epigraphy of Egypt thus displays not only features which mark it as specifically Greek (as opposed to Egyptian) but also traits which distinguish it as being from Egypt. It developed there alongside but separate from a considerable corpus of hieroglyphic texts. The relatively few signs of osmosis between the inscriptions in Greek and those in the native tongue reveal the cultural distance between settler and indigenous populations. One manifestation of the continuity of Greek epigraphical practice in Egypt can be found in the various decrees through which councils or associations honored high-ranking protectors and in which a list of the dedicators' names, each with its patronym, follows the text of the decree proper. In the Greek tradition, the lists aim to commemorate the members of the group individually, to lend concrete recognition to their power of decision, and to immortalize the mutual solidarity which binds patron and beneficiaries (Bingen 1989: 18–19). One such honorary decree is recorded in the inscription put up by the military *politeuma* ("garrison" or "club," Lewis 1986: 30) of the Idumaeans and the Idumaeans in the city of Memphis, in which the Semitic group, assembled in the temple of its god Qos–Apollon, decrees lifelong honors to its benefactor Dorion and celebrates its motion through a sequence of names (*OGIS* 737). There exists no Egyptian equivalent to this type of inscription, since neither the form of decision-making nor the mutual publicity derived by dedicator and dedicatee is given comparable expression in that cultural group. The Semitic corps' adoption of a Greek epigraphic practice bespeaks that group's deliberate attempt to set itself in the Greco-Macedonian sphere, a reflex mirrored in the growing number of Greek names among the descendants of the mercenaries (Thompson Crawford 1984: 1071–3).

On the other hand, *proskynemata*—inscriptional acts of religious adoration performed before a divinity on behalf of oneself or for a beloved one far away—are Greek inscriptions found exclusively in Egypt, beginning around the middle of the second century BCE (Geraci 1971: 12–26). These documents, whose origins and significance are rooted in demotic epigraphy, seem to "translate" what the Greeks saw the Egyptians do. The inscriptional monument thus takes on an additional dimension, absent from classical Greek epigraphy and derived from the decoration of the local temple or tomb where the prayer occurs: the inscription becomes a physical substitute for the worshipper performing the act of devotion, and the lasting remembrance desired is that of the divinity and not solely that of the passerby who might stop and read the text (Geraci 1971: 23 and Bingen 1989: 19–20).[12] The following late Ptolemaic example is typical, though many are much more succinct: "I, Achilleus, son of Lagon, have come to our mistress Isis and have performed the act of adoration for my parents, my wife and my children. 19 October 89 BCE" (*IPhilae* 1.34).

The epigraphic corpus of Egypt cannot be dissociated from the other major body of documentary evidence native to its land, comprising papyri, *ostraka*, and mummy tags, each amply documented in Greek, Latin and Demotic.[13] Papyrology and epigraphy are often mutually complementary in domains ranging from onomastics and prosopography to economic and religious life. Several archives have now been reassembled from documents written on different materials and in several languages. One such is that of Paminis and his son Parthenios, businessmen established at Coptos in the Thebaid and active in the early Principate, whose double lives can be pieced together from three separate dossiers, one comprised of Greek inscriptions, another of hieroglyphic and demotic inscriptions, and the third of Greek *ostraka*. The first two sets of texts reveal the religious role which these affluent Greco-Egyptians played in the cults of their native Coptos, while the third shows them engaged in the transport of goods to sites on the Red Sea.[14]

A recent investigation of the inscriptional remains recovered in Egyptian villages—either farming communities or workers' quarters hastily created in the vicinity of quarries and necropoleis—points to a similar coexistence of inscriptions written in Greek and in Demotic (the former sometimes commissioned by Egyptians, the latter by Greeks). In such milieux, where official texts are rarely posted, the epigraphic corpus comprises religious dedications, mostly to local deities but sometimes to rulers; epitaphs, which often combine Greek conventions and themes in the text with native elements in the decoration; and graffiti, scratched or painted, in many cases originating with travelers or military personnel. The survey reveals a great disparity in the epigraphic habit of Egypt among both regions and villages: the Oxyrhynchite nome, a region bountiful in papyri, has yet to reveal a single inscription; within the villages, whereas few inscriptions signal recent (Ptolemaic) settlement, ample inscriptional documentation regularly points to pre-colonial development. The epigraphy of Egypt is primarily an urban phenomenon and a cultural manifestation shaped to a great extent by political and economic factors (Wagner 1993: 101–15).

Vernacular Latin

Latin, a language originally spoken in Latium from around 800 BCE, spread together with Rome's power and became the common language of Italy by the time of Augustus, then of the western Mediterranean and the Balkan regions. While most Latin-speakers spoke a colloquial ("vulgar") form of Latin, the dialect now known as classical Latin developed from forms of the language fashioned for specific purposes such as legal codes, ritual texts, public oratory, and pontifical records. The earliest Latin texts, literary and epigraphic, reveal a language which, though distinct even from its immediate neighbors, Oscan and Umbrian (Palmer 1954: 33–73), nonetheless displays traits acquired from its relationships with the local non-Latin Italic dialects (Vine 1993). Since almost all regions of Italy were primarily Latin-speaking by the Augustan period (Harris 1989: 178–9), most of the inscriptional remains documenting the various dialects are of Republican date, with the exception of Oscan (in Campania) and Etruscan, which continue to be written in the first century CE.[15]

Britain

The linguistic landscape of the Roman world can be approached from Britain, the province now judged to be "the main source of new Latin" (Adams 1992: 1). Recent British finds include over 250 inked wooden leaves from the beginning of the second century CE unearthed during excavation at the fort of Vindolanda near Hadrian's Wall (Bowman–Thomas 1994; Bowman 1994: 15) and 130 curse tablets recovered from the sacred spring at Bath, ranging from the second to the fourth centuries CE (Tomlin in Cunliffe 1988). While some of the Vindolanda tablets are recessed pieces of wood once coated with wax and written upon with a metal stylus (the familiar form of writing tablet), most are wafer-thin leaves, "between 1 and 3 mm thick and about the size of a modern postcard," (Bowman 1994: 15) cut from the outer sapwood of green timber (alder, birch, occasionally oak) and made to bear writing in ink on one or both of their surfaces (Bowman–Thomas 1983: 26–31).

The tablets concern auxiliary units—the Ninth Cohort of Batavians and the First Cohort of Tungrians, along with their respective commanding officers, have been securely identified—garrisoned at Vindolanda before Hadrian's Wall was built. They comprise letters and personal and administrative documents discarded as the fort was enlarged, rebuilt, and re-occupied over time. The military records preserved at Vindolanda document the detailed assignment of individuals or groups of soldiers to building and construction work, the manufacture of shields and swords, and the scrupulous recording of cash sums, receipts, and lists of commodities and foodstuffs dispensed and purchased. A rare picture of the diet of Roman soldiers in the pre-Hadrianic period emerges from lists recording barley (*hordeum*), fish sauce, pork fat, vintage wine (*vinum*), sour wine (*acetum*), salt, young pig, ham, and Celtic beer (*cervesa*) (*Tab.*

Figure 2.1 Letter from Niger and Brocchus to Cerialis, from Chesterholm (Vindolanda), England. Wood diptych (17.8 × 9.1 cm), 95–105 CE (*Tab. Vindol.* 1.21 = *Tab. Vindol.* 2.248, inv. no. 188).

Vindol. 2.190, 191). At the same time, an inventory of household objects (including side-plates and egg-cups, *Tab. Vindol.* 2.194) suggests a high degree of sophistication in the commanding officer's residence, and a list of clothing (*Tab. Vindol.* 2.196) reveals that the officers and their families could avail themselves of a variety of footwear and a wide range of garments and woven textiles.[16]

The records and letters, official and private, from Vindolanda also document the character and role of literacy in a military outpost on the northern frontier (Bowman 1994: 82–99). The remarkably large number of individual hands represented among the official documents and private letters reveals that their authors—whether clerks in the unit's record office, individual officers and members of their households, or correspondents from other places—commanded basic literacy skills. Although most of the extant letters were written by professional clerks and scribes, the authors normally added the closing greetings in their own hands, thus lending some individuality and, at times, elegance to the messages (as in the closure of Claudia Severa's birthday invitation to Lepidina, *Tab. Vindol.* 2.291). The language of the texts shows how Latin was spoken and written by the natives of northern Gaul (Batavians and Tungrians) whom Rome, following a sustained process of acculturation under Augustus and the Julio-Claudians, later used as instruments of domination in Britain (Figure 2.1). The erasures which mar one of the draft letters written in the hand of the prefect Flavius

Cerialis, for example, suggest that the polished Latin of which he was ultimately capable did not flow naturally from the Batavian officer (*Tab. Vindol.* 2.225). Generally good, the Latin these people wrote shows signs of the common colloquial usages of the time, such as the gemination of *s* in *missit*, for *misit*. Spellings such as *debetor* for *debitor* or *it quot* for *id quod* reflect changes in pronunciation which the writers recorded phonetically (Bowman–Thomas 1983: 724; Adams 1995: 89, 91).

The Vindolanda tablets shed light on the history of the years 85–122 CE on the northern frontier of the Roman empire, from the recalling of the governor Agricola to Hadrian's visit to Britain, a period lacking any literary treatment and otherwise poorly documented in inscriptions. The language which they reveal both complements the colloquial Latin known from Pompeian graffiti (Väänänen 1966, 1967) and supplements it with a few features not otherwise known from the period. And as the largest dated collection of letters in Latin recovered outside Egypt, the Vindolanda material has made an important contribution to the study of the history of Latin handwriting, showing that the script known as Old Roman Cursive employed in most texts is the same as that found in letters written on papyrus in Egypt at about the same time.[17]

The extensive body of vernacular Latin contained in the Bath curse tablets belongs to a different geographical and social milieu, and to a much later period: the texts reveal the names and speech of members of the urban middle and lower classes (the town's minority of shopkeepers, craftsmen, and laborers) in the third and fourth centuries CE (Figure 2.2). Inscribed on lead and tin for local visitors to the sacred spring, many of the tablets record a theft of property and contain an invocation prompting the deity to torment the thief until the stolen goods are recovered. Much in these texts is typical of the common stock of vulgar Latin, especially the phonetic spellings—a mark of the lack of a literary education, not easily obtained by Latin speakers born in Britain in the fourth century, rather than necessarily a sign of lower socio-economic status (Adams 1992: 24). But the tablets also reveal features characteristic of the Latin of Britain, such as the use of *hospitium* for "house" (in 99.23), the opening of *e* to *a* before *r* (as in *Matarnus* for *Maternus* in 30.3)—a phenomenon well documented in Latin loan-words in Welsh (*taberna* > *tafarn*, *Paternus* > *Padarn*) (Adams 1992: 12)—and the use of the Germanic loan-word *baro* (originally "warrior," "valorous man" but in the tablets, four times, simply "man" as opposed to *mulier*, "woman"), a term introduced to Britain either by Germans serving in the Roman army or by other travelers from the mainland, where the noun enjoyed wide currency by the late Empire (Adams 1992: 15–17). Whereas the tablets

Figure 2.2 Curse tablet from Bath, England. Lead (45 per cent) and tin (55 per cent) (5.9 × 8.8 cm), c. 100–400 CE. The tablet, folded five times, records a list of names. (*Tab. Sulis* 9(a), inventory number 612.)

fail to reveal what the mass of British peasants spoke, they do preserve some hints of the Celtic tongue (through the numerous Celtic names, for example) and may include one continuous text in Celtic (no. 14). Comprised of four conjoining fragments preserving the top left corner of a tablet, this tantalizing text inscribed in the Latin alphabet in an admixture of capital and cursive scripts contains several Celtic name-elements and non-Latin combinations of letters and may be "the first text to interrupt the argument from silence that British Celtic was *never* written" (Tomlin in Cunliffe 1988: 129).[18]

Gaul

In his search for traces of the vernacular-speaking population among the *instrumentum domesticum* (inscribed portable objects such as bricks, vases, lamps, and amphorae), Harris (1995: 19–27) observes that, though numerically dominant in most regions of the empire, local languages appear very little in this material; he suggests that the Latin and Greek words inscribed on these mass-produced commodities were written by and for a small, affluent, market-oriented minority comprised of skilled employees, commercial entrepreneurs, and firm owners. The mixed Gaulish Celtic and Latin texts read on kiln dockets recovered at the important ceramic production site of La Graufesenque in southeastern France document such a professional milieu in the first century CE and show this milieu's limited and specialized use of writing, both in the local idiom and in the international business language of the day.

These ceramic dockets, most of which begin with either the Gaulish formula *tuθos luxtos* or the Latin equivalent *furnus oneratus* ("oven loaded"), were evidently written as the pottery to be fired was loaded into the kiln, from ground level up, according to size, after which the lists were checked for accuracy and were fired with the goods as authenticating pieces. They record, for each firing, the names of the potters whose artifacts are processed, the names of the pots, their dimensions, and the number of items to be fired (Marichal 1988: 103–5; Figure 2.3). Although broadly divided into Gaulish and Latin, the texts are all written in vulgar Latin, the designations "Gaulish" and "Latin" reflecting merely the degree to which the Celtic substratum is apparent in them (Marichal 1988: 56). In the former, for example, the rare verbs, adverbs, and conjunctions are Gaulish; the numbers, often, are in the native tongue; some vase types are designated by indigenous nouns and adjectives; and the intrusion of Latin is limited to proper names, vase names, and the designations of measures of capacity, which are treated as indeclinable nouns, or are spelled phonetically, or are written as if they were Gaulish words, with the final *m* omitted, for example, since Gaulish lacks such an ending (Marichal 1988: 101).

Unlike Britain, where the epigraphic habit took hold only after the Roman conquest, Gaul has yielded inscriptions, in Greek letters (Lejeune 1985b), which may go back to the third century BCE. While literary testimony establishes that Gallic was spoken widely—and beyond the

Figure 2.3 Kiln docket from La Graufesenque, France. Terracotta (diam.: 18 cm),
c. 15–65 CE (Marichal 1988: 132 no. 12).

uneducated peasant class—until late antiquity (Harris 1989: 183), the relatively few surviving texts written in the native idiom (Schmidt 1983: 990–5)
document the people's participation in modes of commemoration and
forms of communication which bear the Roman imprint. The internal
memoranda from La Graufesenque are telling witnesses to the coexist-
ing and competing forces of custom and acculturation: they show the
clerks recording kiln contents not only expertly using the Latin alphabet to write their own language but sometimes producing dockets in Latin,
though they know little or no Latin and write texts with little diffusion
beyond the immediate circle of local potters and customers. The latter

practice apparently bespeaks an awareness among the few Latinized Ruteni, who naturally acted as interpreters and translators, that the language of business, administration, and the courts was Latin and that texts drafted in Latin conveyed an official character (Marichal 1988: 102).

Africa

Excavation at the military outpost of Bu Njem in Tripolitania (modern Libya) has yielded 158 *ostraka* (restored to 146 documents: Marichal 1992) whose Latin bears witness to the interaction between the vernacular tongues of the area and the garrison's official language. The best documented indigenous languages of Roman Africa are Punic and the rather elusive "Libyan." A Semitic language related to Phoenician, Punic is known to have been spoken fairly widely until late in the imperial period and is documented in inscriptions, many with parallel Latin texts, up to the beginning of the third century CE (MacMullen 1966: 1, 12; Millar 1968: 130–2). Libyan, distinct in script and form from Punic, is attested epigraphically throughout North Africa, alone or in combination with parallel texts in Punic or in Latin, though the extent of its ordinary use remains uncertain (Millar 1968: 128–30; Adams 1994: 88–9).

The unit documented in the *ostraka* was posted at Bu Njem (Golas in the Latin texts) in the 250s, fifty years after the original legionary detachment was dispatched to this North African frontier to build a fort. Essentially official in content, the texts comprise 43 letters concerning various aspects of daily life in a desert outpost sent to Bu Njem by members of the garrison away on duty. Written in the isolation of the hinterland by people with established ties to Africa (65 per cent of the *cognomina* reveal African connections and 45 per cent of the Latin *cognomina* are specifically African), they provide palpable evidence of a coexistence of cultures in a way that monumental inscriptions are unable to convey.

Here again, as in the texts from Vindolanda and Bath, the distinctive forms of the colloquial Latin suggest that some of the writers were vernacular speakers and learners of Latin, their imperfect learning resulting in broken or irregular speech (Adams 1994: 90). For example, the abnormal *quere ad tessera* (for *quaere tesseram*, "ask for the token") in *ostrakon* no. 95.2–3 may be owed to the writer's native tongue, since the direct object in Punic is regularly marked by a pseudo-preposition placed before the object: seeking a Latin equivalent to the mark which he construes as a preposition, the writer selects *ad* and creates a phrase for which there is no structural parallel in Latin (Adams 1994: 92).[19] Another possible regionalism in the Latin written in the area of Bu Njem is the repeated use of the nominative for the accusative, an "error" perhaps prompted by the absence of case inflections in Punic (Adams 1994: 96–102). A further instance of creative Latin syntax turns up in no. 77, a letter in which the sender, wishing to refer to the consuls who will follow the current ones, writes *consules futuros post Thusco et Basso co(n)s(ulibus)* in lines 6–7, taking the ablative absolute of the consular date as a fixed, indeclinable unit to which he prefixes the preposition *post* ("the consuls to be after the consulship of Tuscus and Bassus"). Since it has been shown that the fort at Bu Njem was laid out according to the Punic cubit and not the Roman foot—and that, therefore, its surveyor was Punic—it is both reasonable to assume that local recruits had entered the ranks of the Roman army and natural to find Latin influenced by the native language of some of its new users (the Punic sound system thus could also explain why *Thusco* is written for *Tusco* in the consular date above).

Palmyra

Lastly, a group of trilingual inscriptions from Palmyra documents a pattern of cultural and linguistic interaction that moves counter to those discussed thus far, in that the texts illustrate how Greek and Latin terminology and concepts found expression in a Semitic language. When Latin entered the Near East, Greek was the primary language of communication throughout the area and, as such, came to function "as a medium of transmission between the various Semitic languages used in the region on the one hand, and Latin on the other" (Schürer 1979: 20–8; Millar 1993: 232–4; 1995: 404). Transliterations of Roman official terms (military and administrative) into Semitic languages were thus generally derived from their hellenized forms (e.g. *legio*, λεγεών in the New Testament, and LGYWN' in Palmyrene) or were coined directly from Greek translations (e.g. *duumvir* → στρατηγός → 'STRTG).

Palmyra as an urban center was created in the first century BCE, and as it developed into a Greek city, acquiring Greek organs of government and offices in the second half of the first century CE, it also entered the sphere of the Roman province of Syria (Millar 1993: 319–36, 1995: 408–9). Unlike in other Greek cities in the region, its people continued to use their native Palmyrene, an Aramaic dialect, in both official and funerary inscriptions, although public texts tended to be bilingual in Greek and Palmyrene. Five trilingual inscriptions, spanning the years 52–176 CE, exhibit Latin, Greek and Palmyrene in parallel texts which echo one another through translation and transliteration from the original Greek, the latest one possibly displaying one Palmyrene word transliterated into Latin (Millar 1995: 413). Paradoxically, there are no Latin inscriptions dating to the period when Palmyra was granted the status of *colonia* in the early third century. Bilingual and Greek inscriptions of the colonial period, however, clearly establish how Latin terminology and Roman concepts of status deeply suffused the social and political structure of Palmyra *qua* Roman colony: six inscriptions commemorating members of a prominent local family refer to those of Roman senatorial rank with words such as συγκλητικός, transliterated SNQLṬYQ', λαμπρότατος, the Greek translation of *vir clarissimus*, and πάτρων (= Latin *patronus*) (Millar 1995: 414–19).

It is hoped that these pages, which have taken us from Greece to Rome and then from West to East again, have illustrated how inscriptions can touch up the ancients' ideological and literary images of cultural cohesion and uniformity with nuances of linguistic and cultural diversity. They restore to Clio some of the rouge she naturally wears—not the artificial color of stylistic and rhetorical effects applied by the literary authors of Greece and Rome but the true and vibrant shades of the variegated voices of the people.

Chapter 3

Names and identities
Onomastics and prosopography

Olli Salomies

My task is to say something about Greek and Latin inscriptions as applied to the study of onomastics and prosopography. Contemplating the subject, I observed that it would hardly be possible to discuss the uses of inscriptions for onomastics and prosopography without saying quite a lot about onomastics and prosopography in general. Both can, however, exist also where there are no inscriptions at all, and this means that in this chapter there will necessarily be some talk both of phenomena not necessarily dependent on the existence of epigraphical sources, and of the uses not of inscriptions, but of onomastics and prosopography. Then there is the problem that the uses of inscriptions for both disciplines are so manifold that it seems quite impossible to give a comprehensive and organized account of the subject; instead, I have had to content myself with illustrating the matter with some chosen examples. I must also mention one important aspect which I can touch upon only in passing here and there, namely the methodological problems inherent in all epigraphical sources (see above, pages 34–6, 46–7).

It may be useful to begin with a definition of "onomastics" and "prosopography" and with an explanation of their uses for the study of ancient culture and history. The very fact that this book includes a chapter dealing with the two subjects perhaps requires some justification, since a similar collection of papers on the historical evidence for another period would not necessarily include a section on the two disciplines. There is also the question why the two subjects are to be treated under the same heading.

Prosopography

Let us start with "prosopography." Of this term, from the Greek πρόσωπον (in later Greek, from Polybius onwards, "person") and γραφεῖν ("to write"), the earliest attestation I know of is the title of the three-volume *Prosopographia Imperii Romani* (*PIR*) published in 1897–8. In the preface it is said that the word "prosopographia" is "*receptum*" (although "*non optimum*"), and so it appears that this was not the first time the term was used. The same expression was used a few years later by J. Kirchner in his similar work on Attic prosopography (Kirchner 1901–3).

As used in the title of these two works, "prosopographia" means a listing, in alphabetical order, of persons of a certain rank or occupation and belonging to a certain period, in which each entry contains a full enumeration of the person's offices and other accomplishments and of all the relevant sources. The same expression, whether in Latin or in some other language, has subsequently been used in many works of the same basic conception (some employing a chronological rather than an alphabetical order). Any group of persons may be taken under consideration in works of this kind: one thus finds prosopographies listing royal envoys of the Hellenistic Period (Olshausen 1974), Roman senatorial women (Raepsaet-Charlier 1987), Roman Epicureans (Castner 1988), and worshippers of Isis (Mora 1990). A special type is that listing persons mentioned by some author (e.g. Ferguson 1987 on Juvenal). Under this heading may be included, besides works labeled as "prosopographies," similar works that use other definitions in their titles—lists of Roman provincial governors, for instance, which tend (for reasons outside the scope of this chapter) to be called "fasti" (e.g. Birley 1981, Piso 1993). Some authors identify works of this type in their titles simply with key words such as "governor" or "senator" in the plural (e.g. Vogel-Weidemann 1982).

In popular usage, however, "prosopography" denotes not only lists of people but also "applied" prosopography, that is, more general studies using prosopographical material and, in a more abstract sense, the method used in these studies. Books commonly combine the various meanings of the term, with emphasis varying according to the author's own predilections. One thus finds books conceived as prosopographies that include in addition studies of a more general nature based on the prosopographies themselves (e.g. many of the books listing Roman provincial governors, which often make general statements on the governors' careers, backgrounds, etc.) or, alternatively, books on a variety of subjects that include prosopographical appendixes listing the known individuals belonging to a certain group or period (e.g. Ghiron-Bistagne 1976 on Greek actors, Leppin 1992 on Roman actors, Wilmanns 1995 on Roman military doctors).

Prosopography as a method basically means using the material gathered in "prosopographies" to acquire knowledge of certain aspects of (in this case) the ancient world. Prosopographical lists are obviously most useful for the editors of the hundreds of new Greek and Latin inscriptions that are published each year who want (and are of course expected) to check if a person mentioned in a new text is already known from other sources: editors of inscriptions referring to Greek actors, for instance, need to look up the lists of Ghiron-Bistagne 1976. Without prosopographical reference works the identification of persons mentioned in new inscriptions would be very difficult and in many cases perhaps impossible.

On a somewhat more complex level, prosopographies and studies based on prosopographical material, especially those dealing with the upper levels of ancient societies, can give us invaluable information on those societies, the nature of the information depending to a large extent on the nature of the sources—whether literary or epigraphical—of the prosopographical material. A thorough study of the leading personalities of Alexander's empire, for example, has shed light on numerous aspects of the actual functioning of the empire (cf. Bengtson 1975: 165 on Berve 1926). In general, however, the Greek world (or at least pre-Roman Greece) does not offer very good opportunities for prosopographical studies (Berve's book is on a special, short, and perhaps atypical period in Greek history). Studies belonging to this category (e.g. Habicht 1972; the eight papers in Habicht 1994: 323–53), which tend to be of a more limited range than those on Roman society, often aim at establishing connections between persons of the same name attested in different sources but usually do not reveal further details about the structure of Greek society. For several reasons a prosopographical approach has more uses and greater potential in the Roman world (Habicht 1972: 103–4). Because of the nature of the sources on the one hand and of Roman society and politics in general on the other, prosopographical studies of Republican politicians usually try (with results thought of by some as controversial) to establish the existence, and to identify the members, of "parties" active within the senate, and to interpret Roman politics in these terms; but such studies are based mainly on literary sources and so must be passed over rapidly in this context.

During the Empire, inscriptions largely replace literary sources in prosopographical studies and so there is a notable shift in the nature of the information available. A typical prosopographical study of the imperial period collects the sources, mostly epigraphical, on certain officials (e.g. the governors of some province, as in Vogel-Weidemann 1982) and tries to find out what kind of people they were (cf. Pflaum 1972: 320, cited in n. 1, on what one should expect of lists of officials). Often it is possible, by complex combinations of prosopographical data, to get a bit farther, and this kind of research can lead to illuminating insights into the organization of government, the hierarchy of offices, the areas of recruitment of certain officials, the composition of (and mutual ties among) the aristocracy, and so on. The study of the local origins of Roman senators of the empire, for instance, has revolutionized our view of the composition of the Roman ruling class: we now know that already by the turn of the first and second centuries a significant number of senators were Greek—a fact of great importance for understanding the nature of the Roman empire, but one which nineteenth-century historians of Rome probably would have thought unbelievable. And it is only on the basis of a detailed study of thousands of epigraphically attested senatorial careers that a clear picture has |emerged of the personnel recruitment policy of the imperial regime and of the manifold patterns of advancement that existed in the Roman state bureaucracy.[1]

Prosopographical observations can also be used to illuminate military or administrative history. That the *legio IX Hispana* was destroyed early in the reign of Marcus Aurelius can be established by prosopographical arguments, and the same goes for investigations concerning the changes in status (from senatorial to imperial or vice versa) of provinces such as Sardinia, Bithynia–Pontus or Baetica.[2] That some studies employing a prosopographical approach are overly optimistic in what they promise or somewhat outsized for their results cannot be denied, and in general the flourishing of this genre seems in recent years to have been on the wane. This may, however, be because our material has already been studied from all possible angles rather than because more and more scholars have started to think that prosopography is worthless; for it cannot be denied that studies using a prosopographical approach have in many cases greatly enhanced our knowledge of the ancient world. At the same time, the value and possibilities of prosopographical studies have been seriously called into question, with skepticism focused particularly on those that claim to illustrate more than just personal history.[3] Whatever the outcome of these debates may be, as long as the discovery of new inscriptions continues to supply new names and persons every year, the practical utility of prosopographical studies will never become entirely obsolete.

Onomastics

Let us turn now from prosopography to onomastics. As with "prosopography," the term "onomastics"—from Gk. ὄνομα ("name") and thus by definition a field of study concerned with names, especially personal names—can cover a wide range of scholarly activities. One can, for example, study onomastics from a purely philological point of view and concern oneself mainly with the etymology, meaning, suffixes, etc. of names. On the other hand, observing the geographical or chronological distribution of certain names and then putting this knowledge to use (for instance by saying that because of his name, someone probably comes from a certain city or area, and then basing demographic observations on this) will take us to another level of onomastics which we may call "applied" onomastics and which in fact in many cases comes close to prosopography. This is where the two disciplines overlap. In order to illustrate to what use this "applied" onomastics can be put, it will be convenient to concentrate on Rome, because personal names in Rome, consisting of several parts and constantly in evolution, offer in general much more material for historical interpretation than do those of classical Greece.[4]

First of all, the fact that the Romans had a hereditary gentile name is useful for establishing relationships between individuals. If two persons of about the same social level and period have the same *nomen*, and even more if they share the same *praenomen* or *cognomen*, it may be suggested that there was a relationship between them; and although assuming this can be risky (some *nomina*, e.g. Iulius or Valerius, were extremely common), this is often the only way one can proceed, since in many cases there is simply no other evidence to work with. When G. Alföldy studied the consulships of fathers and sons in the Antonine period, he had to establish relationships between fathers and sons in almost every case on the basis of names alone (Alföldy 1977: 84–94, 323–6). Furthermore, the fact that in Rome women kept their original *nomen* after marriage is also useful; for instance, the name of the wife of a consul, if known, provides the possibility of finding out the wife's father and other relatives (most of the fathers and relatives listed in Raepsaet-Charlier 1987 owe their listing to no more than their names). This again in some cases provides the possibility (often problematic, it is true) of studying family alliances and other relations within the upper classes of Roman society. Also, "polyonymous" nomenclature—two or more *nomina*, of which one is that of the natural father and the other (or others) that either of an adoptive father, as in the case of Pliny the Younger, or of the maternal family, or simply of some relative or friend (see Salomies

1992)—appears mainly among the upper classes during the Empire and offers ample material for studies (or at least speculation) about social and other relations within the Roman upper classes, studies, in fact, of a sort hardly imaginable without inscriptions and onomastics.

But there is more to Roman names than this. A famous article by Ronald Syme on the origins, development, and structure of the official nomenclature of the emperor Augustus, "Imp(erator) Caesar Divi f(ilius) Augustus" (Syme 1958), for example, shows how important aspects of the ideology and self-representation of the first Roman emperor are reflected in his name, which is carefully constructed to combine traditional elements with innovative features underlining Augustus' special status and pointing to the future. For another, concrete example of how onomastic observations can be of use to the historian, observe the establishment of the date of the appearance of equestrian officials in charge of the four different taxes and duties collected in the province of Africa, the *procuratores IIII publicorum Africae*. Until quite recently, scholars tended to date the appearance of these officials to the time of Hadrian (who is often regarded as a great innovator). But in an article published in 1989, W. Eck pointed out that in an inscription mentioning a procurator in charge of this area of operation (*CIL* V 7547 = *ILS* 1407) the father of the procurator does not have a *cognomen* (Eck 1989), and that this means the inscription cannot be later than about the middle of the first century CE (cf. Salomies 1987: 346–53). Since the decoration of the monument also implies an early date, Eck then drew the only possible conclusion, namely that the establishment of this procuratorship must be dated about 100 years earlier than was previously assumed—a conclusion of great interest for historians of the organization of government in imperial Rome.

Sometimes a person's origin can be deduced on the basis of his or her name, especially if the tribe in which he is registered also is known.[5] C. Seius M. f. Quir(ina sc. *tribu*) Calpurnius Quadratus Sittianus, a senator whose career ended with the proconsulship of Gallia Narbonensis, died and was buried in Praeneste near Rome in (probably) the late second century (*CIL* XIV 2831). Since he exhibits the tribe Quirina in his nomenclature, rather than the tribe Menenia of Praeneste, the man was not buried in his home town. A first clue to his origin is the *cognomen* Sittianus, derived from the *nomen* Sittius. This is a rare *nomen* everywhere in the Roman world—except in North Africa. Now the tribe Quirina was common in African cities, and since the *nomen* Seius, when combined with Sittius and the tribe Quirina, also points in that direction, it is easy to suggest an African origin for the senator (so Syme 1984: 1108; 1988: 211 n. 58). But one can go further: the combined areas of distribution in Africa of the tribe Quirina and of the *nomina* Seius, Calpurnius, and Sittius definitively point to Cirta (the home of many Roman senators), a city assigned to the tribe Quirina with an abundance of Sittii and a good selection of Seii and Calpurnii. This man, then, is to be added to the list of senators from Cirta (Salomies 1992: 112–13).

This is applied onomastics, a form of prosopography, and I hope what has been said above will have demonstrated sufficiently why I am treating the two subjects together in the same chapter. Before turning to my subject proper (starting this time with names and then moving on rather quickly to prosopography), I must remind the reader that one can of course use inscriptions for the study of names and individuals only for those periods in which there are inscriptions. In the Greek world, one finds inscriptions from the eighth century BCE onwards, but they start to be numerous only in the fourth century, the "epigraphic habit" now quickly spreading. In Rome inscriptions start to appear in larger numbers in the second century BCE and become more common in the first century BCE, but it is only in the time of Augustus that an "epigraphic revolution" takes place; what survives from the period of the Republic represents only a tiny fraction of the total number of Latin inscriptions. Onomastic and prosopographical studies of archaic Greece and early Rome are therefore mainly based on sources other than inscriptions.[6]

Names

The uses of inscriptions for onomastics are in the main twofold. First, there is simply the quantitative aspect. Both in Greece and in Rome inscriptions let us know the names of thousands of individuals unknown from other sources, especially those belonging to the lower strata— soldiers, shopkeepers, slaves and the like—who rarely figure in other sources. But inscriptions are often our only source of knowledge also of more highly placed persons, especially in poorly documented periods: for instance, without inscriptions we would know absolutely nothing about many of the leading men of imperial Rome (see below, pages 87–8). The first two published volumes of the *Lexicon of Greek Personal Names* (Fraser–Matthews 1987; Osborne–Byrne 1994) mention 66,486 and 62,360 individuals, respectively, and the total number of different names in volume two seems to surpass 8,000. Volume three (on the

Peloponnese and the Greek mainland), of which only the first part (IIIA: covering the Peloponnese, western Greece, Sicily and Magna Graecia) has appeared (Fraser–Matthews 1997) will, when complete, include a further 75,000 persons (E. Matthews in Osborne–Byrne 1994: vi). Only a small number of these names is known from sources other than inscriptions, and even in the case of those known also from literary sources, the bulk of attestations comes from inscriptions (e.g. of 68 Athenian men called "Demosthenes," only two or three seem to be known only from literary sources: Osborne–Byrne 1994: 110–11). In Rome, the situation is the same: without inscriptions, we would know perhaps less than one per cent of all *nomina* and *cognomina*, and books such as those of Schulze (1904) and Kajanto (1965) could never be written.

It is, however, important to keep in mind that even though many thousands of ancient inscriptions survive, and even though hundreds of new ones are published every year, we do not know all Greek names or Roman *nomina* and *cognomina*, yet alone all Greeks and Romans who once lived. Although there are more than 40,000 inscriptions from the city of Rome from the first three centuries CE, it has been suggested that we know only about four tenths of one per cent of those who lived in the city during this period (Duncan-Jones 1978: 195); of the population of Roman Dalmatia during the same period we know perhaps only one tenth of one per cent (Wilkes 1977: 751–2). Women and children are always underrepresented in epigraphical sources (of the 62,360 individuals in Osborne–Byrne 1994, only 5,691 are women: E. Matthews, ibid. p. vi.); and some people (usually, perhaps, those on the lower rungs of the social ladder) were never commemorated in tombstones (Meyer 1990: 77 n. 22, with references to papers by W. Eck). These calculations of course concern the whole population; if one concentrates only on special groups at the higher levels of society, the numbers are much better. An interesting paper on Roman senators by W. Eck (1973), for example, shows that the higher the office, the more office-holders are attested (usually, of course, only epigraphically). Of those who held the quaestorship, the lowest office, between 69 and 138 CE, we know nine per cent; of proconsuls of Africa or Asia during the first three centuries CE, on the other hand, we know 50 per cent (Africa) and 70 per cent (Asia—but "new" proconsuls of Asia seem to crop up in inscriptions every two or three years); of those who held the consulship twice, we know practically all.

Secondly (to get back to names), we generally learn more about them from inscriptions than from literary sources. In Greece this is perhaps not so important as in Rome, but here, too, inscriptions can be very useful.

Greek names

In classical and Hellenistic times, Greeks normally had only one name, e.g. "Perikles" or "Platon." However, it was in many circumstances customary to add the "patronymic," the name of the father (most often in the genitive). When abroad, it was not uncommon to add a reference to one's home, usually in the form of an adjective ("Athenaios," "Milesios," etc.). In Athens, citizens normally added their "demotic"— a reference to the "deme" ($\delta\tilde{\eta}\mu o s$) to which they belonged, this roughly indicating the place of origin within Attica (and thus useful, e.g. for demographical studies). The use of the demotic became obligatory in official registers and the like in 403/2 BCE, but one can find isolated instances even earlier (Lazzarini 1976: 66; Meyer 1993: 110 nn. 25–6). Whereas individuals are often referred to in literary sources by only one name, inscriptions tend to give the full nomenclature, especially if the person is relevant to the contents of the inscription (i.e. is not simply mentioned in passing, as in a date).[7]

Consequently, we often have additional information from inscriptions about individuals mentioned also in literary sources. For instance, of the brothers Eurykleides and Mikion, the Athenian politicians of the 230s and 220s BCE, only their names are known from literary sources; from epigraphic evidence we learn that they were sons of Mikion and from the deme Kephisia (*PA* 5966, 10188). On the other hand, there is much variation in naming practices in literary sources, as in inscriptions (cf. n. 7): in historical narratives, for instance, one name only is generally used for persons whose identity is certain, whereas in other types of source (e.g. speeches, not to mention biographical works), one observes a tendency to add the patronymic or the deme or both, in some cases for the sake of clarity, but often simply because it was not abnormal to do so even in everyday speech. Thus Cicero can refer to Epicurus as *ille Gargettius*, "that man from (the deme) Gargettos" (*Fam.* 15.16.1), this no doubt reflecting an Athenian custom, and even today, as in antiquity, we speak of the Athenian politician as "Demetrius of Phalerum." Of Demetrius we know not only his deme but also his patronymic from literary as well as from epigraphic sources, and the same goes for other prominent Athenians of roughly the same period, such as Demosthenes and Epicurus (see *PA* 3455, 3597, 4855; Figure 3.1).

Figure 3.1 Statue base from somewhere in or near the theater of Dionysus in Athens, now in the park of the archaeological site of the theater, close to the entrance. Pentelic marble (117 × 82 × 80 cm), c. 115–60 CE (*IG* II/III² 3609). The inscription was set up by two Athenians, the brothers Tiberius Claudius Demostratus and Tiberius Claudius Leonides, to honor their brother Tiberius Claudius Lysiades from the deme Melite, of whom it is said that he was the son of the *dadouchos* (a priest of the mysteries at Eleusis) Sospis, grandson of the *dadouchos* Lysiades, great-grandson of the *dadouchos* Leonidas; that he had held the eponymous archonship; and that he had acted as *panegyriarch*. At the end of the text Demostratus and Leonides specify that the setting up of the statue had been approved by the city of Athens. The archonship is dated to the reign of Hadrian or Pius by Follet 1976: 511, 514. The text gives us useful information on an important Athenian family in the first and second centuries CE, of which at least some members already possessed Roman citizenship, this being made clear by the prefix "Tiberius Claudius."

Roman names

Greek epitaphs, the most common type of Greek inscription before Roman times, seldom offer more information on the deceased than just the name, whereas in Latin funerary inscriptions it was common to include such details as the age at death and in many cases also the occupation. For this reason, and because in Latin inscriptions a sharp distinction is drawn between freedmen and the freeborn, they are in general somewhat more useful for further study than their Greek counterparts—not only for social history but for onomastics, for it is good to know what kind of people had certain names.

In the Roman onomastic system of the classical period, which was based on the family name common to all members of the family, each male had at least a first name, the *praenomen* (usually abbreviated), and a family name, the *nomen* (*gentilicium*), e.g. "M. (i.e. Marcus) Tullius." In addition, some Romans had a third name, the *cognomen*, e.g. "M. Tullius Cicero." Women did not usually have *praenomina* (see Kajava 1995a), but beginning in the first century BCE a woman could have a *cognomen*. The use of *cognomina* by men, sporadic as late as the first century BCE, quickly became more and more common under the early Empire: by the middle of the first century CE the absence of one was exceptional (for this evolution see Salomies 1987: 277–99). It is important to note also the evolution of the nature of the *cognomen*. During the Republic, when the *cognomen* was in use mainly among the higher classes, a *cognomen* was usually hereditary and as such became in practice a further family name: all sons of a M. Tullius Cicero, for example, inherited the two names "Tullius Cicero" and were distinguished from each other only by *praenomina*. But when, from the first century BCE onwards, the use of a *cognomen* began to spread among the rest of the population, the new *cognomina* were normally personal, each son being given his own distinctive *cognomen*.

This was an important evolution, for in the course of time the personal *cognomen* superseded the old personal name, the *praenomen*, which now gradually lost its importance; accordingly, from the second century one observes the *praenomen* being omitted more and more often, even in funerary inscriptions; at the end of the third century CE it was altogether abandoned (Salomies 1987: 346–413). Knowledge of this evolution is useful for those dealing with epigraphy, for nomenclature is often the only criterion for dating Latin inscriptions. And although a close dating on this basis is impossible, at least one can say that an inscription in which a man who does not have a *cognomen* is mentioned should be "early," probably before the middle of the first century CE (cf. above on *CIL* V 7547), whereas an inscription in which *praenomina* are omitted must be "late," second century CE or probably even later. (Names offer many other clues for dating, which we cannot go into here.)

A Roman name in its fullest form contained two further items: the filiation recording, after the *nomen*, the *praenomen* of the father (sometimes also that of the grandfather and occasionally even those of more distant ancestors), usually in the form "M(arci) f(ilius)" (freedmen here referred to their former owners, e.g. "M(arci) l(ibertus)," "freedman of Marcus": see Figure 3.2); and, after the filiation, the *tribus* or "tribe," originally the voting district in which a Roman citizen voted, of which there were altogether 35 (see Taylor 1960). Abbreviated usually with three letters (Qui(rina), Pal(atina) etc.) and to be understood most often in the ablative case, the tribe had lost all political meaning by the time of the Empire, but it remains useful for scholars wishing to study people's origins, for some tribes point to certain cities or regions: Quirina for instance was the tribe of many African cities (cf. above), Voltinia that of many cities in Narbonese Gaul (cf. E. Birley 1951: 161–2). Both filiation and tribe tend to be omitted in inscriptions from the second century onwards—another clue to their date.

The full nomenclature of a Roman citizen, then, would look like this: "M(arcus) Tullius M(arci) f(ilius) Cor(nelia sc. *tribu*) Cicero." This is not, of course, a form normally used in literary sources. Latin authors rarely mention the filiation or the tribe and have a tendency to refer to persons by a pair of names. During the Republic, the pair would normally consist of the *praenomen* and either the *nomen* or the *cognomen* (e.g. "C. Marius" or "L. Sulla"; cf. Salomies 1987: 252–5). From the time of Augustus onwards, with the personal *cognomen* gaining in importance and gradually superseding the *praenomen*, authors begin to favor a style of nomenclature consisting of the pair *nomen* and *cognomen* ("Albius Tibullus," etc.).

Literary sources, then, do not always supply the information on personal names one would like to have. This is where inscriptions come in, for inscriptions tend to record a formal, full nomenclature, at least for persons important within the text (e.g. the deceased in epitaphs or the honorands in honorific inscriptions). Indeed, without inscriptions we would not even know the names of all the 35 tribes. In many cases inscriptions mention the *praenomina*, filiations, and tribes of persons of whom literary sources use only the *nomen* and *cognomen*: the governor of Pannonia known from Tacitus (*Ann.* 12.29.2) as Palpellius Hister, for example, in fact turns out to be a Sex(tus) Palpellius P(ubli) f(ilius) Vel(ina) Hister

Figure 3.2 Roman funerary plaque commemorating members of a household of Cn. Quintii and A. Livii. Marble (85.9 × 68.8 × 5.1 cm), c. 50 BCE–50 CE (Treggiari 1982: 181–4). The epitaph presumably came from the façade of a free-standing monumental tomb in which the ashes of the 16 persons named were deposited. The names, disposed in two columns read top to bottom, left to right, identify 14 freedmen and freedwomen, several jointly manumitted by two or three (or, in one case [lines 22–3], four) Quintii and Livii, one a *concubina* (a common-law wife: lines 4–5), and two freeborn but illegitimate children ("Sp(urii) f(ili/ae)": lines 12, 17). Several of the ex-slaves were freed by women, as is normally indicated by a reversed "C" (for "Gaia", the Roman "Jane Doe" or "any woman"), sometimes, because women generally lacked *praenomina*, by the *nomen gentilicium* (Quintia) spelled out (lines 9, 15, 18, 20, 26), once (lines 22–3) by both. (The J. Paul Getty Museum, Malibu, California, unknown artist, Roman funerary inscription, first century BCE (?). CA.Malibu.JPGM.L.80.AA.62.)

(*ILS* 946, from Pola in Histria); Dillius Aponianus, a legate of the Third Legion (Tac. *Hist.* 3.10.1) is a C. (i.e. Gaius) Dillius L(uci) f(ilius) A(uli) n(epos) Ser(gia) Aponianus (*CIL* II²/7 275, from Corduba). In these instances the inscriptions provide an additional bonus by disclosing the origins of the senators, inasmuch as the tribe in both cases coincides with that of the findspot. In others, inscriptions add names not attested in literary sources: the nomenclature of Pliny the Younger can be reconstructed as "C. Plinius Secundus" on the basis of literary evidence, but inscriptions (below, pages 88–90) disclose, in addition to his filiation and tribe (of Comum, of course), that he also bore the *nomen* "Caecilius" of his natural father ("Plinius" being that of his adoptive father). Silius Italicus the poet, consul in 68 CE, acquires a *praenomen* and two further *nomina* from *MAMA* 8.411, in which he appears as "Ti. Catius Asconius Silius Italicus."

The fact that Pliny and Silius Italicus had more than one *nomen* brings us back for a moment to "polyonymy," a phenomenon referred to earlier (see page 77). Without inscriptions we would hardly even suspect that such a thing existed, for polyonymous nomenclatures have left very few traces in literary sources, in which during the Empire persons are usually referred to by *nomen* and *cognomen* alone. A man who appears in some inscriptions as "Q(uintus) Roscius Sex(ti) f(ilius) Qui(rina) Coelius Murena Silius Decianus Vibullius Pius Iulius Eurycles Herclanus Pompeius Falco" is called simply "Pompeius Falco" by Pliny and Fronto (Salomies 1992: 121–2, where it is noted that there is much variation in the number of names used of this man in inscriptions also).[8] Sometimes inscriptions not only supplement but also correct literary sources; for instance, two equestrian prefects in office under Tiberius at the time of the Sejanus affair are called by Cassius Dio (or by manuscripts of Dio, at 58.9.2–3) "Naevius Sertorius Macro" and "Gracinus Laco," but inscriptions (again, also revealing the two men's origins) name them "Q. Naevius Cordus Q. f. Fab(ia) Sutorius Macro" (*AE* 1957, 250, Alba Fucens) and "P. Graecinius P. f. Pob(lilia) Laco" (*ILS* 1336, Verona). Because of *ILS* 960 and *AE* 1987, 163, the *nomina* of Pontius Fregellanus (Tac. *Ann.* 6.48.4) and Sextius Paconianus (*Ann.* 6.3.4; 39.1) have to be corrected to "Pontilius" and "Sextilius," respectively.

Sometimes, it is true, inscriptions do not help, if they are too fragmentary; a notable example is that from Hippo in Africa in honor of Suetonius (*AE* 1953, 73). Furthermore, inscriptions do not normally use the full nomenclature of persons mentioned only incidentally; the only inscription to mention Tacitus (*OGIS* 487, from Mylasa) does not settle the question of his *praenomen* because he is referred to simply as the proconsul of Asia in a date and thus simply as "Cornelius Tacitus." What is more, late inscriptions tend to omit *praenomina*, filiation, and tribes even of honorands; accordingly an inscription from Tyre set up in honour of the Severan jurist Domitius Ulpianus (*AE* 1988, 1051) does not tell us more about Ulpian's nomenclature than we already know from literary sources. (We still await epigraphical finds mentioning authors such as Cornelius Nepos and Albius Tibullus, of whom only these names are known.)

In some cases inscriptions, instead of being useful, only introduce trouble, as for instance in the case of the father of the emperor Antonius Gordianus I (238 CE): in the *Historia Augusta*, the collection of imperial biographies much in disrepute because of its tendency to fabrication and invention, the father is said to have been called Maecius Marullus. It used to be thought that this was another of many fictive characters (see *PIR²* M 56), but an inscription, possibly of the third century, found near Rome not far from the place where the Gordians had a villa, now in fact mentions a [M]aecius Marullus *v(ir) c(larissimus)*, i.e. a senator (*AE* 1971, 62). Is this really the father, as some scholars have thought? If so, one wonders why he does not have the same *nomen* as his son. Or is the identity of names simply a coincidence? Or has the author of the *Historia Augusta*, when inventing a father for the emperor, simply used an existing person's name? We cannot know.

Roman careers

On the other hand, to move from the sphere of onomastics to that of prosopography, epigraphical sources also mention a large number of persons unknown from other evidence—and not only those belonging to the so-called lower classes: in periods not well documented in literary sources (in Rome this means much of the Empire) even consuls and other state officials may find themselves omitted from the literary tradition. A look at a few pages of the *Prosopographia Imperii Romani* (*PIR*) or of lists of provincial governors (such as Alföldy 1969) is enough to show that only a minority of Roman consuls and governors are known from sources other than inscriptions (and in some cases coins). In periods covered only by inferior historical sources, such as the *Historia Augusta* (cf. n. 9), that is, in the second and third centuries CE, even very highly placed senior statesmen and generals may pass unnoticed by the authors whose work we happen to have. Under the Empire, a group of an especially high status comprises those who held the consulship twice and who were also urban prefects of Rome. A catalogue of such men from the period 70–160 CE (Vidman 1982b: 302–3) lists at least three— Q. Glitius Atilius Agricola (*cos. II* 103), Ti. Iulius Candidus (*cos. II* 105) and M. Lollius Paullinus Valerius Asiaticus Saturninus (*cos. II* 125)—not mentioned by any extant writer (the latter two appear as "Candidus" and "Asiaticus" in late antique consular lists) and of whose existence we would know nothing or practically nothing if we had to rely on literary sources alone. Luckily, all three are known from quite a few inscriptions, from which we can derive the whole career (and filiation and tribe) of Atilius Agricola (*PIR*² G 181 and below, page 90) and Valerius Asiaticus (*PIR*² L 320) and many details of the career of Iulius Candidus (*PIR*² I 241 with *IEphesos* 810).

That we know any details of the lives of these men is of course due to the fact that the inscriptions from which Romans of some status are known in many cases offer more information than just the name. Honorific and funerary inscriptions of higher officials of the imperial government often set out the whole career of the honorand, and Romans of higher status are often known not from one but from several epigraphical texts which supplement one another and which, when combined, constitute complex personal dossiers. Almost all kinds of inscriptions can offer information useful for prosopographical studies (Figure 3.3). From military diplomas, dated to the day, one can extract information on governors and military commanders; besides mentioning consuls not known from other sources, they often supply the date of consulships otherwise not datable. Provincial building inscriptions, often dated, may mention governors. Votive inscriptions set up by soldiers sometimes refer to governors or legionary commanders. Funerary inscriptions of slaves and freedmen often mention their patrons (see below, page 90, for the funerary inscription of a philosopher accompanying Salvius Iulianus to Germany). In some cases one finds useful information on Roman functionaries in inscriptions of their relatives or other officials: that the Vespasianic consul C. Arruntius Catellius Celer was *curator operum publicorum* in the early 80s is known from inscriptions referring, not to Celer, but to his equestrian assistant, L. Vibius Lentulus (*IEphesos* 2061, 3046); a Spanish inscription of a young senator recording that he had held a minor office "in the consulship of his father Aemilius Papus and of his father-in-law Burbuleius Ligarianus" discloses not only that Papus and Ligarianus were consular colleagues but that the young man had married Ligarianus' daughter (*AE* 1983, 517).

Pliny the Younger, about whom we know quite a lot from literary sources, especially his own letters and the *Panegyricus*, is a special case. Pliny is known also from a number of inscriptions, several of which add onomastic details not known from the literary sources (the name of his father, his tribe, and his additional *nomen* Caecilius). From three honorific inscriptions in particular—all from the period after Pliny's consulship in 100 CE, but before his mission to Bithynia (*CIL* V 5263 and *AE* 1972, 212 from his home city, Comum; *CIL* V 5667, set up by the

Figure 3.3 Statue base *in situ* in the middle of the first row of seats in the theater of Dionysus in Athens. Pentelic marble (56 × 83 × 83 cm), 111–12
CE (*IG* II/III² 3286 = *CIL* III 550 = *ILS* 308). The monument was set
up in honor of a 35- or 36-year-old Roman senator with a bright
future, namely P. Aelius Hadrianus, the later emperor Hadrian. A
man thought by some to have been rather too interested in Greece
and Greek things, Hadrian held the Athenian archonship in 111–12
CE, this being the occasion of the setting up of the monument. The
main text is in Latin, whereas the archonship and the dedicators
—the Council of the Areopagus, the Council of Six Hundred, and
the *demos* of the Athenians—are given in Greek. The main text
gives Hadrian's full name—P(ublius) Aelius P(ubli) f(ilius) Serg(ia)
Hadrianus (we thus learn that this father was also called Publius and
that he belonged to the tribe Sergia which, as we know from other
sources, was the tribe of his home town Italica in Spain)—and his
complete career, ending with a suffect consulate in 108 CE. The career
enumerated in this inscription confirms the description of Hadrian's
career given in the beginning of Hadrian's *vita* in the *Historia
Augusta*, but includes some items omitted in it.

people of Vercellae, from the territory of Mediolanum [Milan])—one
gathers that Pliny may have been the patron of Vercellae and that he
possibly owned a villa where that inscription was found. Pliny further
appears in the nominative, i.e. as the dedicator, in two inscriptions
enumerating his whole career: *CIL* V 5262 (*ILS* 2927), from Comum,
recording Pliny's building of baths and further benefactions there, and
CIL XI 5272 (fragmentary), from Hispellum in Umbria, set up after his

death, which shows that Pliny had bequeathed a considerable sum to Hispellum to fund some (unidentified) building, this again implying close contact with a town, where he may have owned land, as he did in another Umbrian city, Tifernum. Finally, although it could be deduced from Pliny's *Panegyricus* that he was consul in September 100, it is good to have this confirmed by the discovery in 1969 of a fragment of the inscribed consular list of Ostia pertaining to that year (Vidman 1982a: 45).

Q. Glitius Atilius Agricola, Pliny's contemporary and an important senator, although never mentioned in literary sources, is known from a large number of honorific inscriptions, many now fragmentary, set up by various dedicators in his home city, Augusta Taurinorum (Torino) (*CIL* V 6974–87; two are included in *ILS* as 1021 and 1021a). *CIL* V 6974 and 6975 enumerate the career up to Agricola's first consulship under Nerva; the rest are from a later period and go on with the governorship of Pannonia (following on the consulship) and a second consulship; the latest text (6980) adds the prefecture of the city of Rome, Agricola's highest office. Exact dates are furnished by other kinds of epigraphic evidence: the first consulship is dated to 97 CE by the Ostian *fasti* (Vidman 1982a: 45), the Pannonian governorship to 102 by a military diploma (*CIL* XVI 47), and the second consulship to the end of January 103 by another diploma (*CIL* XVI 48). Finally, Agricola is mentioned in the funerary inscription of one of the slaves from his household in the capital (*CIL* VI 14740).

The epigraphic dossier on Salvius Iulianus, consul in 148 and a lawyer mentioned in many literary sources, consists of several documents (cf. Salomies 1992: 41 on the varying name forms). *CIL* VIII 24094 (= *ILS* 8973), an honorific inscription from Pupput in Africa, enumerates Iulianus' complete career up to his highest office, the proconsulate of Africa. Since Iulianus was an "ordinary" consul (that is, one entering office on January 1), many sources, both epigraphic and literary, mention his consulship in 148; an inscription from Rome, *CIL* VI 855 (cf. also *AE* 1968, 25) telling us that Iulianus, as *curator aedium sacrarum*, gave permission to erect some monument (not identifiable) in September 150, gives an exact date for this office. Two inscriptions from lower Germany refer to Iulianus' governorship of the province: *CIL* XIII 7791 mentions a soldier who served under him; *CIL* XIII 8159 (*ILS* 7776) records a philosopher who accompanied him and no doubt reflects his intellectual interests. Finally, an inscription of late 168 or early 169 (*ILTun* 699) recording the dedication of the *Capitolium* of Thuburbo Maius in Africa by Iulianus as proconsul of Africa settles the date of his proconsulship.

These instances may suffice to show that we often have quite a lot of information on Roman functionaries, coming from many kinds of epigraphic source. Although it is true that, even in those cases in which we have various epigraphic information on certain individuals, we do not get to know all we would like to—and perhaps should—know (note Millar 1983: 131–4); what information we do have can be used for a wide range of observations, many of which come under the general heading "prosopography" but which in fact surpass the limits of "personal" history. We have already seen that in periods poorly documented in literary sources inscriptions often let us know not only the names of leading men but also the fact that they were indeed leading men. This is very important extra information indeed. Of course epigraphical sources also regularly offer information additional to, or in some cases corrective of, what we know from other sources (cf. above, on names, and Cox 1995 on prosopographical information derived from private orations of fourth-century Athens). Collecting and studying the inscriptions mentioning priests who belonged to the priesthood of the *sodales Augustales, Flaviales, Hadrianales* in the time of Antoninus Pius, men of very high standing, and comparing this group with that of the correspondents of the senatorial author Fronto, and finding that not one *sodalis* appears in the latter group, allows us to determine more precisely Fronto's social position (Pflaum 1972: 319).[9] A study of an inscription from Delphi shows that Iunius Gallio, governor of Achaea, must have been in office from 51 to 52 CE; this in turn allows a new dating of the apostle Paul's stay at Corinth (Reynolds 1971: 144 on an article by A. Plassart). A governor of Lycia, Marcius Priscus, seems (especially from *IGRR* 3.659, as reread by W. Eck) to have governed the province continuously from Nero to Vespasian, from which it follows that "Suetonius cannot quite mean what he seems to say when he states that Vespasian withdrew freedom from the Lycians (*Vesp.* 8.4)" (Reynolds 1976: 185 summarizing an article by Eck). Prosopographical information coming from inscriptions can also be used to supplement and correct papyrological sources; for instance, more than 30 prefects of Egypt are known from both papyri (the main source material in Egypt) and inscriptions, the two sources in many cases supplementing each other (cf. Pflaum 1981: 258–68 for further information on Roman officials in Egypt emerging from inscriptions).

An exemplary governor

It may be appropriate to conclude with a somewhat more detailed summary of a remarkable demonstration of how and to what extent an inscription, when combined with other literary and epigraphical evidence, can lead to important prosopographical observations that in turn illuminate Roman history more generally.

Until recently, the senator M. Cornelius M. f. Gal(eria) Nigrinus Curiatius Maternus was known from two inscriptions, *CIL* II 3783 and 6013, set up in his honor in his home town of Liria in eastern Spain and specifying that he had been consul and governor of both Moesia and Syria (the latter a very high distinction). Estimates of this man's date varied widely; E. Hübner, the editor of *CIL* II and a most distinguished epigraphist, thought that the letter-forms of no. 6013 pointed to a third-century date. The question was settled in 1973 when a large fragment of another inscription in honor of Cornelius Nigrinus from Liria was combined with a known fragment of the same text (*CIL* II 3788) and was published in a definitive way (Alföldy–Halfmann 1973, with references to earlier publications). The new text, setting out the whole career of the man up to his governorship of Syria, specified that he had won military awards in a war which can only have been "Dacian" ([*bello Da*]*cico* in lines 7–8)—in theory, then, under either Domitian or Trajan. Since the emperor giving the awards is not named, only a war fought under Domitian can be meant, for it is only Domitian whose name is omitted in similar circumstances. Furthermore, the text elsewhere refers to two emperors (by whom Cornelius Nigrinus seems to have been "adlected" into the senate), the traces of whose nomenclature clearly point to Vespasian and Titus. We are thus dealing with a man who held senatorial offices between the 70s and the 90s of the first century CE.

The inscription tells us that, after minor offices, Nigrinus was legate of the Eighth Augustan legion (in Strasbourg), governor of Aquitania, and, subsequently, legate of Moesia; between the last two offices he must have held a (suffect) consulship, since a governorship of Moesia required consular status. The editors point out that M. Cornelius Nigrinus must be identical with a man of whose name only the beginning "M. Co[" has been preserved in an inscription dated to 83 CE, in which he is mentioned as (suffect) consul (*CIL* XIV 4725). As for the governorship in Moesia, we know that when the Dacians invaded Moesia in the mid 80s, the governor Oppius Sabinus was killed in battle; it used to be thought that this happened in 86, but the editors now suggest 85. Since Nigrinus' governorship of Moesia followed on his consulship in 83, it appears that he was Oppius Sabinus' successor. The Dacian war was going on, and in about 86 the province was divided, no doubt for strategic reasons, into "lower" and "upper" Moesia. Since we know that a certain L. Funisulanus Vettonianus was governor of upper

Moesia from about 86, Nigrinus must have continued as legate of lower Moesia, a province of higher status. The governors of the two Moesias evidently did their jobs well, for both were awarded military decorations (for Nigrinus see above, for Vettonianus see *ILS* 1005), which, to judge from the imperial acclamations of Domitian, must have happened already before the end of 86. Since Nigrinus, unlike Vettonianus, had received an exceptional number of awards, it appears that he fought with success also in the Dacian campaigns of 88 and 89 and must have stayed in Moesia at least until 89, perhaps even later.

This is very good new information indeed. But knowing that Nigrinus then went on to govern Syria, and that we can now date this office, provides us with perhaps even more interesting insights into Roman history at the end of the first century. All the governors of Syria from the 80s until late 94 or early 95 and again after 100/101 are known, and Nigrinus is not among them; he must then have been in Syria between 94/95 and 100/101, a period which would fit two average governorships of about three years. The governorship of another known legate of Syria, L. Iavolenus Priscus, must also be located in this same period, and many indications (not only the fact that he was consul three years after Nigrinus) suggest that Priscus was in Syria after, rather than before, Nigrinus. It follows that Nigrinus must have been governor of Syria between 94/95 and ca. 97—in other words, precisely at the time Domitian was murdered (September 96) and was succeeded by the weak and elderly emperor Nerva, who was unable to stabilize his position until he adopted Trajan, a man in his forties with a distinguished administrative and military career, in late October 97.

Now from a letter of Pliny datable to the earlier part of 97 (*Ep.* 9.13.10–11), it emerges that there were at the time *magni dubiique rumores* about the plans and aspirations of an (unnamed) eastern governor who had an *amplissimus exercitus* at his disposal. Since this can only mean the legate of Syria, it follows that Pliny was referring to Cornelius Nigrinus. All this means that the rather smooth picture of the events of 96/97 emerging from the meager literary sources—Nerva after a crisis adopting Trajan, agreed by all to be the most suitable candidate—must be replaced with a much more nuanced reconstruction of events: it now appears that, when it had become evident that Nerva was not going to manage by himself, there must in fact have been a fierce competition between the possible candidates to be chosen as his colleague: Trajan, governor of upper Germany, had a serious rival in the governor of another important province, Syria, this man too, like Trajan himself, a Spaniard (Alföldy–Halfmann 1973: 363–7).

How exactly Trajan prevailed in the end over Cornelius Nigrinus must remain unknown, but two inscriptions setting out the career of another senator, A. Larcius Priscus (Alföldy–Halfmann 1973: 364), and establishing that in about 97, as an ex-quaestor of Asia only in his twenties, he was named legate of the Syrian legion *IV Scythica* and interim governor of the whole province, seem to imply that Nigrinus, instead of becoming emperor, had to leave Syria in a hurry. Although there remain details we would like to know, we can say that in this case prosopographical observations based on a few honorific inscriptions have led to at least one page—an interesting page—of Roman history being rewritten.

Chapter 4

The family and society

Richard Saller

D M
ANNIAE SATVRNINAE
Q VIXIT ANN XVII M V
D XII L EVHELPISTVS VXOR
B M F

(*CIL* VI 11818)

"To the sacred shades of Annia Saturnina, who lived 17 years, five months, 12 days, Lucius Euhelpistus made this (monument) for a well-deserving wife" (Figure 4.1) This funerary inscription from the city of Rome, which contains the standard elements of a Roman imperial epitaph, would appear to be too brief and formulaic to be a very promising source for the study of family and society in the Greco-Roman world. Nevertheless, for want of better documents for most of the ancient Mediterranean, the social historian must rely heavily on inscriptions, most of which are no more informative than this dedication.

The historians who wrote in antiquity from Herodotus on took as their main subject the public sphere—that is, the men's world of politics and war. When Tacitus in the early second century CE had to recount the sordid domestic affairs of the imperial family, he did so not because he was interested in family life in general but because the public life of the Republic had degenerated to meaningless, hypocritical forms, leaving real power to the emperor's household. In genres other than history, classical literature was written overwhelmingly by elite men for elite men and offers us a view of ancient society that is very limited socially, geographically, and by gender.

Without the same limitations of interest as their ancient counterparts, social historians today search for classical source materials to broaden

Figure 4.1 Epitaph of Annia Saturnina from Rome. Marble, c. 75–200 CE (*CIL* VI 11818). The dedication is notable only for its typicality, containing the standard elements of an imperial epitaph: names of deceased and commemorator, their relationship, the age of the deceased, and a stock epithet (in this case, "well-deserving"). (The Vatican Museums, Galleria Lapidaria, *paries* 3, 46, inventory number 8972.)

these horizons. If they had at their disposal the notarial archives and parish records available to late medieval and early modern historians, then the hundreds of thousands of inscriptions from antiquity would constitute no more than a sidelight in the study of ancient society. Without other documents, ancient historians are driven to give close attention to the usually brief, often fragmented, inscribed stones.

The subject of this chapter is the body of inscriptions from the private sphere, excluding civic and religious texts. A few of these inscriptions provide texts longer than a dozen lines, but most are short, formulaic funerary commemorations. The longer inscriptions can be read and interpreted in a hermeneutical manner similar to literary works. For instance, the acephalous memorial from a senatorial husband to his beloved wife tells a story of her life through the turbulent years of the civil wars following the assassination of Julius Caesar (see below). The brevity of the vast majority of inscriptions, however, leaves the historian with no story and requires a different method of study: since each in isolation is insignificant for the purposes of social history, these inscriptions must be studied in aggregate to identify patterns that permit meaningful conclusions. That is to say, the facts that Annia Saturnina died at age 17 years, five months, and 12 days, and was commemorated by her husband are not of much interest except as part of a body of data to reconstruct patterns of social bonds, ages at death, and the culture of commemoration. The use of inscriptions for such generalizations, however, raises difficult methodological questions that do not arise in traditional military and political histories of discrete events that are each significant in their own right.

This chapter is biased in favor of the Latin-speaking regions of the Roman empire. The bias is partially a reflection of my personal research interests, but also a result of the inscriptions themselves. As Fergus Millar has noted, the cities of the Greek East produced proportionately more public inscriptions which "tend both to be fuller and more revealing individually . . . and to come in denser concentrations" (1983: 113). Conversely, the private ancient tomb-inscription with age at death and commemorator is characteristic of the Latin West of the Roman Empire; but Millar has little to say about their value as source material, owing to their methodological difficulties (1983: 134–5).

Family life from inscriptions

Inscribed memorials to the dead by living family members are so pervasive in human societies as to seem almost banal. Such a dismissive attitude, however, misses the fact that in diverse societies the deceased and their social bonds with the living have been represented in different ways that reflect cultural concepts and social realities. But the reflection is not simple and direct, and the historian must confront several interpretive issues.

As Ian Morris has rightly stressed, funerary inscriptions are just one enduring element of a cultural complex surrounding death, including burial, mourning, disposition of property, and so on. To be interpreted properly, epitaphs must be understood as related to the other practices and beliefs. Unfortunately, the evidence is hardly ever available to the historian to place particular inscriptions in the context of the ephemeral rituals performed by those connected to the deceased. Indeed, in most cases the inscriptions have been detached from the burial itself. Even though the epitaph should ideally be interpreted within its archaeological context, that often turns out to be impossible. And with the loss of context, the historian loses valuable information about dating and grouping of burials (Morris 1992: 156).

The Greek family

Funerary artifacts and practices have long been used by classical scholars to understand Greek and Roman family and society. Perhaps the most famous effort was N. D. Fustel de Coulanges' *The Ancient City*, originally published in 1864. Fustel argued that the early family of the Greeks and Romans was a social construct based on religion, not on biological reproduction or natural affection. Central to this religion was the worship of dead ancestors, a corporate group defined by the agnatic lineage. It was crucial that each father have a son to whom he could transmit both the sacred duty of sacrifice to the *manes* of male ancestors and the family estate on which these ancestors were buried. The sanctity of the family tomb in perpetuity provided the foundation for Greco-Roman ideas of private property. In Fustel's reconstruction, then, ancestor worship along agnatic lines, memory of the dead, the structure of family and kinship, and the inheritance of private property all coincided; and, consequently, evidence for one aspect could be used to shed light on another. It would follow that if inheritance was so tightly linked to commemoration of the dead, evidence for patterns of commemoration could be used to detect patterns of inheritance.

For his reconstruction Fustel drew on very widely scattered literary passages, written over a period of more than a millennium and over the area from India to Rome. Despite its intuitive appeal, Fustel's evolutionary scheme had a weak evidential base. A systematic analysis of Athenian funerary inscriptions enabled S. C. Humphreys to mount a convincing critique of Fustel's position. The social organization imagined by Fustel should have produced large burial groups of agnatic lineages scattered across the countryside. A major obstacle to demonstration of the existence of such burial groups is that familial bonds among the buried can be identified only with the aid of inscriptions indicating relationships. As Humphreys points out (1980: 98), with the exception of the Kerameikos (and more recently Rhamnous), historians usually do not have precise information about burial groups identified by inscribed markers, and the extant epitaphs published in the standard collections often cannot be linked to a specific archaeological context.

Despite the shortcomings of the evidence, however, Humphreys is able to discern significant features of the Athenian family which do not conform with Fustel's interpretation. The stress in the epitaphs is not on the representation of the deceased as a member of an agnatic lineage. In the sixth century, Attic inscriptions commemorate individual qualities of the deceased—his goodness, his military prowess, or his beauty (*IG* I² 976 = I³ 1194 *bis*; *IG* I² 984 = I³ 1200; *IG* I² 982 = I³ 1277). Of the 20 inscriptions noting the commemorator's relationship, nearly half (nine) are dedications from father to son; of the remainder, four others are also from parent to child, two more from parent and spouse, three from a sibling, and two from children to father. Only the last category, the two dedications to a father, corroborates Fustel's scheme of sons burying and memorializing their patrilineal ascendants in return for inheritance of the patrimony (Humphreys 1980: 104–5 with n. 18).

Funerary inscriptions from fourth-century Attica are far more plentiful and again, like those of the sixth century, memorialize close family relationships. The motifs of some monuments convey to the reader a poignant sense of loss of a family member. Humphreys' count of the relationships commemorated (1980: 116 n. 48) reveals husband and wife to be most common (88 examples); both parents with a child form the next largest group (50 + ?15), followed by father and son (30 + ?13), brother and brother (7 + ?3), mother and daughter (5 + ?4), brother and sister (5 + ?1), father and daughter (4 + ?2), and mother and son (2 + ?1). Notably rare among the Attic epitaphs are broader groups including relatives beyond the immediate family. That is to say, the sense of loss expressed in fourth-century epitaphs and the desire to evoke memories of the dead were heavily concentrated within the nuclear family. Within that family group, patterns of a gender bias in favor of sons over daughters emerge, but the fact that the conjugal bond is the most common relationship represented is decisive against Fustel's assertion that the structuring principle was agnatic.[1]

The Roman family

The standard funerary inscription of the Roman imperial era has survived by the thousands, to be gathered by historians into large corpora. The typical elements of these epitaphs include the name of the deceased with an indication of status, the age at death, the name and relationship of the dedicator, and an epithet to describe the deceased. Each of these elements has been studied in detail by historians. The status indicators in the names have been discussed in the preceding chapter on nomenclature (see above, pages 84–5).

The ages at death would seem to offer some insight into mortality patterns in the Roman world. Annia Saturnina, whose epitaph was quoted at the beginning of the chapter, died very young, at age 17. If the corpora of funerary inscriptions included a large proportion registering premature death, then the historian might conclude that the Romans had a low life expectancy caused by poor living conditions.

Unfortunately, methodological problems preclude such arguments. Hopkins demonstrated that those Romans commemorated with an age at death cannot have been a cross-section of all deceased (1966; 1987; also Éry 1969 and above, pages 35–6). In all regions of the Latin-speaking empire, newborns are rare in funerary commemorations, even though they must have accounted for a very large proportion of the deaths, perhaps a quarter to a third, to judge from comparable pre-industrial societies. Furthermore, in most regions only some of the epitaphs give an age at death. It can be shown that youths in Rome who died in their teens and twenties were more likely than their elders to have their age noted, probably because the age was felt to be more noteworthy and poignant in cases of premature deaths (Parkin 1992: 5–19; Saller 1994: 15–18). The historian must be cognizant of the fact that, despite inclusion of age, the funerary monuments were not the equivalent of census returns, and that commemorative customs must be taken into account in any sociological interpretation.

The Roman jurists provide explicit testimony about the meaning attached to burial and commemoration in the title of the *Digest* "Religious Things, Funeral Expenses, and the Right to Conduct Funerals" (11.7). Performance of the funerary rites was closely associated with inheritance and was assumed to be a sign of willingness to take up the estate of the deceased (*Dig.* 11.7.3–5, Ulpian). The jurists stress that the assumption was not always legally correct, but in a way that reveals a strong popular belief. The jurists further reveal that in the absence of an heir the responsibility for burial devolved upon a close family member.

What social patterns emerge from the thousands of commemorative relationships preserved on stone? A broad study of inscriptions from Rome, Italy and the Latin-speaking provinces (Saller–Shaw 1984) concluded that although some regional variations are observable, the commemorative relationships are predominantly within the nuclear family—that is, between husband and wife, parent and child, or siblings. As in the Attic inscriptions, extended kin are uncommon—usually about five per cent of all relationships. Furthermore, the few extended kin represented— grandparents, uncles, aunts—do not fall into any clear pattern or structure along paternal or maternal lines, despite arguments to the contrary (Saller 1997, *pace* Bettini 1991).

How should these commemorative patterns be interpreted? The jurists' comments on the popular meaning attached to performance of burial rites suggest that in these patterns we see a reflection—albeit imperfect—of lines of inheritance and bonds of affectionate duty (*pietas*).[2] Those bonds are heavily concentrated within the nuclear family of husband, wife, and children; they are bilateral and exhibit little generational depth.

This understanding of the tombstones has been met by methodological objections—in particular, that the aggregate counts take the dedications out of their ritual and archaeological context. Morris (1992: 156–63) argues that in order to interpret the patterns the historian must know the full ritual process that generated the texts collected in *CIL*. A richer understanding of the ritual would certainly be desirable, but is not in most cases possible or essential. The epitaphs were inscribed to perpetuate the memory of the deceased into future generations and to represent his or her closest relationships to passersby who had no knowledge of the burial ritual. One of the archaic Greek epitaphs quoted by Humphreys is quite explicit: "Whoever was not present when they buried me, let him mourn me now. *Mnema* of Telephanes" (*IG* XII, 8 396 = Pfohl 1966: no. 18). In other words, as texts to be read by future generations, epitaphs were explicitly or implicitly composed with a view to a detached reader such as a traveler along the Appian Way, who knew no more of the family and kin of the deceased than is represented in the written text as read by the present-day historian.

Another methodological issue arises from the fact that not all burials found in a well-preserved archaeological context were marked by an inscribed stone. For example, the excavations beneath St Peter's in the Vatican provide the historian with the rare luxury of epitaphs *in situ* (Toynbee–Ward-Perkins 1956). Within the house-tombs there, some burials are marked by dedications preserving the memory of a relationship, while other graves are unmarked (Eck 1988). The latter suggest that for some social strata burial was anonymous and, consequently, that funerary inscriptions do not represent a cross-section for the population. It is certainly true that inscribed memorials do not capture the full population nor the full range of relationships within the social groups who erected them. But whereas the biases of selection create insurmountable obstacles for mortality studies, the choices that Romans made are precisely the aim of a socio-cultural study of commemoration. The facts that within the house-tombs Romans chose to highlight certain bonds in writing, especially husband–wife and parent–child, but left others without a lasting memorial, reveals something important about hierarchies of duty and affection within the household.

Yet another criticism of the tabulation of commemorative relationships is that the analysis does not take adequate account of the life course.
That is to say, a parent-to-son dedication might be interpreted differently, depending on whether the son was an unmarried 15-year-old
or a 30-year-old married man. Through an analysis of age-at-death
and commemorative relationship, it is possible to trace patterns through
the life course. Males were most commonly commemorated by parents
through their early twenties, and then by a wife or children after age
30. Females were usually commemorated by parents through their
early teens, and then by husbands after age 20 (Shaw 1987, Saller 1994:
25–41). Though some variations can be detected, this pattern is broadly true of the Latin-speaking population with the epigraphic habit. The
most satisfactory explanation for the shift from parent to spouse as preferred commemorator is the marriage of the deceased. (In most regions
parents disappear too quickly from dedications of deceased women
around age 20 and deceased men around age 30 to be explained solely
by the increasing likelihood that the parents will have died as their children age.) The commemorative pattern, then, offers a general reflection
(albeit imperfect) of typical ages at first marriage—late twenties for men
and late teens for women. This pattern of late male/early female marriage is common in later Mediterranean societies and has important
implications for fertility, the shape of the family, and the paternalistic
tone of the conjugal relationship (Saller 1987a, 1994).

In many inscribed texts the only other descriptive element is an
epithet to characterize the deceased—for instance, *benemerens* ("well-
deserving"), *dulcissimus/a* ("sweetest"), *carissimus/a* ("dearest"), and *pien-
tissimus/a* ("most devoted"). The most common epithets were so routine
that they were abbreviated; *benemerens* was regularly shortened to *b.m.*,
as in Annia Saturnina's epitaph. Their routineness may incline the historian to treat the epithets as banal, but certain conclusions may be drawn
from their study. First, the stock epithets are so standardized that we
may doubt whether they provide a realistic description of particular family relationships. Nevertheless, they do provide a general guide to how
the Romans imagined the happy, virtuous family, and thus they provide a check on some of the more exotic interpretations of the Roman
family. Against assertions that the Roman family was about property
rather than affection, or that commemoration was about testation, it may
be said that the most commonly-inscribed epithets represent family
relationships as loving (*carissimus*), pleasurable (*dulcissimus*), and reciprocal
(*benemerens*, *pientissimus*). A more detailed study leads to other interesting
conclusions by disaggregating the body of epitaphs by age and relationship

(see especially Nielsen 1997, which is more sophisticated than Curchin 1982). Whereas *benemerens* is the single most common epithet and applicable to all household relationships, *pietas* is a quality ascribed more selectively: parents, children, and siblings are frequently described as *pius*; wives only occasionally; and household dependents only very rarely. The common attribution of *pietas* to parents as well as children is particularly interesting, because cultural historians have conventionally thought of *pietas* as a hierarchical virtue of obedience particularly appropriate to children to show to their fathers. The funerary inscriptions reveal that it would be more accurate to define it as a reciprocal quality of affectionate devotion valued in parents and children alike.

A few longer epitaphs provide some of the most detailed glimpses available of women, family relations, and gendered values from classical Rome. Two famous inscriptions include part of the funeral eulogy (*laudatio*) for two elite women of Rome. Ironically, the longest commemoration, the so-called *Laudatio Turiae*, is fragmented and missing the names of both the deceased and her aristocratic husband-commemorator, so that the inscription now serves not as a memorial for an individual but as a nameless expression of praise for a wealthy woman (*CIL* VI 37053 etc.; cf. Gordon 1983: no. 28). The opening of the preserved section of the *laudatio* narrates in some detail the heroic efforts of "Turia" through the violent years of the civil wars (44–30 BCE) to preserve her father's estate according to the terms of his will. In so doing, she displayed *pietas* toward him and his last wishes. "Turia" then used this wealth to support her female relatives in her house and to provide them with dowries—another outstanding display of *pietas*. During the civil war "Turia" supported her husband in exile and afterwards remained married to him for decades. Such a long marriage uninterrupted by divorce is praised as "rare" and elevated by "Turia's" wifely virtues, including chastity, obedience, companionship, wool-making, religion without superstition, and *pietas* toward her *familia*. The *laudatio* departs from the expected in its account of "Turia's" inability to bear children and her offer to invite another woman into the house to produce children for her husband. Her husband proclaims to the world that he angrily refused the offer, and the couple lived together as husband and wife to the end of her life (on this inscription and its uncertainties, see Wistrand 1976, Horsfall 1983a, Flach 1991).

Since historians have no *laudatio feminae* preserved in a classical literary text, this epigraphic text is very valuable despite its damaged condition. It casts a life story into an idealized eulogy in a fashion that reveals much about the peculiar position of Roman women. The recurrent theme is "Turia's" *pietas*—toward her parents, her mother-in-law, her female kin, and her husband. Devotion toward her father and husband included obedience, but the property rights of Roman women opened space for "Turia" to act on behalf of her husband during the war and to bestow dowries on her relatives. And yet the inscription also suggests that "Turia" willingly gave up some of her independence of property rights by allowing her husband to manage her estate, which had to be kept separate from his under Roman law. The stress on child-bearing as the purpose of Roman marriage is painfully evident in the details about the couple's disappointment—the husband's hopes for descendants and the "wife's failure." Like Latin literature, these eulogies supply us with the men's voice.

The Augustan eulogy for Murdia by her son also offers a combination of stock idealization and awkward realities (*CIL* VI 10230 = *ILS* 8394; Horsfall 1982). Like "Turia," Murdia received praise for chastity, obedience, wool-working, and devotion to her natal and conjugal families. As with "Turia," much attention was given to Murdia's display of devotion in her disposition of family property. Murdia's problem was rather different; instead of no children, she had children by two husbands, the first of whom left her a widow. Her eldest son, the eulogist, praised her love and fairness in dividing the property from her side of the family equally among all of her sons (with a portion for her daughter) and in specifying that the property from her first husband go only to the offspring of that marriage, that is, her eldest son (the speaker) (Humbert 1972: 255). The eulogy further praises Murdia for "obedience" and "propriety" in remaining in the marriages to the "distinguished men" arranged by her parents. This text gives historians a sense of how the legal freedoms of a Roman woman after her father's death—to initiate divorce, to make her own choice of a husband, and to dispose of her own property—were constrained by the cultural values of obedience (*obsequium*) and fairness in the distribution of her estate. The situation of the propertied woman in classical Rome was not a simple one either of patriarchal oppression or of liberation, but was a complex outcome of the tension between sometimes contradictory legal rights and cultural values.

The elite Roman household (*domus*) was a large amorphous social unit ideologically centered on the *paterfamilias*, *matrona*, and their legitimate children (Saller 1987b). It included slaves and free(d) dependents sometimes numbered in the hundreds. Funerary inscriptions provide crucial evidence to illuminate the social organization of the hierarchical household. Commemorations reveal that even though Roman law did not acknowledge the right of slaves to marry, in reality slaves in large households formed *de facto* family units (Flory 1978). Furthermore, the family lives of masters and slaves interacted in numerous ways: funerary dedications by (former) masters to (ex-)slave wetnurses (*nutrices*) and childminders (*pedagogi*) reveal an affective attachment that may have partially masked the harsh exploitation (Bradley 1991: 13–75). If Roman ideology drew a sharp contrast between the honorable legitimate children and the honorless slaves, inscriptions draw attention to a broader social spectrum in the *domus*—in particular, to *alumni* or "fosterchildren," who appear in an intermediate status, described with some of the epithets associated with legitimate children (*dulcissimus, carissimus*) but not others (especially *pientissimus*, see Nielsen 1997; Rawson 1986).

Finally, funerary dedications provide an important reminder that legitimate marriage (*iustum matrimonium*) was the prerogative of Roman citizens and was thought to be appropriate between honorable men and women of more or less comparable status. In the very many cases where one partner did not have the legal right or where the low status of the woman made honorable marriage inappropriate, concubinage was an acceptable, even preferred, alternative. Analyses of the dedications to *concubinae* show that they were invariably of humble status, usually slave or freed (Rawson 1974; Treggiari 1981; Figure 3.2). Roman mores did not approve of relationships where social and gender hierarchies were not congruent—that is, a relationship between a socially inferior man and a superior woman. Such relationships no doubt existed, but powerful norms suppressed their overt expression on public funerary monuments.

Among the most difficult tasks for family historians is to document variation of practices by status and region and over time. Broad assertions have been advanced that the affectionate family began only in the early imperial era and spread gradually from the senatorial elite in Rome down to the slave class (Veyne 1978, Foucault 1986). The epigraphic evidence is impossible to reconcile with any strong form of this hypothesis. A well-known late Republican monument portrays a husband and wife holding hands and celebrates the conjugal bond of a freed couple, the butcher Lucius Aurelius L.l. Hermia and Aurelia L.l. Philematium (*CIL* I² 1221 = VI 9499 = *ILLRP* 793 = *ILS* 7472 = *CLE* 959; Figure 4.2). The marital values depicted in the text—Aurelia's chastity, modesty, and "fidelity to a faithful husband"—show that the stock Roman virtues of domestic life were not imperial innovations nor the preserve of the senatorial elite (cf. Warmington 1940: 22–5, no. 53). Other "family portraits" and epitaphs of freedmen in the triumviral period corroborate

Figure 4.2 Funerary relief of L. Aurelius L.l. Hermia and his wife, Aurelia L.l. Philematium, from the Via Nomentana, Rome. Travertine, c. 75–50 BCE (*CIL* I² 1221 = VI 9499 = *ILLRP* 793 = *ILS* 7472 = *CLE* 959; cf. Warmington 1940: 22–5, no. 53). The stone commemorates a freed butcher from the Viminal hill and his wife and is unusual for its size and detail. The text and iconography are notable as evidence of conjugal ideals among humbler Romans of the late Republic. The bas relief shows the wife grasping her husband's right hand. The inscriptions praise the marital ideals of chastity, affection, and fidelity. (The British Museum.)

these points (Kleiner 1977). Variations by class were probably more subtle. Among the propertied elite, dedications from child to parent are especially noticeable, whereas dedications to humbler men and women in Rome came more often from their spouses. This class difference may be related to the greater significance of patrimonial transmission among the elite (Saller–Shaw 1984: 138).

Regional variations in the patterns of commemoration are discernable, but hard to interpret with confidence. For instance, in epitaphs from the Iberian peninsula women (especially mothers) appear more frequently than in other regions. Furthermore, the very gradual decline in parental commemorations through the life course suggests that, in contrast to other regions, Spanish parents continued to assume responsibility for funerary dedications for both sons and daughters after marriage. It is tempting to hypothesize that these patterns reflect different family relationships and roles for women, but difficult to substantiate without better evidence of other kinds. More generally, comparative evidence from Roman Egypt (Bagnall–Frier 1994) and from later Europe (e.g. Herlihy–Klapisch-Zuber 1985) should lead us to expect basic differences in household composition between town and country. Since the bulk of the epigraphic evidence comes from urbanized areas, it cannot be used to demonstrate a contrast.

Roman funerary inscriptions were not generally dated, thus limiting their value in tracing changes in family life over the centuries. However, a broad comparison between pre-Christian and Christian commemorations reveals several trends. The cultural influences of urbanization and Christianization in the western empire seem to be associated with an increased propensity to commemorate women and young children (Shaw 1991); at the same time, Christian commemorations were increasingly focused on the deceased's relationship with God and were likely to omit the name and relationship of the dedicator (Shaw 1984: 467–8).

The basic continuities in patterns of burial commemorations from archaic Greece to late imperial Rome are perhaps more striking than the changes over the millennium. Religious beliefs such as Christianity and other cultural preferences influenced the likelihood of the expression of a commemorative relationship, but where relationships between deceased and living were memorialized, they were predominantly within the nuclear family. Nowhere do we find epitaphs that singly or collectively emphasize the lines of agnatic descent or broader kin groups that Fustel de Coulanges made the center of his scheme of social evolution in antiquity.

Social status and labor

Status

The historians in classical antiquity and the Roman jurists were inclined to base their remarks about social status on a dichotomy between the honorable citizen-soldier and the honorless cowardly slave (Finley 1981: 116; Hunt 1998). This political ideology essentialized citizen/slave categories in a way that sometimes made movement between the two difficult to accommodate. The difficulty was acutely felt at times in Rome, where slaves formally freed by citizen masters became Roman citizens. Despite the legal transition to citizenship, however, the original lack of honor was not forgotten—hence, the stereotype of the boorish freedman portrayed most memorably in

Petronius' caricature of Trimalchio. Inscriptions from the Greco-Roman world permit historians to move beyond the ideological antinomy and the stereotypes to get a sense of the social reality of a slave society and to catch glimpses of the rich complexity of statuses between slave and free citizen.

Slavery has been very common in premodern societies, but in only a few have slaves been numerous enough to have a major role in economic production. Social historians have attempted to use inscriptions to estimate the magnitude of slavery in the various cities and regions of the ancient Mediterranean basin. But these attempts face the same obstacle as the use of epitaphs to delineate the age structure of ancient societies—that is, the epitaphs do not constitute a representative cross-section of the population. The densest concentration of epitaphs comes from the great capital city of Rome and holds out hope of a better understanding of the largest urban center in Europe before 1800. Tenney Frank in 1916 published a controversial epigraphic study interpreting one of the most striking features of the thousands of inscribed monuments. By Frank's count nearly 90 per cent of the residents named on these stones were of slave stock, and most of those slaves came from the eastern Mediterranean. This finding, then, became the foundation for his racialist interpretation of the decline of Rome: the native Roman stock was gradually replaced by "oriental" slaves and their descendants, who did not share the hereditary virtues of the old Roman farmers (1920: 124).

Frank's conclusions provoked criticisms on various grounds. In particular, it was argued that one of his primary indicators of servile status or background, a Greek *cognomen*, was not a reliable guide, since Greek foreigners and children of native Romans might also have Greek names. Lily Ross Taylor's classic study, "Freedmen and Freeborn in the Epitaphs of Imperial Rome," answered some of the criticisms and concluded that "it is likely that most of the Roman populace eventually had the blood of slaves in their veins" (1961: 132). The significance of this debate rests on the assumption that there was some genetic difference between "native Roman stock" and "servile blood." Once these essentializing assumptions about pure origins and contamination of blood lines are abandoned, the debate can be shifted into more meaningful socio-cultural terms.

Taylor herself recognized that the epitaphs did not represent a cross-section of the urban populace, but were artifacts of particular cultural values. She argued that the overwhelming predominance of freedmen and women in the lower-class epitaphs of Rome, and the rarity of poor freeborn, were a result of the special incentive for the freed to record their achievement on funerary monuments (1961: 129). "The success of the freedmen in securing much of the burial space not in the hands of men of rank is an indication of the numbers, the wealth, and the initiative of the entire class" (1961: 131). The invisibility of the burial of the freeborn poor in a society that valued the honor of monumental self-representation after death is noteworthy. By contrast, whatever their precise numbers, freedmen and women were central to non-elite society of imperial Rome to a degree which the historian might underestimate from literary sources, as no traveller leaving ancient Rome through the closely packed monuments of freedmen and women could (see Figure 3.2).

Beyond Rome and Italy, the evidence for the scale of slavery in Rome's provinces is scarce outside of Egypt. The distribution of slaves and ex-slaves in provincial inscriptions has been interpreted as evidence that slavery in the northern and western provinces was concentrated in the urban centers (MacMullen 1987). However probable the conclusion, the case depends on a dubious argument from silence. Since field slaves in the countryside were unlikely to be manumitted and even less likely to be mentioned in inscriptions, their absence from the epigraphic record outside of cities cannot be taken as significant (Samson 1989: 100).

Elite authors were not much concerned with the interactions among the freeborn poor, the freed, and the slaves of Rome, but the corpus of inscriptions allows some broad generalizations. Whereas in Roman law and ideology the boundary between slavery and freedom was sharp and powerful, in social reality the boundary was constantly crossed by manumitted individuals and by family bonds between slave and freed. From *CIL* VI from the city of Rome, Beryl Rawson gathered 1,500 lower-class epitaphs with two parents and offspring, encompassing 4,795 names. The rarity of freeborn families in this group—only three—is notable. The vast majority of these families are composed of slave, freed, and freeborn: 73 of the freed children have two slave parents; 751 have one slave and one free(d) parent; 122 freed children come from families broken up when the child was sold to a different master; and 591 were born of parents already free(d) at the time of birth (1966: 73). These numbers are not representative of the whole population, but the large number of children born of one slave and one free(d) parent serves as a forceful reminder that urban slavery in Rome, with frequent manumission, amounted to a form of lifecycle servitude and that manumission of members of a servile family was often spread over time, with the result that at any one moment these families straddled the slave/free boundary.

The numerous children born of already freed parents were regarded as *ingenui* or "freeborn," and after another generation of free birth the stigma of slavery was sufficiently diluted to make entry into the highest imperial orders permissible, at least in law. That is, the boundary between freed and freeborn was permeable over time. And yet the patterns of conjugal bonds in the funerary inscriptions suggest that the social boundary between freed and freeborn poor was palpable—a fact that might not be expected in view of the lack of color distinctions or other overt markers. Among the hundreds of marriages, Rawson only occasionally discovered a union between a freeborn husband and freed wife, and only rarely one between a freeborn wife and freed husband. In another study, Weaver estimated that a maximum of 15 per cent of *liberti* and 10 per cent of *servi* in the Roman inscriptions had freeborn wives, and probably the proportion was much lower (1974: 126). This stands in strong contrast with the high-ranking slaves of the imperial household, the *Caesaris servi*, the majority of whom (66 to 75 per cent) had freeborn wives in the period 41–235 CE. These marriage patterns in the inscriptions show that the wealth and power of imperial slaves and freedmen, decried so bitterly by elite authors, in reality translated into social prestige that enabled them to marry women of higher legal status (Weaver 1974: 127). A mid-first-century law, the *senatus consultum Claudianum*, provided that a free woman living in a conjugal arrangement with a slave without his master's consent could be enslaved along with her children, but the inscriptions show what could not otherwise have been guessed—that the terms of the law were often not enforced (Weaver 1986: 166).

Not only was the slave/free boundary repeatedly crossed, but the polarity between slave and free—the characteristic development of classical Greece and Rome—remained complicated by a variety of intermediate statuses (Finley 1981: 67–122). Although Roman law provided clear avenues for full, formal manumission, many slaves in the Republic were informally freed and left in an ambiguous status by their masters. Augustus attempted to clarify their situation with a law setting rules for formal manumission and establishing a different status, Junian Latinity, for slaves not manumitted according to the formal conditions. Among the conditions for full manumission and citizenship was a minimum age of 30 years for the slave. Informally manumitted slaves, Junian Latins, were given a means of acquiring full citizenship by presenting themselves to the Praetor as the parents of a one-year-old child. If Junian Latins failed to acquire citizenship, then their property reverted to their masters upon their death. Their situation is conceptually important, because it obscures the neat class distinction between poor free Romans, who at least owned their own bodies and labor, and slaves, who did not own their labor (de Ste Croix 1981: 63–65).

The question about Junian Latinity that cannot be answered from legal texts is: was it a common status or a fringe condition? On the basis of funerary inscriptions, Weaver (1990) has argued that Junian Latins were far more common than previously suspected. Of those ex-slaves commemorated in Italian cities, 65 per cent had been manumitted under the age of 30, and 35 per cent under the age of 20. In the provinces 40 per cent of commemorated ex-slaves had been manumitted under the age of 30. Unless we imagine the Praetor promoting thousands of Junian Latins individually to full freedom each year, it seems likely that a very large proportion of ex-slaves lived out their lives in this intermediate status.

From the eastern part of the Roman world, the Delphic manumission inscriptions describe a different and harsher intermediate status, one not allowed in Roman private law. Nearly one thousand inscriptions from the period 200 BCE–100 CE document more than 12,000 manumissions at stated prices; of these, about one-third were conditional manumissions or *paramone* contracts. The large number of comparable inscriptions offers the historian a time-series of information with unusually rich possibilities for analysis (Hopkins 1978: 133–71). Suffice it to say here that these texts provide the fullest evidence that many slaves in the eastern Mediterranean paid very large sums (more than 300 drachmae) to secure their full freedom only at some future time, typically upon the death of the slave's master. Before that time, the manumitted slave was required by the agreement to continue to serve the former master and—it is stressed in the document—to be subject to punishment for failure to obey.

The extreme cruelty of servile punishments emerges from literary texts of various genres. The routineness of these punishments is perhaps most chillingly revealed by an inscription from Puteoli with the text of a municipal law [*De munere publi*]*co libitin*[*ario*], which specified contractual terms of the duties of the municipal undertaker (*AE* 1971, 88, with Bodel 1994: 72–80). The law, probably of late Republican date, lists among other tasks infliction of private punishment on slaves at the master's bidding. The fee is a modest four sesterces, payable to those who carry the gibbet on which the slave is bound, to those who apply the whipping, and to the executioner (II.8–10). The inscription is testimony to the fact that the vicious, even crippling punishment of slaves depicted in Latin literature cannot be dismissed as literary exaggeration.

Labor

Social historians know more about the lives of slaves than those of the far more numerous free rural laborers outside of Egypt. The status and conditions of labor of the latter are briefly illuminated by a few, scattered inscriptions. For instance, from Asia Minor we have the inscribed letter of 253 BCE from king Antiochus II to Metrophanes regarding the sale of a royal estate at Pannucome to the divorced queen Laodice (Welles 1934: no. 18). The estate includes the *laoi* or peoples, along with their households and property. The inclusion of the *laoi* in the sale points to a system of dependent labor, but the debates over how to categorize the labor—serfdom? some form of "oriental production"?—stem from a lack of more precise evidence about the systems of land tenure (de Ste Croix 1981: 157).

The development of the classical *polis* in Greece and Rome largely suppressed non-slave, dependent forms of rural labor, at least in law. Yet in reality the rights of citizen peasants were not always observed, as evidenced by a long inscription from the *Saltus Burunitanus* in Roman North Africa (*CIL* VIII 10570 + 14464 = *ILS* 6870). The text is a copy of a petition to the emperor Commodus (ca. 180 CE) from tenant farmers on an imperial estate, complaining of serious abuses by the contractor Allius Maximus, in collusion with the emperor's procurators. On the great imperial estates of North Africa, land was rented to a chief lessee, who in turn subleased plots to tenant farmers. The petition indicates that the tenants were obligated by a law of Hadrian to provide two days of labor three times per year for plowing, cultivating, and harvest on the central unit of the chief lessee. The tenants claim that they were forced to work more than the required number of days by physical force applied by soldiers at the disposal of the procurator. The worst aspect of the outrage was that the free tenants, "even Roman citizens," were "beaten with rods and cudgels"—punishment fit for slaves, not citizens.

Commodus responded with a reassertion of the six-day obligation, and the petition and imperial rescript were duly inscribed and posted. The public inscription was no doubt intended by the tenants to restrain the activities of the procurator, soldiers, and chief lessee within legal bounds. Without an enforcement mechanism, however, the efficacy of the rescript depended on its "sanctity," stressed by the tenants. And yet, since the sanctity of Hadrian's earlier, publicly inscribed law did not so restrain the procurator and chief lessee, we may wonder whether this inscription provided the desired protection.

The imperial tenants' petition provides the social historian with a rare and precious glimpse of rural working conditions, showing how the legal regulations of tenancy could be circumvented by relationships among the powerful. Such texts are so rare that it is tempting to overgeneralize from them, but in truth these inscriptions are so few that they leave us with no knowledge of the status and conditions of the vast majority of the agricultural population of the Roman empire.

Greco-Roman writers drew ideal gender distinctions, in addition to status distinctions, in regard to labor. Articulated by authors such as Xenophon in his *Oeconomicus*, the ideology assigned domestic labor inside the household to women in contrast to men's labor outside the house in the fields and in the public sphere. The epigraphic record from the Latin-speaking West of the Roman empire indicates that the ideology is a little too neat to describe reality, but that it did in fact influence the kinds of work that urban working women undertook (Kampen 1981). Dedications to women reveal that they worked in crafts and trades. The ideal of domesticity appears to have affected this labor in at least two ways: they are often associated with their husbands in business (Treggiari 1979: 76), and they are disproportionately represented in clothing production and food service, traditionally domestic occupations (Treggiari 1979: 78; Kampen 1981: 133). The epigraphic survey of Treggiari (1981: 78) showed that women are identified in inscriptions with only 35 of the 225 occupations attested for men. Although one should not argue from silence that women never worked in the other 190 types of job, the pattern of attestation may be taken as a general guide to the gendered nature of occupational choice in the ancient world.

Social mobility

The social hierarchy in the Roman empire was steep, officially sanctioned and enforced, and publicly displayed in many ways, including inscribed monuments. Its oppressiveness depended in part on opportunities for mobility.

The hundreds of career inscriptions provide the most systematic evidence for mobility in Rome, most of it within the elite orders. With the passing of the Principate, the career inscriptions gradually became more standardized as the hierarchy of offices became more fixed. To give an example, one of the most spectacularly successful careers is recorded in an honorary inscription dedicated to Marcus Bassaeus Rufus, who rose from the centurionate to be Praetorian Prefect under the emperor

Marcus Aurelius. His posts are listed in reverse order, beginning with his prefectures and consular decorations, through his four procurator-ships, down to his numerous military posts (*CIL* VI 1599 = *ILS* 1326; Pflaum 1960–1, no. 162).

The career inscriptions of senators and equestrians have been subjected to many close studies (e.g. Pflaum 1950, Alföldy 1977) in order to understand Roman imperial administration and the men who staffed it. It must be remembered, however, that the career inscriptions alone have certain limitations. The inscriptions were not bureaucratic administrative documents, but texts designed to honor elite men upon some signal success or after their death. Consequently, the inscriptions do not give important information about the content of the jobs or the reasons for appointment. Historians have been inclined to interpret these inscriptions in terms of a narrative of increasing bureaucratization of the empire, with promotion based on seniority and specialized merit. But the lists of offices do not in themselves reveal how promotions were achieved. And, finally, studies of cursus inscriptions often fall into the trap of failing to account for those careers that were less successful and less likely to be honored with a grand inscription. Only through statistical argument, not through reading of individual inscriptions, can we know how exceptional Bassaeus Rufus must have been: fewer than one in a hundred centurions can have reached the pinnacle of the equestrian career, the Praetorian Prefecture. (For critiques of the standard cursus studies, see Saller 1982: ch. 3, Hopkins 1983: ch. 3, Flaig 1992: 569–73.)

Most cursus inscriptions tell historians only of mobility within the elite orders from municipal aristocracies to the equestrian or senatorial orders. Upward movement into the local aristocracies is harder to document. However, M. L. Gordon was able to use tell-tale names of freedmen to discover the promotion of their sons into the local senate. Through an analysis of more than a thousand inscriptions recording names of decurions, she concluded that as many as a third of the decurions in Italian port cities were of servile descent, while in inland cities the proportion was much lower, perhaps one-eighth. Literary texts indicated a deep prejudice among aristocratic Romans against such mobility, while the honorific inscriptions point to the motive for setting aside the prejudice. As Gordon concluded, local senates were ready to swallow their distaste where the wealthy freedman was in a position to donate lavishly in return for his son's promotion. "The inscriptions which record the honors attained by 'new men' are oppressively full of their expensive benefactions" to the community (Gordon 1931: 74).

An inscription from the reign of Marcus Aurelius suggests a similar tension between social ideals and realities in Roman imperial Athens. The emperor reiterated the rule that membership on the council of the Areopagus be conditional on three generations of good birth and expressed the hope that there were enough good old families to allow adherence to the rule. At the same time, Marcus acknowledged that circumstances had caused sons of freedmen to be admitted to the Areopagus and that they should remain if they had been recruited before Marcus' letter (Oliver 1970: 2.57–68).

If freeborn humble men were able to achieve mobility into the curial order, their successes are almost impossible to identify because their names do not mark their origins, as freedmen's names do. From North Africa comes one exceptional inscription recording the arrival of a freeborn laborer, known as the "Mactar harvester" (*CIL* VIII 11824 = *ILS* 7457). The head of the inscription is lost, and with it the name of the deceased. In the surviving text the honorand tells his life story in 29 lines of verse, beginning with his rise from a family possessing "neither property nor a *domus*." After years of work as a harvester "under the fierce sun," he led a gang of harvesters in Numidia for 11 years, accumulating the wealth to acquire "*domus et villa*" and to take a place in the curia of Mactar. Though notable as an exception, the formulation of this story—from propertiless to *dominus*—illustrates the symbolic terms in which Roman provincials cast success, in particular, the centrality of the well-appointed *domus* as a symbol of status available for purchase by the new rich. This inscription offers some sense of the meaning of social mobility, but individual examples cannot tell the historian how often social promotion into the leisured elite occurred.

Social relationships

Ancient political theorists regarded the family as the fundamental unit of society. Beyond the family, Seneca argued, benefactions established relationships that held society together with the glue of reciprocity. Among the ways that a grateful recipient could thank his benefactor was an honorary inscription. Most of these thank-you texts are frustratingly brief: some are explicit that the inscription is in return for favors bestowed (*CIL* VIII 20684) and a few specify that the favor was support for candidacy for an official position (*CIL* VIII 25382). The Thorigny Marble provides the fullest text describing exchange of favors in a patron–client relationship. The monument was erected in honor of a Gallic magnate, T. Sennius Sollemnis, by the provincial council in 238 CE. Two faces of the stone contain the texts of two letters concerning Sollemnis, written by two grand imperial officials, Claudius Paulinus and Aedius Iulianus, who had governed the province of Lugdunensis. The letters reveal that Sollemnis had used his local standing to block an initiative to charge Paulinus with maladministration. By way of thanks, Paulinus later bestowed on Sollemnis a six-month tribunate on his staff in Britain, accompanied by a salary and a collection of luxurious gifts (*CIL* XIII 3162, with Pflaum 1948). What is notable about this *quid pro quo* is not so much that it occurred as that it was thought perfectly appropriate to advertise the facts on a public monument. Since historians have suggested that the importance of patronal bonds waned as the imperial bureaucracy developed, these inscriptions are valuable evidence that provincial administration continued to be embedded in a network of personal friendships and patron–client relationships stretching out from the imperial capital, and that civic ideology did not condemn this patronage as our modern ideology does (Saller 1982).

Instead of membership in local councils or grand friendships, the humble artisans of the Roman world, including slaves, gathered to form clubs or *collegia*, based on a common craft or neighborhood or religious cult (Waltzing 1895–6; Ausbüttel 1982). Whereas senatorial literature took a suspicious view of the subversive potential of these humble clubs, the epigraphic evidence shows that *collegia* served basic non-political needs of the humble and replicated the hierarchical premises of Roman society (Patterson 1994). Furthermore, the clubs were often linked to upper-class society through the sponsorship of aristocratic patrons (Clemente 1972).

The fullest *collegium* inscription (*CIL* XIV 2112 = *ILS* 7212 = *FIRA* III no. 35) gives the rules of a burial society in Lanuvium, as approved by a *senatus consultum* of 136 CE. The purposes of the *collegium*, to judge from this offical text, were decent burial for its members after death and regular banquets of a humble sort before death. The *collegium*, like the city, had its magistrate, the *quinquennalis*, who received extra portions at the banquets and whose honor was protected against members' insults by stiff fines. The club and its magistrate were ceremonially integrated into the wider imperial and cosmic hierarchy through religious offerings to the goddess Diana and the deified imperial companion Antinous on their birthdays. This text is valuable insofar as it suggests that ordinary Romans adopted and mimicked the hierarchical ideology of their social superiors, rather than resisting it. Other, shorter inscriptions from other Italian towns point to similar functions of burial and communal dining (Hopkins 1983: 211–17; Patterson 1994).

Conclusion

The fact that ancient Greeks and Romans habitually chose to represent themselves and their social relationships to posterity through the medium of inscribed texts offers the social historian special opportunities. Though much shorter than literary texts as a rule, inscriptions provide a range of evidence over space, time, and social class that classical literature cannot match. As a result, epigraphy is especially valuable in helping the social historian to understand the margins of society (actually the majority) as defined by literate aristocratic men—the childless senatorial woman, the successful harvester, the beaten imperial tenants, the mixed families of slave and freed, and the slave partially freed by a *paramone* contract.

The inscribed texts can be roughly divided between the brief, formulaic epitaphs and the longer inscriptions, each of which presents methodological difficulties for the social historian. The latter are richer in content to provide a deeper understanding, but also are unique or nearly so. The uniqueness makes it hard to judge the typicality of the social experience or relations described. For instance, if there were any reason to believe that the economic and social success of the Mactar harvester was common throughout the empire, it would require a major revision of our view of the hierarchical quality of Roman society. But no other comparable inscription exists. Even the most common type of inscription, the simple epitaph, does not represent a cross-section of the population; and as a result generalizations from this evidence must be circumscribed. Nevertheless, that caveat is true of all genres of evidence for ancient societies and should not deter historians from attempts to describe and analyze the broad characteristics of ancient society.

Chapter 5

Civic and religious life

James Rives

In the Greco-Roman world, the *sine qua non* of true civilization was the city. It was a defining characteristic of barbarians that they were nomadic, like the Scythians, or dwelt in scattered households and small villages, like the Germans. The Greeks and Romans, on the other hand, prided themselves on their cities. Yet the Greek or Roman city was much more than a simple population center: it also had to possess a number of particular elements, both physical (particularly amenities like theaters, gymnasia, or baths) and institutional. The latter included what we would call the local government, i.e. the town council and a selection of magistrates, as well as public cults, a variety of public and semi-public associations, and above all a certain style of social organization and interaction.

This civic life, in all its richness and variety, informed many of the literary works that have come down to us from antiquity, and by studying these texts we can build up a fairly detailed picture of it. Nevertheless, literary texts have several significant limitations as source material. First is the simple fact that they were for the most part concerned not with technical and everyday matters but with aspects of "higher culture." Consequently, although they provide us with portraits of great men and accounts of great events, with discussions of political theory and speculations about the divine world, by and large they contain only incidental references to basic civic and religious institutions. The chief exceptions are scholarly and antiquarian works, a few of which have fortunately come down to us complete (such as Aristotle's *Constitution of Athens* and Pausanias' *Description of Greece*), a few in more literary reworkings (such as Ovid's *Fasti*), but most in mere snippets preserved by later writers like Athenaeus and Macrobius. Inscriptions play a vital role in filling in these gaps, and in giving us a view of civic life at ground level as well as from the heights. A second limitation of literary sources is that they focus very largely on the major cities of the ancient world, Athens and Rome above all. Rome, in particular, was the center of the intellectual as well as the political world for at least three centuries. Yet although the inhabitants of the capital no doubt dismissed those who lived in "the provinces" in much the same way as Londoners and New Yorkers dismiss those who live in "the north" or "the midwest," the fact remains that the latter constituted the majority of the population. Inscriptions provide us with an insight into their lives that literary texts are simply unable to provide.

It is perhaps useful to distinguish two different aspects of what inscriptions can tell us about civic life, although in practical terms the two are inseparable. On the one hand, they can provide answers to simple factual questions: what magistracies existed in Karystos? What were the public cults of Narbo Martius? On the other hand, inscriptions can reveal something of the texture of civic life. By providing examples of habitual and day-to-day matters, of the regular and recurring features of civic affairs, they give us a feel for normal civic life that we can get only rarely from other sources. In this chapter I will try to illustrate both types of information. The range of inscriptions that deal with civic and religious life, however, is very wide; moreover, by examining the same inscription with different questions in mind we can extract from it very different sorts of information. Although it is impossible in one chapter to cover this huge range of material even cursorily, I hope to suggest something of its variety, by looking in turn at civic institutions, religious institutions, and associations.

Civic institutions

A discussion of civic institutions proper is the best place to begin, not only because these provided the basic framework for civic life in general, but also because this area demonstrates so well the extent to which our knowledge depends on epigraphic sources. Perhaps the most splendid examples come from the Roman side, where we are fortunate to have substantial remains of several inscribed town charters, i.e. sets of regulations concerning public and private law that were granted either to Roman colonies at their foundation or to native communities on receiving Roman municipal status. The most important of these come from Spain. One, from the town of Urso, is that of a Roman colony founded on instructions of Caesar in 44 BCE. Three others are those of towns that became Roman *municipia* under the Flavians; these three present many similarities and seem to derive from a common archetype.[1] Together

Figure 5.1 Tablet three of the town charter from Urso (Osuna), Spain. Bronze, c. 75–100 CE (*CIL* II 5439 = I² 594 = *ILS* 6087 = *FIRA* I² no. 21 = *RS* no. 25). The three columns of text on this tablet begin in the middle of chapter 91 (upper left-hand corner) and end with the beginning of chapter 106 (bottom right). The first sentence of each chapter extends into the margin; beneath it is a numeral indicating the number of the chapter. Remains of the molding that framed the tablet survive on three sides; that on the left hid the joint between this tablet and the immediately preceding one. (National Archaeological Museum, Madrid.) (For a larger reproduction, refer to page 179.)

they provide extensive information about the details of public law and administration in towns of the western Roman empire. The Urso charter is the longest: out of the original document, which contained at least 134 paragraphs, 50 are either wholly or partially extant (Figure 5.1). They cover an extremely wide range of topics: for example, paragraphs 66 through 68 provide for local *pontifices* and *augures*; paragraphs 70 and 71 establish annual games in honor of Jupiter, Juno, and Minerva and of Venus; paragraphs 73 and 74 ban burials and cremations in or within the immediate vicinity of the town; paragraph 93 forbids magistrates from accepting gifts from public contractors; and paragraph 99 reserves the right to the community to build aqueducts through privately owned land.

The Spanish municipal charters are an extremely rich source of information, but they are also very unusual documents. Other types, less detailed but still of great interest, are much more typical. One of these, characteristic of Athens and Rome in particular, is the list, either of magistrates or of the members of a particular public body. These are especially common in Athens, where we find lists of archons, councilors, *prytaneis*, ephebes, and priests.[2] These take different forms: a few, like those of the archons, are lists pure and simple, while others are incorporated into various sorts of public inscriptions. Of the latter, the most common are joint dedications to a deity made by the group as a whole, or inscriptions recording honorific decrees which the city as a whole passed in praise of the particular group. Such inscriptions add a depth to our understanding of Athenian institutions that we would otherwise lack, even though the literary sources for the Athenian constitution, thanks above all to Aristotle's *Constitution of Athens*, are better than those for almost any other ancient city. We may consider two particular institutions discussed by Aristotle, the *prytaneis* (*Ath. Pol.* 43.2–44.3) and the *ephebeia* (*Ath. Pol.* 42). Both are well illustrated by inscriptions. In fact, almost 500 inscriptions relating to the *prytaneis* have been found in the agora of Athens, more than any other type of inscription except for epitaphs. These range in date from 408/7 BCE to 231/2 CE, with the majority belonging to the period 307/6 to 86 BCE. Similarly, there are hundreds of inscriptions relating to the Athenian ephebes, the members of the publicly organized training association for young men, ranging in date from the latter half of the fourth century BCE to the third century CE.[3] These inscriptions supplement Aristotle's description with additional details, by listing, for example, all the various officers and sub-officers of the council. More importantly, they reveal the continuity of civic institutions over the centuries despite significant changes in the status of Athens, a continuity that helps us to understand the survival and even the vitality of Greek cities in the Hellenistic and Roman periods.

The Roman world also provides us with lists of magistrates. Perhaps the most famous and important are the so-called *Fasti Capitolini*: two lists, one of consuls from the beginning of the Republic and one of triumphators from the founding of the city, that were engraved during the reign of Augustus somewhere in the Forum Romanum.[4] These inscriptions, like the statues of great Romans in the Forum Augusti, were no doubt part of the general Augustan scheme of glorifying Rome's past and, by implication, present and future. Many other examples of consular *fasti* are also extant, from many different parts of Italy. The fact that many of these were associated with calendars suggests that they were used largely for chronological purposes. The fragmentary *fasti* from Ostia, for example, which cover the period 49 BCE to 154 CE, list for every year the consuls of Rome, the chief magistrates of Ostia, and brief notices of the year's notable events (Degrassi 1947: no. 5; see also Vidman 1982a). Nor were municipalities the only other institutions to make use of the form: so too did private associations of all types. A striking example is the *collegium* of the household staff of an imperial villa at Antium, which follows the entry of the annual consuls with that of the annual officers of the group (Degrassi 1947: no. 31).

Another type of list is the *album decurionum*, the inscribed record of a local town council. The two best examples are from Canusium in Apulia, dating to 223 CE (Chelotti et al. 1985: no. 35 = *CIL* IX 338 = *ILS* 6121; cf. Horstkotte 1984), and from Thamugadi in Numidia, from the mid-fourth century CE (*ILS* 6122 = *CIL* VIII 2403 and 17824; cf. Chastagnol 1978). They list all the members of their respective councils, grouped according to their rank, in a manner reminiscent of the senate in Rome, and give us insight into the social hierarchies in these sorts of towns. The album of Canusium, for example, begins with a list of civic patrons, divided into men of senatorial and equestrian status (Figure 5.2). Among the former are some fairly grand figures: the eponymous consul of 224 CE, the prefect of Egypt, and the legate of Lower Moesia. The patrons of equestrian status, while not quite so impressive, seem to have had closer personal ties with the town, since several had held high public office there. The other holders of high office evidently constituted the local gentry: important men locally, but minor figures within the empire as a whole. We can thus see the spectrum of connections that a small town could have with the elite, ranging from the relatively small fry who managed most of the day-to-day affairs to very distinguished men whose local involvement was probably slight, but whose patronage contributed to civic prestige.

The vast majority of inscriptions that deal with civic institutions are highly formal documents. But there are occasional exceptions, such as the lively electoral graffiti from Pompeii. One candidate, L. Ceius Secundus, for the chief magistracy of the town, the duovirate, received endorsements from Primus the fuller, Felicio the lupine-seller, and Euhode the bath-attendant (*ILS* 6404 = *CIL* IV 3478, 3423, 840); a man named Genialis supported Q. Bruttius Balbus, because "he will maintain the treasury" (*ILS* 6405 = *CIL* IV 3702). The muleteers backed C. Iulius Polybius who, according to one campaign slogan, "brings good bread" (*ILS* 6412 = *CIL* IV 113, 429). M. Cerrinius Vatia, a candidate for the aedileship, received the perhaps dubious backing of "the late-drinkers" (*seribibi*) and "the sleepy-heads" (*dormientes*) (*ILS* 6418 = *CIL* IV 581, 373), while Cn. Helvius Sabinus, "an eminently deserving young man," got more respectable support from the worshippers of Isis (*ILS*

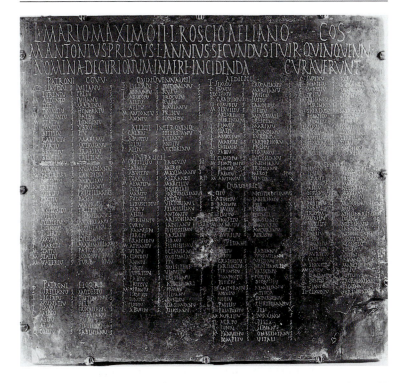

Figure 5.2 Album decurionum from Canusium (Canosa), Italy. Bronze (66 × 74 cm), 223 CE (Chelotti et al. 1985: no. 35 = *CIL* IX 338 = *ILS* 6121; cf. Horstkotte 1984). The first line records the Roman consuls and the second the chief local magistrates, for dating purposes. The first column on the left side lists the patrons of the town, divided according to senatorial and equestrian status. The members of the council are listed in descending rank, from left to right. The final letters (usually S, sometimes X or O) of the *nomina* and *cognomina* have been separated and aligned to create a series of decorative borders to the columns of names. (National Archaeological Museum, Florence.)

6420 = *CIL* IV 787). These endorsements, not engraved but simply painted on the walls of buildings, provide a colorful supplement to the formal, even stuffy, official inscriptions, while a careful analysis of them yields interesting insight into the culture of the times. The graffiti we have seem to cover a period of nine years, during which time all candidates for the duovirate ran unopposed. This suggests that the graffiti did not function in the same way as electoral advertisements in our own society, i.e. to persuade voters to support one candidate over another, but were simply a form of self-promotion, perhaps intended to provide long-term prestige for the candidate's family.[5]

Although I have so far singled out some of the more striking types of inscriptions, we are by no means limited to them when seeking to learn about civic life. We can in fact select almost any town at random, and learn things about it from inscriptions that we would never learn from literary evidence. Take for example Karystos, on the southern tip of Euboea: a few references in Herodotus, Thucydides, and Livy give us the main facts of its external relations, but say almost nothing of its internal history. From two brief inscriptions, however, we learn that in the second and first centuries BCE the town had not only the usual magistrates such as archons, secretaries, and grain-buyers (σιτῶνες), but also a board of "harbor-guardians" (λιμενοφύλακες), a term otherwise unknown.[6] This unusual magistracy not only shows the importance of the harbor to Karystos, but also reveals that the town had its own distinctive organization, and was not simply derivative of other Euboean cities like Eretria. Another inscription gives us a glimpse into its financial organization. *IG* XII,9 7 is a record of public debts owed to various private creditors in other cities, five men in Thebes and one in Histiaia. The amounts indicate that Karystos was borrowing rather large sums of money at this time, about 370 BCE, presumably for some major municipal project. The public treasurers responsible for managing this debt constituted a board of six men, who held office for half a year and then turned over the accounts to the next board; such an organization was clearly designed to include a number of people in the management of the public finances, suggesting a democratic constitution (Wallace 1962 and Migeotte 1976). Although Karystos is by no means particularly well represented in the epigraphic record, these three inscriptions alone give us significant glimpses into its civic organization.

The more numerous the inscriptions from a particular city, the more easily we can trace the development of its civic organization. In the cases of cities that underwent Hellenization or Romanization, the changes can be quite dramatic. Although Lepcis Magna in North Africa lacks anything as comprehensive as a municipal charter, the surviving inscriptions, mostly dedications of various sorts, allow us to trace its evolution from a Punic to a Roman city. Throughout the first century CE the inscriptions are typically bilingual in Latin and neo-Punic. From these we learn that the chief magistrates were two *sufetes* (*IRT* 319, 321–3, etc.), the Latinization of the *shûfêtim* found in the neo-Punic versions (*IRT* neo-Punic 12, 27, etc.); the latter also mention two *mûhazim*, probably translated as *aediles* in the Latin texts (*IRT* 99, 599). Under Trajan the city received the status of a Roman colony, and thereafter we find typically Roman civic institutions: the *ordo decurionum, duoviri, quinquennales, aediles*. It is interesting to note, however, that there was somewhat greater continuity in religious institutions. In the first century CE we find a priesthood described in neo-Punic as *addir ʿazarim* (*IRT* neo-Punic 27, 30, 32) and translated into Latin as *praefectus sacrorum* (*IRT* 319, 321–3, 347), which continued to exist after the grant of colonial status (Reynolds–Ward-Perkins 1952: 79–82).

The preceding should give some idea of the varied data that we can obtain from inscriptions, even those that at first glance may not seem particularly promising. It is important to remember, however, that this evidence does not speak for itself. We as investigators must work to bring forth its richness. Perhaps the most obvious task is that of accumulation: by setting inscriptions against one another and studying them as a whole we can learn much more than we can from individual examples. This is the case with the inscriptions from Lepcis, which reveal the internal development of the city only when taken together, and also with the inscriptions concerning the *prytaneis* and the ephebes in Athens. But we must also set in a broader context the simple data provided by inscriptions and develop their implications. We may, for example, consider in more detail paragraph 62 from the Urso charter, which deals with the staff assigned to the local magistrates. Each of the *duoviri*, the chief magistrates of the colony, has the right to two lictors, an *accensus*, two scribes, two messengers, a copyist, a herald, a *haruspex*, and a flute-player. These attendants, or *apparitores*, are all citizens of the colony and receive certain benefits during their period of service—notably, exemption from military service and annual pay ranging on a scale from 1,200 sesterces for the scribes to 300 sesterces for the copyists, heralds, and flute-players. On further investigation, we find that this list of *apparitores* helps reveal the day-to-day activities of the *duoviri*: the scribes and copyist were needed for record-keeping and for drawing up formal decrees; the herald and lictors for public proclamations and for clearing the way; the lictors also for arrests and for the exercise of coercive power; the *haruspex* and flute-player for the performance of public sacrifices. We also get a sense of the prestige of the *duoviri*, who would on all public occasions be accompanied by several of these attendants, as well some insight into local finances, since the staff of the *duoviri* alone cost the city 13,000 sesterces a year. Lastly, we can on reflection discern here a social class almost invisible in literary sources. The *apparitores* were obviously not elite, yet at the same time held defined and respectable positions in civic life:

they received a public salary and enjoyed benefits similar to those of the magistrates. It is easy to imagine that such men might have been of considerable importance in their own social circles (cf. Purcell 1983).

Not only the content but also the actual form of an inscription can provide insight into the nature of ancient civic life, as with the *prytaneis* inscriptions from Athens. As noted, the bulk of these date from the third and second centuries BCE, from the restoration of the democracy after Demetrius of Phalerum until the conquest of Sulla. During this time it was the normal practice to inscribe an honorary decree for each group of *prytaneis* after they had served their time in office. The features of these decrees changed over time, but in their developed form they were fairly elaborate (Figure 5.3). There was first a decree of the people commending the work of the *prytaneis* and citing by name their treasurer and secretary; this was followed by a decree of the council awarding olive garlands to these two officials, as well as to the priest of that tribe's eponymous hero, and to the secretary, the undersecretary, the herald, the flutist, and the treasurer of the council (Meritt–Traill 1974: 9–10). We need to imagine these documents in context, as marble plaques on display in the agora, one of the centers of public life in Athens. Their existence there meant that popular participation in the civic life of Athens was not simply an intangible ideal, but was embodied in the mass of these inscriptions. Everyone could see for themselves the numbers of those who had served in the council and had received as their due this public and permanent form of recognition. These inscriptions thus not merely recorded civic life in Athens, but also contributed to its unique texture.

Religious institutions

To treat civic and religious institutions separately is perhaps somewhat misleading, since in the ancient Mediterranean both were integral parts of a single civic organization. For example, we have already seen that the Urso charter deals with public priesthoods and sacrifices at the same time as magistracies and public finances; indeed, the latter necessarily included the expenses of the public cults. But it is convenient to consider the inscriptions that deal primarily with religious institutions apart from those that deal with civic institutions, especially since the Greek material in particular has been gathered in distinct corpora, the various collections of so-called *leges sacrae*.[7] There are between two and three hundred examples dating mostly from the fourth century BCE to the second century CE, although some go back to the classical or even archaic periods. Although they are all conventionally classified as *leges sacrae*,

Figure 5.3 Decree from Athens honoring *prytaneis*. Pentelic marble, broken at the bottom (102 × 49 cm), c. 20 BCE (inv. no. 807; cf. Meritt–Traill 1974: no. 293). In the center two garlands surround the names of two officials; the councilors are listed on either side. At the bottom remains of other garlands are visible.

they in fact take a number of forms: some are formal decrees of the local council or people; others are inscribed temple regulations; still others are more mundane documents such as contracts, inventories, and records of various kinds. A few, like the fragmentary archaic inscription from Selinous, deal with more esoteric matters like rituals of purification (Jameson–Jordan–Kotansky 1993; see above, page 44). Most of them, however, deal with the same sorts of topics, so that we can make some generalizations about the information they provide. The Latin material presents some broad similarities to the Greek, but is with a few exceptions much less rich and has consequently not been gathered into special collections.[8]

One of these exceptions is the inscribed calendar: while there are only a dozen or so Greek examples, there are 42 Latin examples. All the latter date from the Augustan and Julio-Claudian periods, except for one of late Republican date, and all come from peninsular Italy, again with one exception from Sicily. Although no individual example is complete, they allow us to reconstruct a fairly complete calendar for this period, and so to learn a great deal about the temporal organization of civic life in Rome and in other towns of Italy. One important feature of these calendars is that they combine civic and religious data. They are full calendars, listing every day of the month, and noting whether public business is allowed or prohibited and also the public sacrifices and festivals that are to take place.[9] The Greek examples are very different. For one thing, they are not really calendars at all, but rather lists of sacrifices by date. Consequently, much less is known about the workings of the actual calendars. That of Athens, for which the most evidence survives, has been painstakingly reconstructed from the preambles of public decrees, although not without a measure of controversy.[10] Secondly, at least in some cases, they go into considerable detail about the actual conduct of the sacrifice. For example, a fourth-century BCE calendar from Cos devotes over 60 lengthy lines to a single month; unfortunately, the records for only one month survive fairly complete, with smaller remains of three others (*LSCG* 151 = *SIG*[3] 1025–7).

All other types of *leges sacrae* are much better represented on the Greek side. One of the most common is the regulation of the cult place, whether temple, altar, or sacred grove. Such regulations cover a range of topics. Some of them lay out the ritual requirements for people who wish to enter the sacred area; we commonly find instructions to be free from sexual relations, mourning, or childbirth for a certain number of days. Sometimes these also include outright bans on particular groups, such as slaves or women. Another common type of temple regulation deals with the sacred property. A first-century BCE inscription from Smyrna, for example, concerns the sacred fish in the sanctuary of an unnamed goddess. It opens with an injunction not to harm, maltreat, or steal the fish, followed by a curse on those who disobey ("may they be eaten by fish"), instructions that any fish that dies of natural causes be presented on the altar that very day, and lastly a blessing for those who maintain and increase the goddess's fishpond (*LSAM* 17 = *SIG*³ 997). More typical is this third-century BCE example from Loryma in Caria: "Do not remove any dedications from the temple; do not damage anything; do not disturb the arrangement of tablets, nor bring in others without the priest" (*LSAM* 74). An example of this sort of inscription dating to the classical period comes from the town of Arkesine on Amorgos and records a decree prohibiting people from kindling fires within the temple of Hera (*LSCG* 100 = *IG* XII,7 1). One of the few extant Latin *leges sacrae*, the dedication of a temple of Jupiter Liber in 58 BCE in the Sabine village of Furfo, falls into this category, since most of it consists of detailed conditions for the use and sale of temple property (*CIL* I² 756 = *ILS* 4906; cf. Laffi 1978; Gordon 1983: no. 19). Similarly, an inscription from Spoletium of the mid-third century BCE records the regulations of a sacred grove: nothing is to be removed from it nor any wood cut except during an annual festival; infractions must be expiated by a sacrifice and, if committed intentionally, by a fine (*CIL* XI 4766 = *CIL* I² 366 = *ILS* 4911; see Bodel 1994: 24–9. For a Greek example, see *LSCG* 116 = *SIG*³ 986 = *CIG* II 2214c).

Another important category of *leges sacrae* is of those that deal with civic religious festivals. Inscriptions like these are particularly enlightening, because they allow us to understand the practical significance that a civic religious festival had for the inhabitants of a city. For example, we find instructions that schoolboys be released from lessons and household slaves freed from their tasks for the duration of the festival, or that various sorts of public, legal, and business transactions be suspended, or that the entire population wear garlands. Other inscriptions regulate the religious processions that often constituted a part of a festival, defining which civic groups should take part and in what order. In a festival for Zeus Sosipolis in Magnesia, for example, the procession consisted of the local council, the priests, the various magistrates, the youth associations, and the victors at various games, all organized in particular groups (*LSAM* 32 = *SIG*³ 589 = *IMagn.* 98). As several scholars have pointed out, such regulations give us insight into the way the citizens of these cities conceptualized themselves and their place in the civic structure.[11] One of the most detailed inscriptions is that regulating the mysteries of

Andania in Messenia, dating to 92/1 BCE. Pausanias (4.33.5) regarded these as second only to the Eleusinian mysteries in sanctity, and like them they were a civic responsibility. The inscription describes among other things the oath and the garments of the initiates, the procession, the selection of victims, the management of the funds, and fines for various infractions (*LSCG* 65 = *IG* V,1 1390; English translation in M. W. Meyer 1987: 51–9).

From the imperial period we have several inscriptions regulating the local imperial cult, like those from Gytheion in the Peloponnese (*SEG* 11 922–3; English translation in Sherk 1988: nos 31–2; cf. Price 1984: 210–11). One of the longest Latin *leges sacrae* deals with the celebration of the imperial cult in Narbo Martius. It consists of two inscriptions on different faces of an altar: one describes the organization of the cult under the presidency of three *equites* and three freedmen, and details the sacrifices to take place on the various imperial anniversaries; the other records the dedication formulae. This inscription is of great interest for what it tells us not only about the organization of a public cult in a city of the western Empire, but also about the roles of different social groups in civic life (*CIL* XII 4333 = *ILS* 112; English translation in Sherk 1988: no. 7.I.C; cf. Cels Saint-Hilaire 1986).

Lastly, there is a whole range of *leges sacrae* that deal with priesthoods. From these we can learn what sorts of honors and privileges civic priests might enjoy. They were often entitled to wear special robes and crowns, to take precedence in civic processions, and to sit in privileged seats at public performances. They also received more practical benefits, including portions of all animals sacrificed in their temples or to deities over whose cult they presided. This particular benefit seems to have been a matter of great interest, since we encounter it in many different inscriptions and often in very specific and carefully discriminated forms; from Athens, for example, we have the inscribed accounts of money received from the sale of skins of sacrificial victims (*SIG*[3] 1029 = *IG* II 741). More substantial benefits included immunity from taxes and various liturgies, which again could be enumerated in careful and exact detail. Inscriptions also shed considerable light on how people acquired priesthoods: some by election, some by cooption, some by inheritance, and many, it seems, by sale. One particularly interesting inscription from Erythrai is a record, covering a number of years, of the sale and re-sale of some 35 or 40 priesthoods, together with the names of their purchasers and the prices paid (*LSAM* 25 = *SIG*[3] 1014).

Although, as noted above, the Roman material is in general much less rich, one of the largest single dossiers of inscriptions concerning ancient religion comes from Rome: the *acta* of the Arval Brothers, an archaic priestly college revived by Augustus. Their activities originally centered on the cult of the Dea Dia, an ancient earth goddess, but in their revived form they also engaged in many rituals of imperial cult. Detailed records of all their activities throughout the year were inscribed in their sacred grove. Extensive fragments are extant, representing the reigns of almost every emperor from Augustus to Gordian III. The vast bulk of these inscriptions consists of a detailed description of their rituals—both regular rituals, such as the sacrifices to the Dea Dia and those on behalf of the emperor and his family, and occasional rituals, such as various expiatory rites and vows for the emperor's safety in times of danger. But there are also records of the cooption of new members and the appointment of new attendants and servants. Because of their great detail and the large span of time that they cover, one scholar has aptly described these inscriptions as "the most precise and extensive source for the religious history of Rome and even of the western empire."[12] Similar in some ways to the *Acta Arvalium* are the *acta* of the Atiedian Brothers in the town of Iguvium. These records, inscribed on seven bronze tablets, are not in Latin but in Umbrian, an ancient Italic language, and strictly speaking have nothing to do with Roman religion proper. Yet they represent another strain of the Italic religious tradition of which Roman religion was a particular example, and represent it in a detailed form during a period for which the Roman sources are considerably scantier. Although the dating of the tablets is controversial, the oldest seem to go back to the early third century BCE, while the most recent can be no later than the mid-first century BCE. Like the *Acta Arvalium*, they contain mostly prescriptions for particular rituals, but they also include contracts between the brotherhood and other civic bodies as well as decrees concerning the privileges and duties of the chief officiant.[13]

Again, the importance of inscriptions for the study of civic religion is not restricted to lengthy *leges sacrae*. The vast majority of inscriptions touching on religion are much briefer and less detailed, but even these can be quite informative. The most common type of religious inscription is the dedication, marking the consecration of a shrine, an altar, or some smaller offering to a god. Although at their most basic dedications can consist of nothing more than the god's name, they usually include the name of the dedicator and some indication of the circumstances of dedication. The latter can often be quite revealing. For example, some Latin dedications include the formula *decreto decurionum*, sometimes abbreviated to *d. d.*, "by decree of the decurions;" this indicates that the dedication was made with the formal authorization of the local council, and suggests that the deity in question was the object of an official civic cult. Dedicatory inscriptions on buildings tend, not surprisingly, to be more elaborate and to include not only the names of the deity and the dedicator (whether an individual or a city) but also the date, various details about the construction process, and even its cost. For an extensively excavated site, such as Aphrodisias in Asia Minor or Thugga in North Africa, inscriptions allow us to catalogue most if not all of the official cults of the ancient city, and so to recreate in some detail its religious life.

Associations

Although the official civic and religious institutions of a city provided the basic framework of civic life in the ancient Mediterranean, they were not its only constituents. Another important aspect was the huge range of smaller associations that existed within the larger framework of the city. Although literary sources give us occasional glimpses of these groups, it is only from inscriptions that we learn of their number and variety, and get some sense of the enormous importance they must have had for many of the inhabitants of Greek and Roman cities (Poland 1909; Ausbüttel 1982). These associations were of all sorts, so many and so varied that any attempt to catalogue them tends to be overly schematic. We may, however, usefully distinguish different types of associations on the basis of their nature or goal, such as professional associations, religious groups, ethnic associations, youth groups, and social clubs. These categories are by no means discrete, but instead display considerable overlap. Many ethnic groups, for example, were made up of merchants and tended also to function as business associations. Similarly, most groups, no matter what their primary *raison d'être*, had a patron deity to whom they would offer regular sacrifices, while virtually all groups had a social aspect.

Although all of these associations played an important part in ancient civic life, some were more fully incorporated into the formal organization of cities than others. In terms of their official status, there seems to have been a full spectrum, ranging all the way from important civic institutions to groups that were by definition excluded from civic life. An obvious example of the former is the Greek *ephebeia*, which functioned to integrate the young men into civic life as they reached adulthood, and thus played a vital role in the organization and maintenance of the community (Pélékidis 1962). There were also youth groups in many towns of the western Roman empire, usually described as *iuvenes* or *iuventus*, that seem to have been roughly similar in nature. Their focus was not military training, as was the case in Athens, but rather competitive sports, especially horseback riding and sword-fighting. A number of inscriptions attest to the games that they performed in the circus or amphitheater, variously described as *Iuvenalia* or *lusus iuvenum*. Like their Greek counterparts, they also took part in religious activities, and some of them were actually named after particular deities, among whom Hercules was a favorite (Jaczynowska 1978; cf. Ladage 1979).

Very common in the western Roman empire were the groups known variously as *Augustales* or *seviri Augustales*. Their importance in civic life is indicated by the sheer number of inscriptions in which they appear— some 2,500. This is in dramatic contrast to their absence from literary texts, among which they appear only in the *Satyricon* of Petronius (30.2 and 71.12). Despite a certain amount of local variation, most of the groups display the same broad characteristics. Although their formal purpose was the celebration of imperial cult, their most important function seems to have been to provide wealthy freedmen, who were barred by their status from holding municipal magistracies, with an opportunity to acquire public prestige. *Augustales* often acted as civic benefactors, funding entertainments and building projects, and were in turn entitled to various privileges similar to if lesser than those of the civic magistrates and priests (Duthoy 1976 and 1978). Somewhat similar to the *Augustales*, but much less common, were other groups that took their names from various deities. In various towns of Italy, for example, we find *Apollinares* (*CIL* IX 815–16 and XI 845 = *ILS* 6478–9 and 6669), *Mercuriales* (*CIL* IX 23, 33–4, and 1707–10), and *Minervales* (*CIL* V 7462 = *ILS* 6748). These groups seem to have had a status somewhat like that of *Augustales* elsewhere, and are in fact sometimes associated with them. In several towns of North Africa, including Carthage, there were groups known as *Cereales*, which seem to have been similar. For example, in the small town of Bisica they joined with the decurions in erecting a memorial to a local notable (*CIL* VIII 12300 = *ILS* 6829; cf. Rives 1995: 159–61).

Religious associations with some sort of formal public standing seem to have been less common in the Greek world, although there are exceptions. In Miletus there was an association of men responsible for ceremonial songs, the *Molpoi*, that was closely integrated into the town's formal civic organization. We have a body of material, probably inscribed in the second century BCE but largely dating to earlier periods, that includes among other things various regulations for a civic festival and a list of items to be supplied by the city on that occasion (*LSAM* 50 = *SIG*[3] 57; cf. Robertson 1987). More common in the Greek world were associations that had no defined public standing, but that reproduced on a smaller scale the structures of civic life, as we learn from inscriptions recording their decrees, dedications, and bylaws. Particularly interesting in this connection are the regulations of the *Iobacchoi* in Athens, which date to the latter part of the second century CE (*LSCG* 51 = *SIG*³ 1109 = *IG* II² 1368; English translation in M. W. Meyer 1987: 95–9). These rules cover the entry of new members into the association, the dates and occasions of the meetings, the ceremonies in which the members participate, and the standards of behavior. It is easy to see a number of similarities with civic structures: the group met as a body and elected from their own number magistrates who were charged with carrying out the religious and organizational duties of the group and who in turn received titles and a privileged place in the group. Groups like these were especially popular in Rhodes during the second and first centuries BCE, where inscriptions reveal dozens of different associations. Some had very elaborate names, such as the *Heliostai Athenaistai Hermaistai Aristeideioi*, presumably founded by a man named Aristides (*SIG*³ 1114 = *IG* XII,1 162).[14] These groups seem to have been social groups at least in part, since they are sometimes described as *eranistai* and had as their chief officials *archeranistai*. But it is likely that at least some functioned simultaneously as associations of merchants, similar to the groups of Italian businessmen in Delos who organized themselves as *Hermaistai*, *Apolloniastai*, and *Poseidoniastai* (Hatzfeld 1912).

Similar groups existed in the Roman world as well, and displayed similar characteristics. The *collegium* formed by the domestic staff of an imperial villa in Antium has already been mentioned (see above, page 122). Two similar groups have left copies of their bylaws similar to those of the *Iobacchoi* in Athens: the *cultores* of Diana and Antinous in Lanuvium (*ILS* 7212 = *CIL* XIV 2112) and the *collegium* of Aesculapius and Hygia in Rome (*ILS* 7213 = *CIL* VI 10234), both dating to the 130s CE. Whereas the *Iobacchoi* seem to have been rather aristocratic, the worshippers of Diana and Antinous were obviously of low social status and included even slaves. The membership fee was 100 sesterces and an amphora of "good wine," while monthly dues were only five *asses*; the chief benefit of membership seems to have been that the group would finance and organize the funerals of its members. But, like the *Iobacchoi*, the members elected annual magistrates who had specific duties and privileges. The inscription thus allows us a look into the life of lower-class men, for whom positions as civic magistrates or even *Augustales* were an impossibility, but who could still cut fine figures as the *magistri* of a *collegium*. Moreover, it suggests the pervasiveness of the civic organization as a model for social interaction in a way that literary texts rarely if ever do.

Conclusions

As noted at the start of this chapter, one of the things that defined Greco-Roman civic life was a certain style of social organization and interaction. It is worthwhile in closing to call attention to one important aspect of this style that inscriptions are particularly useful in bringing to life: the importance of prestige and public recognition, and the desire of people to obtain that prestige in any way they could. A huge number and range of inscriptions, both Greek and Latin, were erected to record public honors voted to groups and individuals. The actions that brought forth such honorific decrees were quite varied. Examples from the classical and earlier Hellenistic periods often celebrate what we might call simply good citizenship. A decree from Astypalaia, for example, grants a golden garland to a man who had done a good job as *agoranomos*, the official in charge of the market, and arranges for the honor to be publicly announced as an incentive to others (*SIG*³ 946). Increasingly, however, such honors went to those whose contribution to civic life was much more extraordinary, and usually involved great wealth. It is clear that in the late Hellenistic and Roman periods civic life had come to depend on these great benefactors, who paid for the various buildings and institutions that distinguished civic life from that in villages (Gauthier 1985; Veyne 1990).

We can see this quite clearly in an inscription from the small town of Thugga in North Africa, an honorific dedication to a civic patron named L. Marcius Simplex. Engraved on the base of a now lost statue, it recorded his public career both in Thugga itself and in the metropolis of Carthage. The statue and inscription were decreed by the local council and erected at public expense on account of Simplex's "outstanding munificence" (*CIL* VIII 26609). It is only from another inscription that we learn what specific form that munificence had taken: Simplex had paid for the construction of a Capitol, a striking symbol of Thugga's Roman aspirations (*CIL* VIII 15513). It was this munificence, and not simply the performance of magistracies and other public offices, that won Simplex the honor of a public statue (cf. Rives 1995: 118–24).

Women as well as men could bestow these sorts of benefits and enjoy the sorts of public recognition that went with them. The importance of women in civic life is another aspect of the ancient world that is known almost entirely from inscriptions, since literary and legal sources usually depict women as largely relegated to private life. For example, an inscription of the first century BCE from Priene records a public decree in honor of a woman named Phile, who paid for the city's aqueduct and reservoir. More strikingly, it notes that she was the first woman ever to hold the eponymous magistracy of the city (Hiller von Gaertringen 1906: no. 208; cf. Fantham et al., 1994: 156). This coincidence suggests that the increasing importance of wealth in public life, i.e. the ability to fund important public works, may have played a role in overcoming the traditional ineligibility of women for public offices (cf. van Bremen 1983). A similar but better attested case from the imperial period is Plancia Magna of Perge, who held a number of important public positions, including an eponymous magistracy, the priesthood of Artemis, the patron deity of the city, and the priesthood of the imperial cult. In return, she was honored with two public statues, one dedicated by the civic council and assembly, and the other by the council of elders; inscriptions on the bases list her public offices and describe her as "daughter of the city" (*AE* 1958, 78; *AE* 1965, 209). She also constructed an elaborate monumental gate to the city, adorned with statues of the gods, members of the imperial family, and her own father and brother. Not only the central arch but also the bases of the individual statues were adorned with the name of Plancia as dedicator (cf. Boatwright 1991).

Inscriptions are by far the most important source of information available for studying this fundamental aspect of the Greco-Roman world, the constant exchange of benefits and honors between a city and its elite. Not only that, they are also important physical remains of that phenomenon. For how was prestige embodied in Greek and Roman cities? Partly, of course, in receiving garlands publicly decreed, in being attended by public *apparitores*, in taking a leading place in public processions, in occupying the first rows at public performances. But prestige was embodied to an equal or perhaps even greater extent in the inscriptions that constituted a public and permanent record of those very honors, and of the great benefactions that merited them. All the citizens of Thugga could see the statue of Simplex, but it was the associated inscriptions, not only that on the statue's base but also that on the temple he built, that ensured that a record of his deeds and thus of his prestige would endure for generations to come. Similarly, Plancia Magna's great city gate at Perge was at the same time the gift of her munificence and a monument to her fame and glory. Inscriptions thus not only survive as an essential source of information about civic life, but were at the time an essential part of civic life as it was lived.

Chapter 6

Inscribed *instrumentum* and the ancient economy

Giuseppe Pucci

The art of our necessities is strange,
That can make vile things precious.

Shakespeare, *King Lear*, III, ii, 70

Roman law defines *instrumentum domesticum* as "the equipment necessary to the management and use of a household, furniture, tools, utensils, etc." (Berger 1953: 505); for the modern student of antiquity, however, *instrumentum* primarily means the categories of materials of daily life that Heinrich Dressel gathered in volume XV of the *Corpus Inscriptionum Latinarum*: bricks and other objects in heavy terracotta, amphorae, kitchen- and tableware, lamps, glass vessels, metal objects of various sorts, seals, gems, and rings.[1] Nevertheless this list is scarcely exhaustive, and we can follow Harris (1993: 7) in applying the definition to "most kinds of inscribed portable objects," with the exceptions of coins and materials that function purely as carriers of writing (wooden tablets, *ostraka*, and the like).

Pieces of *instrumentum* are, generally, objects of rather modest economic value. Why, then, are they of interest to the student of the ancient economy? Because, unlike the historian of a post-industrial economy, the ancient economic historian cannot avail himself of records documenting the production and distribution of goods. In all the pages of classical literature that have come down to us almost nothing is found which tells us how a factory worked, what size and what sort of workforce it employed, what its output was, how wholesale and retail sales were transacted, what the costs and profits were.

In order to try to answer questions such as these, the historian of the ancient world can only ask the objects themselves—at least those that, not being of perishable material, have survived. It would seem an obvious approach, and yet it has only begun to be attempted relatively recently. The principal problem is that, in order to study the history of material culture, there is a need, as Voltaire foresaw in his *Fragmens sur l'histoire* (article XIII) (1785), for "men who know something other than books." In our case the historian must know how to handle archaeological objects. But if we look at the history of scholarship on the subject, we must note that the relationship between history and archaeology has not been easy.

When, at the end of the sixteenth century, the great Spanish scholar Augustinus maintained that it was necessary to give more credit "to medallions [i.e. coins] and tablets and stones than to what the writers wrote," he was making a bold statement bordering on heresy (and not only in a figurative sense: it was easy to incur a charge of challenging the reliability of the Holy Scriptures). The emphasis, understandably, was on coins and monumental inscriptions; but already Jacques Spon, speaking of the monuments that contribute to expanding our knowledge of the ancient world, included also *instrumentum*, and his *Archaeographia*, published in 1679, embraced studies both of inscriptions (*epigrammatographia*) and of household goods (*angeiographia*). Later, around the middle of the eighteenth century, the Count of Caylus did not hesitate to proclaim every ancient object, even the most humble, a "bearer of history." And an edict of the kingdom of Naples of 1755, just a few years after the discovery of Herculaneum and Pompeii, urged the use of "care and industry" in the collection of "vessels or implements . . . of marble or clay or metal," because from these were drawn "the greatest benefits . . . both for the understanding of antiquity and for the illumination of history." It seemed that the path had been laid out, but events transpired otherwise. In the course of the nineteenth century the history of art became the dominant academic trend in archaeological studies, at the expense of the study of material culture.[2] Even if they had wanted to use archaeological sources, historians of the ancient economy could not have done so, because the archaeologists were not concerned to furnish them with any. As late as 1869, Blümner could write an essay on the history of crafts in antiquity on the basis of literary sources alone.

One can therefore understand why Dressel's work represented such a gigantic step forward, especially because Dressel knew how to be both an epigraphist and an archaeologist and so studied not only the inscription but also its carrier (Blech 1980: 13). Not only did he create typologies for amphorae and lamps that, with adjustments and revisions, are still today basic tools of research, but several of his observations on the functions of the different types of inscription (e.g. on lamps) have established themselves as standard. To cite a specialist in the field (Pavolini 1980), it can be said not only that the passage of time has not disproved any of Dressel's general conclusions but also (unfortunately) that we know no more than he did about the organization of production and the management of the workshops. According to Pavolini, the two paths of research—typological analysis and epigraphic exploration—"have not been encountered in such unity" since then.

Not even Dressel, however, used inscribed *instrumentum* for a broader study of the Roman economy. Credit for having been the first to employ archaeological materials effectively in writing the economic history of antiquity is generally awarded to Rostovtzeff (1926; cf. Momigliano 1953, 1954). But it is fair to recognize that already ten years previously the Finnish scholar Hermann Gummerus had published in the *Realencyclopädie* of Pauly-Wissowa a long article—really a monograph—on industry and commerce in the ancient Roman world (Gummerus 1916) in which he gathered practically all the available evidence, especially that of stamped *instrumentum*. Even if in the sober columns of Pauly-Wissowa we do not find the capacity, characteristic of Rostovtzeff, of evoking, along with the products, the lifestyle of the producers, the evidence is often presented with a higher degree of elaboration. For example, Gummerus was the first to attempt a quantitative analysis of the servile workforce of the pottery workshops at Arezzo based on the names found on stamps.[3]

Nonetheless, even if it is right to recognize the importance of certain precursors, it was only during the final decades of the twentieth century that *instrumentum domesticum* began to become a truly important source for ancient economic history, thanks to the enormous increase in excavated material, to progress in the study of material culture, and to advances in our understanding of the economic structures of ancient societies.[4] Recent collections of essays by various specialists give a fairly good idea of the state of the art in the Roman world;[5] similarly complete syntheses are thus far lacking for Greece and the East.

From production to distribution

What kinds of inscription are found on *instrumentum domesticum*? What sorts of information can they provide? And what problems do they present? We must in the first place distinguish between inscriptions applied during the manufacturing process and those added at a later stage. Among the latter we must further distinguish between those pertaining to the transportation and distribution of the product and those inscribed during the subsequent life of the object itself. These last, more often than not, are graffiti incised by the owners. Apart from exceptional cases such as the fragment of a cup found in the workshop of Pheidias at Olympia with the famous graffito $\Phi\epsilon\iota\delta\acute{\iota}\bar{o}$: $\epsilon\grave{\iota}\mu\iota$ ("I belong to Pheidias"), they are generally more relevant for social than for economic history.[6] They can tell us for whom certain products were primarily intended, and the names can reveal the social status of the owners, their ethnic origin, and their level of literacy.

Distribution

Far more important for economic history are the inscriptions applied during the distribution process. Sometimes these were inscribed graffiti, sometimes painted texts. On Greek vases, merchants' trademarks are known already in Mycenaean times, but the majority are those found on Attic vases, generally under the footing, where the writing is less obtrusive (Johnston 1979). In addition to personal names, many bear numbers that refer to the counting of the vases and to their price. Unfortunately, the latter are extremely controversial: it is disputed, for example, whether they refer to obols or to drachmae. Amyx (1958) was convinced that we are dealing with obols (one-sixth of a drachma), but as such the prices have seemed to some implausibly low. The prices in themselves, moreover, mean less if we do not know the conditions of production (the fixed costs, the price of manpower, the quantity of objects made) and other parameters of the cost of living (Webster 1972: 270–9; Johnston 1979: 33–5).

Graffiti applied by traders are found also in Roman contexts. One of the most interesting cases comes from the site of Magdalensberg, in Austria. Here numerous objects (vessels of *terra sigillata* and amphorae) exhibit the letters "TK" in ligature. According to Zabehlicky-Scheffenegger (1985), the letters might indicate that one and the same entrepreneur (the hypothesis is that we are dealing with T. Kanius of Aquileia, proprietor of the most important clearing house in the northern Adriatic) transported ceramic ware of Arezzo and the Po valley and Istrian amphorae into Noricum, whence he imported iron back into Italy.

The painted inscriptions (*tituli picti*) found on Roman amphorae are more complex. They concern not so much the container itself as the goods transported (wine, olive oil, fish sauce). The names that appear here seem to be those of persons involved in the sale of the goods, since they almost never coincide with those found in the stamps, which are thought to be those of the manufacturers of the containers (Manacorda–Panella 1993: 56). The amphorae identified as type 20 in Dressel's typology, which carried olive oil from Baetica (southern Spain) to Rome, present a special case: since it was the responsibility of the imperial *annona* to guarantee the supply of olive oil to the capital, the state functionaries assigned to its supervision placed inscriptions on the containers that had been inspected (Rodríguez-Almeida 1984, Remesal Rodríguez 1989).

Vase signatures

The richest information, without doubt, and at the same time the greatest problems come from the inscriptions put on pieces of *instrumentum* at the time of production. In most cases these were stamps impressed with a die, but there were also painted texts. The best known are those found on Greek pottery. In view of the high aesthetic quality of Greek ceramic workmanship, these vase signatures are mainly of interest to the art historian, but here too we are dealing with objects that fall into the category of *instrumentum domesticum* (Immerwahr 1990). Indeed, the social status and economic capabilities of artisans in classical Greece are much-debated subjects (Coarelli 1980), and the signatures on vases are one of the few sources on which the economic historian can rely in order to understand how workshops functioned as productive enterprises (Webster 1972).

The oldest signatures go back to early archaic times; the latest belong to the second half of the fourth century BCE.[7] When the verb ποιεῖν ("to make") is used, as it always is in the oldest inscriptions, we must conclude that the artisan meant to say that he had fashioned the entire vase, both the modeling and the painted decoration. Soon, however, the verb γράφειν ("to depict") came into use.[8] If there can be no doubt about the meaning of γράφειν, about that of ποιεῖν there has been a steady discussion since the last century.[9] At issue is the question whether the term refers to the manufacturer of the object or to the owner of the workshop—persons who, in a developed operation, cannot have been the same. When the two verbs appear side by side in reference to the same subject (e.g. X ἐποίεσεν καὶ ἔγραψεν), the customary interpretation is that the craftsman had meant to say that he himself had fashioned and painted the vase. This happened in four cases certainly and in another two probably. But when ποιεῖν construes with a different subject, according to Cook (1971) it most likely refers to the owner of the workshop. Cook gives much weight to a pair of cases in which two different names are followed by ποιεῖν: whereas it is difficult to see why two different potters would have been involved in making a vessel of modest dimensions (in both cases, a cup), one can well understand why two owners of the same workshop might be named.

This formula is perhaps related to the older one in which no distinction is made between modeling and painting and the same verb ποιεῖν is used for both activities: here the first name would identify the craftsman who fashioned the vase, the second the one who decorated it (Guarducci 1967–78 3.473). Then there is the case of Euphronios, who at first (at the end of the sixth century BCE) signed as a painter and subsequently (from the beginning of the fifth century) with the verb ἐποίεσεν. Since Euphronios was one of the most accomplished painters of his era, it seems odd that he would have gone back to the less prestigious activity of modeler (at least if he had not been constrained to do so by the deterioration of his eyesight, as has been suggested). Conversely, it has been thought that, thanks to the proceeds of his activity as a painter, he became the owner of a workshop. That would explain also the dedication around 470 BCE by this same Euphronios, in his capacity as "potter," of a statue on the Acropolis as a "tenth share" of his profits (*IG* I² 516).

Naturally, it is possible that the owner fashioned the vase with his own hands. The objection that the appropriate verb to describe the operation of modeling is πλάττειν may be dismissed when we remember that sculptors also used the verb ποιεῖν, rather than γλύφειν (to sculpt), to sign their work. Obscurities remain, however. It is not clear, for example, why the percentage of signed works is so low: of 132 vases (broken and intact) attributed to Onesimos, for example, only one is signed. If the signature of the potter was indeed a trademark for commercial use, as our modern logic leads us to suppose, we might expect examples to have been more numerous.

Stamps

The problems increase when we come to consider the stamps impressed by dies into objects in the course of production. In general we must distinguish between containers—amphorae, jars, bottles, *urcei*—and products in themselves—building materials, table- and kitchen-ware, lead pipes, and so on.[10] The common feature is that these are not unique pieces, as in the case of the individually signed Greek vases, but objects produced in quantity, on which the same text was reproduced mechanically by means of a die made of metal, wood, terracotta, or other material. Some of this category of materials are known in very many examples, which enables the economic historian to calculate on the basis of a statistically significant sample—an exceptional circumstance in the ancient world.

The first stamps in Greece appear in the archaic age on roof tiles and bricks. The words δαμόσιον or ἱερόν and, later in the Hellenistic age, βασιλικόν indicate that the objects belong to a public building, a sanctuary, or the king, and serve primarily to prevent illegitimate misappropriations, but also perhaps to regulate production. Sometimes the entrepreneur had the materials necessary for fulfilling a contract stamped in his name, but true and proper trademarks appear only in the Hellenistic age (Orlandos 1966: 93–5, Siebert 1978a: 121–2).

Stamps appear on Greek amphorae in the second half of the fourth century BCE (at Thasos around 340, at Rhodes around 330, and at Cyprus a little later). In the West the oldest amphora stamps are those of the so-called Greco-Italic type, between the end of the fourth and the first half of the third century BCE.[11] The first Roman amphorae with stamps are the late Greco-Italic type, beginning in the second half of the third century BCE (Manacorda 1989).

As for tableware, in Greece the oldest examples, from the second half of the third century BCE, are found on some glazed vases and on the so-called Megarian vases (Courby 1922, Siebert 1978a), which were in fact made in many localities in Greece. In the West the phenomenon appears to be older. The transition from "artist's signature" to "trademark" (Siebert 1978b) came in black-glazed pottery between the end of the fourth and the beginning of the third century BCE. The custom fell almost completely out of use after the Second Punic War, at the beginning of the second century BCE.[12] During the second century BCE so-called Italo-Megarian pottery was stamped, as was Italic *terra sigillata* beginning around the middle of the first century BCE. In the first century CE stamps are found also on the *sigillata* made in Gaul, Spain, Pannonia, and, more rarely, in the East (Eastern *sigillata*). The practice of stamping tableware fell off toward the middle of the second century CE in Italy and in the third century in the provinces.

Glassware was stamped from around the middle of the first century BCE, when the technique of glass-blowing was discovered. Some objects were stamped as tableware, others as containers (generally of perfumes) (Sternini 1993, 1995). Lamps were stamped, especially in Italy, from the first century BCE to the third century CE. As for building materials, Roman bricks and roof tiles were stamped sporadically beginning in the first century BCE, extensively during the second century CE, infrequently during the third century, and widely under Diocletian and Constantine (Manacorda 1993).

Even from this schematic list it seems clear that, whatever reasons there may have been for stamping, they cannot have been equally valid for all the products in all periods. It is enough to remember that Italic or Gallic tableware was stamped, but African *terra sigillata* (African red slip ware) almost never was stamped for the entire five centuries in which it was produced (from about the end of the first century CE to about the end of the fifth).

Before asking what stamped *instrumentum* can tell us about the ancient economy, the economic historian must therefore first address the question: why was it stamped? It seems obvious that a stamp, as a text destined to accompany a product permanently, publicly fixes responsibility on an individual or a group of individuals or on a public or private entity. Like a signature, it establishes a link of ownership and/or responsibility between a work (generally a product) and its creator (Siebert 1978b, Manacorda 1993). But one never puts a signature or stamps a name for oneself; always it is done for someone else. Before being set into an economic context, the stamp must therefore first be seen in a social and cultural dimension.

Like any text, a stamp is a message that a sender entrusts to a particular medium so that it will be received by a recipient. The two extremities of the semiotic chain are strictly related, and we can only understand each side of the link to the extent that we understand the other. Was the recipient the purchaser? Sometimes the answer would seem to be yes. A pot made at La Graufesenque (ancient Condatomagus) in southern Gaul has the stamp *Scottius fecit Aretinum*. In this case, as in similar instances, it seems that the potter wanted to advertise his merchandise to potential customers by declaring that it had all the characteristics of a pot made at Arezzo, the Italian city famous for its red tableware, which was exported throughout the empire. If we accept this explanation we must admit that the target at which this message is aimed is a literate consumer well enough informed to know the value of pots from Arezzo and capable of appraising a piece according to established standards of quality, unless the targeted consumer is perhaps simply considered to be susceptible to the call of fashion. There are also, however, stamps on *terra sigillata* that have no true letters but only a sort of imitation of alphabetic characters. The target here is therefore a customer who cannot read. But perhaps in this case the message is the medium: the guarantee of quality exists in the presence itself of an inscribed mark (Pucci 1983: 110, Pucci 1993a: 75).

On the other hand, there are other types of stamps which the average man on the street would have had great difficulty in deciphering.

On Greek amphorae, for example, the stamps exhibit a variety of complicated symbols and are often poorly impressed. Specialists think they were made not so much to be read as to be seen and recognized by persons of a certain experience, such as shop overseers or official functionaries. Stamps of this type would have had the value of signifiers rather than of the signified. To use comparable terms familiar to today's consumers, they would more closely resemble barcodes than price tags (Garlan 1993b).

Amphorae

The case of amphorae requires further consideration. It is by now regarded as certain that the names appearing in amphora stamps refer to the container and not to the contents. One can therefore imagine that the stamp had three aims, possibly overlapping with each other: to guarantee the durability and soundness of the container (soundness was required in all containers [*vasa*] by Roman law), to guarantee the capacity (*amphora* was also a unit of measurement), and to enable fiscal accounting. In Greek amphora stamps, next to the name of an eponymous magistrate appears another name, thought to be a magistrate or functionary charged with supervising the manufacture of amphorae (Seyrig 1970). But sometimes the name is feminine, and therefore not that of a magistrate. In other cases this second name is accompanied by the verb ποιεῖν or by the term κεραμένς and must therefore refer to the maker of the amphorae (Garlan 1993b).

In general the producer of amphorae could be an independent artisan who sold to the landowner or to merchants who bought wine or olive oil from farmers; the landowner himself, who made the containers for his own produce on his own *fundus*; or a slave or freedman of the landowner who managed a kiln on his behalf in some relation of dependency, according to one of the numerous possibilities offered by ancient law.

Roman amphorae offer the most complex documentation in this respect and provide an important indicator of the level of development of the ancient economy. The ideal of the Roman farmer was self-sufficiency on his own *fundus*, and for this reason every landowner was in theory interested in producing the *instrumentum* necessary for selling his own products; but in fact, in an underdeveloped economy, many, in order to save the expense of permanent installations, preferred to rely upon outside sources. The production of non-agricultural goods on the *fundus* is therefore a sign of greater development. In the case of workshops managed by slaves or freedmen, it is possible to measure the level of

Figure 6.1 Stamped amphora handle from Monte Testaccio, Rome. Terracotta (c. 5 × 2 cm), c. 210–40 CE (*CIL* XV 2605). The abbreviated text is perhaps to be read *P. Mo( ) Cu( )? / (ex) fig(linis) f(undi) Do(ppiani?).* Superimposed on the lower right corner of the textual stamp is a small lentoid stamp (Grinnell College, Iowa: IA.Grin.GC.L.S.730).

mixture of estate revenues and business income in a pre-capitalist society (Figure 6.1).

During the Republic and early Empire the stamps on Italian amphorae contain the names of *ingenui*, even of elevated rank—indeed arguably of Pompey himself (but the case is not proved)—and thus demonstrate the involvement of landowners in commercial activities. The stamps on amphorae produced at Brundisium during the late Republic show a particular intertwining of interests between aristocrats or members of the municipal oligarchies and their slaves and freedmen, wherein *familiae* of slaves are connected to individual *domini* or to partnerships of *domini*. In all likelihood we have in these cases a concrete instance of the possibility provided for by Roman law of *exercere negotiationes per servos*, that is, of entrusting the management of an entrepreneurial activity to slaves with their own funds, *servi cum peculio*, who were liable to third parties only to the extent of the fixed amount of their *peculium* and thus did not put the patrimony of the *dominus* at risk.[13]

The stamps on Spanish amphorae likewise reveal the presence of persons of prominence at the municipal level, whereas nothing similar is found on Gallic amphorae. On the amphorae of Africa Proconsularis the stamps bear the name of the city, perhaps as an indication that production was controlled at the municipal level. In Tripolitania of the third century CE the display of the "clarissimate" (*vir clarissimus* was the title appropriate to senators) on amphora stamps shows the intertwining of politics and the economy, which can be explained also by the fact that olive oil was a provision of the *annona*.

Why, then, did some areas not stamp their products at all? The most striking case is that of the wine amphorae of the Aegean, an area where stamps had previously been employed for centuries. Even within a single area—indeed, within even a single center—of production not all the products were stamped. One hypothesis is that stamps were applied only to the amphorae sold to other producers, not to those made on one's own *fundus* for one's own merchandising. Alternatively, perhaps only a certain percentage were stamped. But in this case we must abandon the explanation of the stamp as a guarantee that would identify the manufacturer in the event of a dispute (Manacorda–Panella 1993). Nor can it be maintained that only amphorae destined for export were stamped, because not all the amphorae exported have stamps.

Barrels and glassware

Other containers offer partially comparable evidence. Wooden barrels were often inscribed. Of 140 known, 40 bear traces of a stamp—branded with a hot iron die or carved—and graffiti. The names that appear on the inside are thought to represent the manufacturers. The stamps on the bungs might refer to the producer of the contents or even to the merchant, as with the stamps on amphora stoppers (Hesnard–Gianfrotta 1989; Baratta 1994).

Glassware was certainly stamped by the glassmaker in some cases, but in general the names are thought to refer to the producer of the contents. Of course, there is always the possibility that they were one and the same. Some stamps on glass bottles of the second century CE—*patrimoni, patrimonium, vec(tigal), monop(oliu)m p(atrimoni) Imp(eratoris) Cae(saris) M(arci) A(ureli) [Ant]onini*—reveal a form of state control. Thought to have carried balsam from the East, the containers were in fact made in Cisalpine Gaul. Perhaps the commodity first arrived from the East and was then packaged and marketed in Italy. The fact that not all the perfume containers were stamped is perhaps due to a practice of stamping only containers for concentrated goods (Sternini 1993, 1995).

Bricks and tiles

The class of *instrumentum* that best allows the legal and economic historian to glimpse the possible internal organization of production is

Figure 6.2 Roman brickstamp from Rome. Clay (diam.: 10.3 cm), c. 150 CE (*CIL* XV 354; cf. Bodel 1983: no. 30). The text, read from the outermost line first, left to right, identifies the brick as *op(us sc. doliare) ex pr(aedi-is) Sabinae Sabinillae, de / fig(linis) Negarianis.* Figured at the center is a *signum* showing a bust of Vulcan wearing a *pileus*, looking right; before it is a hammer, behind it a pair of tongs. (Kelsey Museum of Archaeology, Ann Arbor: MI.AA.UM.KM.L.1206.)

brickwork (bricks and roof tiles). Indeed, the stamps applied to these products were, at least at one time (the second century CE), the most elaborate of all *instrumentum*. Let us look at a typical example (*CIL* XV 290): *ex pr(aediis) T. Stat(ili) Maximi, phig(linis) Maced(onianis), opu(s) Q. Aburni Celer(is).* Here we have an indication of the place of origin (the estate of Statilius Maximus), of the claypits or kiln (or both) (the *figlinae Macedonianae*), and of the name of the *officinator* (Q. Aburnius Celer). The object itself is indicated by the term *opus*, often specified more correctly as *opus doliare*, sometimes as *opus figlinum* (cf. Figure 6.2).

On the basis of this sort of evidence Dressel considered *figlinae* to be production units belonging to the owner of the land and subdivided internally into workshops (*officinae*) directed by *officinatores*. More recently Helen (1975) has maintained that *figlinae* simply means claypits and indicates the place, rather than any particular structure, of production. In most cases, he believes, *officinatores* would have been independent of the *dominus* and would have produced on their own behalf on the basis of a contract of *locatio-conductio* or of *usus fructus*. An active role is attributed to landowners only when an *officinator* is not mentioned in the stamp or is the slave or freedman of the owner. In Helen's view there would not have been any concentration of production in the hands of senators, much less an imperial monopoly. Setälä (1977) for her part maintains that of 150 known landowners (*domini*) only four are certainly also producers. Margareta Steinby (1982), on the other hand, finds it difficult to believe that senators, *equites*, and the emperor had nothing to do with the manufacture of bricks. *Figlinae* in her view can indicate both the claypits and the means of production (the kilns)—and indeed, nothing prevents us from thinking that the phrase *ex figlinis* indicates both the place and the unit of production. The name of the *officinator* thus would have served to distinguish several related activities.

Steinby's most interesting hypothesis is that the stamps should be understood as the abbreviated formulation of the legally stipulated contract between *dominus* and *officinator*. Previously it was thought that this contract had been drawn up as a *locatio rei* (the *res* would have been the claypits or the workshop) and that the *officinator* paid to the *dominus* a sum for using the latter's property. But if, as Steinby believes, the object of the contract is the finished product itself (the *opus*), then it would have been a matter of *locatio operis*: that is, it would have been the *dominus* who paid the *officinator* (who is sometimes defined as a *conductor*) for an agreed-upon quantity of the product, of which in the end he remained the owner. Similar contracts are attested in Egypt of the third century CE (*P. Oxy.* 3595–7).

From the standpoint of economic history, the difference is considerable. In Steinby's hypothesis the *dominus* is no longer a mere landlord (*rentier*) but is himself an entrepreneur. The *officinator*, on the other hand, is not always materially involved in the production process (in some cases, the *officinator* is a woman). Rather, the *officinator* appears to be an entrepreneur who employs his (or her) own dependents, whether slaves or hired workers, and who over time moves from one establishment (*officina*) to another, possibly forming partnerships along the way. Obviously, for Steinby a brickstamp was not addressed to the final user of the product, who would have had a great deal of difficulty and little interest in deciphering its text. Its function is to be explained instead within the *figlinae*. In effect, in a single *figlinae* some *officinatores* might have been slaves or freedmen of the *dominus*, others slaves or freedmen of another person bound to the *dominus* by contract. The stamp would then have served to maintain accountability within the context of each *figlinae* (often each *officinator* is distinguished by a symbol).

Manacorda (1993: 46), however, believes that Steinby's thesis does not completely explain the stamps on bricks. The abbreviated formula of the contract appears only in a late stage in the development of the brick industry, but stamps were also used earlier, without reference to the *opus* and the contracting parties. Why? And why publicize a contract, using legal terminology, if it was a matter strictly relevant to the internal organization of the enterprise?

Even if all is not clear, brickstamps give us a great deal of information for economic history. Among the *domini* we find senators and *equites*, men and women—proof, in one way or another, that the upper classes knew well how to exploit their landed properties. And if in the Severan age the sole producer of bricks was in fact the emperor, it is very likely that this reflects the heavy concentration of agrarian lands in the hands of the princeps. Brickstamps also attest a certain social mobility. We find among the *officinatores* numerous transitions from servile to freed status and in at least one case, that of a certain Vismatius Successus, from the role of *officinator* to that of *dominus* (Steinby 1993).

One objection to Steinby's thesis is that some stamps exhibit only the name of the *dominus* and others only that of the *officinator* (Manacorda 1993: 46). With regard to the first, Steinby (1993) believes these served to distinguish the products of different *domini* who used the same warehouse (*tegularia*); as for the second, she notes that *dolia* were stamped with the name of the *officinator* alone, even when in brickstamps the latter is associated with the name of a *dominus*. Starting from this observation, Steinby asks if the same thing might not happen with the stamps of other types of clay products (lamps, *terra sigillata*, etc.)—if, that is, those named in stamps might not be *officinatores* working for others (Steinby 1993).

Kilns, claypits, and the organization of production

One thing certain is that a kiln fired at the same time the products of more than one potter or brickmaker not linked to one another by a common name. Probably only a few potters possessed all the resources for production and were able to complete the entire cycle of workmanship autonomously. Smaller shops perhaps had to bring their wares to larger establishments for firing and to pay for the use of the kiln, or had to contribute to paying a specialized kiln-master engaged periodically by a contract of *locatio operis*. Or else the owner of the kiln, not necessarily a potter himself, after having sold a batch of fired products to a *negotiator* who had commissioned them, paid the various craftsmen who had contributed to making the batch. In both cases the stamps could have served to facilitate a proportional distribution of the sums that passed from hand to hand.

Nonetheless, we must not forget that the activity of the potter, no less than that of the brickmaker, was tied to the land. As long as he was not himself the owner of the land, the potter had to acquire clay, water, and wood by paying in some fashion. It is therefore easier to imagine that potters, individually or collectively, entered into agreements with landowners—the more so since they easily moved from one place to another, especially in Gaul. On the *fundus* they could also find extra manpower for some unspecialized work, as seems to appear from a well-known graffito from La Graufesenque which speaks of *pueri* leased to potters by a *dominus* (Pucci 1986, 1993b). Bearing this in mind, we must grant that Steinby's model can be adapted not only to amphorae (for example, to the products of Baetica, where the existence of adjacent workshops belonging to the same *dominus* has already been established and where the expressions *ex praediis* and *ex figlinis* also appear), but also, in more than one case, to tableware. A *dominus* could have had economic relationships with one or more *officinatores* (according to Steinby, the formula *ex officina* that appears on Gallic ware can only refer to them), who supplied him with finished products, exactly as in the contracts on Egyptian papyri cited earlier.

Among those who have greater difficulty in accepting Steinby's model *in toto* are those who don't want to underestimate the value of the stamp as a guarantee, a function that Steinby denies. Relevant in this regard are the brickstamps themselves, where consular dates are found on urban examples from 110 to 164 CE. Whereas for Bloch (1947: 1, 324–7; 1959: 234–8) this is to be explained by the need for controls and for stock-keeping within the production process, Boethius (1941) and Mingazzini (1958: 86–8) believe instead that the consular dates certified the seasoning of the brick and thus guaranteed the quality of the tiles. Manacorda (1993), adducing a suggestive parallel in pontifical legislation at Rome in the nineteenth century, insists on the function of the stamp as a guarantee of size and quality and emphasizes its official function, beyond the private relationship between *dominus* and *officinator*.

These arguments, which apply in part also to lead pipes,[14] have less relevance for tableware. In the light of Steinby's model, other elements instead become significant: for example, the fact that some Gallic workshops, or those of late-Italic potters, used the same dies for the moulds of their relief cups. This could easily be explained by imagining adjacent workshops of several *officinatores* dependent upon a single *dominus*. Furthermore, Steinby is correct in saying that the so-called branch workshops (Pucci 1985, 1993a) can easily be seen as different work stations within the same *figlinae* and that the temporary partnerships attested among potters are no different from those among *officinatores* at brickyards.

Steinby believes that the production of amphorae, tableware, and lamps in the Roman world is only apparently parceled out into a myriad of small and mid-sized workshops and in reality culminates in a restricted number of large properties, as happens with urban bricks. But if this were so, what happened to the finished products? Did a system of distribution exist similar to that hypothesized for the process of production, with a series of agents leading to the same *domini* (Di Porto 1984a, 1984b; Carandini 1989)?

The sale, in bulk, of the products of several *officinatores* is probably demonstrated in at least one case by stamps on the cargo of Gallic *terra sigillata* of the wreck of Cala Culip IV. But was the presumed *dominus* the one who placed on the market the products of all the workshops of which he was the head, or was it not instead an unknown *negotiator* who acquired at the source (as was done with wine, which indeed was often bought before the vintage: Tchernia 1993) the desired quantity of pottery and established the assortment, quality, and price? The two solutions are very different from the point of view of economic history (Pucci 1993a).

In sum, stamped *instrumentum* cannot always supply answers to all the questions the historian of the ancient economy would like to put to it, but it can help him to formulate them intelligently, if in no other way by suggesting in what direction he should orient his research. These humble objects will in any case repay those who humbly dedicate their efforts to them.

Appendix

A brief guide to some standard collections

John Bodel

A basic challenge for anyone wishing to consult ancient Greek and Latin inscriptions is knowing where to find them. No one can hope to keep track of all that has been published, let alone of all that has survived, but systematic perusal of the standard corpora (*Inscriptiones Graecae* [*IG*], *Corpus Inscriptionum Latinarum* [*CIL*]), their regular supplements (*Supplementum Epigraphicum Graecum* [*SEG*], *L'Année épigraphique* [*AE*]), and the main epigraphic journals (*Epigraphica, Zeitschrift für Papyrologie und Epigraphik*) will ensure that not much of significance is overlooked. The easiest way to become familiar with the most important material is to read through the larger collections of selected texts (*Sylloge Inscriptionum Graecarum* [*Syll.*³, *SIG*³], *Orientis Graeci Inscriptiones Selectae* [*OGIS*], *Inscriptiones Latinae Selectae* [*ILS*], *Inscriptiones Latinae Liberae Rei Publicae* [*ILLRP*]). For keeping abreast of more recent finds and new interpretations, the invaluable surveys of Greek and Latin inscriptions published annually in *Revue des études grecques* and separately, under its own title, *Bulletin épigraphique* (*Bull. ép.*), and (approximately) quinquennially in the *Journal of Roman Studies* (Latin texts and, increasingly, Greek inscriptions relevant to Roman matters) provide selective but wide coverage.[1]

In practice, one does not always want to consult the material in the way it is organized in the standard collections—normally by geographical region, with subdivisions according to the type of document—but rather according to criteria adapted to the question at hand. Sometimes the aim is to search a wide range of material in order to learn the frequency or distribution or date or pattern of usage of a particular name or title or expression; at others the goal is to find a specific instance of a given term or to locate an individual text. For these various purposes, selective indices are indispensable. Over the years a standard set of epigraphic indices has evolved, but individual corpora and collections frequently vary in their elaboration of details, especially in the subcategories of *notabilia varia*. The most basic set, common to most epigraphic collections, includes registers of names (in the Roman world, of *nomina* and *cognomina*); rulers and magistrates; civic offices; military affairs; gods, goddesses, and religious matters; geographical and topographical locations; private offices; and miscellaneous items (*notabilia varia*). Complete or nearly complete word indexes of any of the larger epigraphic corpora are rare. For Greek inscriptions, the recent index volume to *IG* I³ (fascicle 3) provides a lemmatized *index verborum* for Attic inscriptions down to the end of the fourth century BCE (304 BCE), and the inscriptions of Ephesos are fully indexed in *IEphesos* 8. The closest thing to a comprehensive word index to a broader collection is to be found in volume four of the third edition of Dittenberger's *Sylloge Inscriptionum Graecarum* (*Syll.*³), which contains a lexicon, compiled by F. Hiller von Gaertringen, of most Greek words in the 1,250 inscriptions included in the first three volumes. For Latin texts only the volumes of *CIL* devoted to inscriptions of the Republic (vol. I²) and to the graffiti and painted wall inscriptions of Pompeii and the cities buried by Vesuvius (vol. IV) were designed from the start to include comprehensive indexes of words, and each is now complete only in part. Computerized "key word in context" indexes have subsequently been produced for the inscriptions of Rome (vol. VI), for stone inscriptions from the province of Noricum (see below at vol. III), and, periodically, for the new series of *Supplementa Italica*, covering the Latin inscriptions of Italy published since the time of the relevant volumes of *CIL* (thus far vols 7, 14).

With the advance of computerized technologies, however, the situation is changing. Not only is it now possible to generate "lemmatized" indexes of words electronically (as in the latest index volume to *IG* I³ or in the third fascicle of the computerized word indexes of the stone inscriptions from Noricum: see Panciera 1991a: 432–5), but sophisticated indices specially adapted to specific classes of inscription, such as the line by line, reverse indexes of abbreviated words for brickstamps from the city of Rome produced by Steinby (1987), provide unprecedented access to epigraphic materials previously familiar only to a handful of specialists. What is more, the recent and rapid expansion of the number of epigraphical databases and searching mechanisms available electronically, on CD-ROM and via the Internet, has made it possible to perform individually defined word searches (and in some cases fragment-of-word searches) with relative ease and efficiency. Chief among these are the electronic databases of Latin inscriptions registered in *L'Année épigraphique* mounted on the world wide web by the Epigraphische Datenbank Heidelberg (see *AE* below) and of Greek documentary texts distributed on

CD-ROM by the Packard Humanities Institute (see *IG* below), which not only report but in many cases revise and correct the editions in the standard corpora. These new tools promise to change some of the ways in which epigraphic research is conducted, but it will be some time before the level of accuracy attained by the best of the traditional printed indexes is widely achieved, and if the impact of computerized concordances and databases on the study of ancient literary texts provides any guide, the new electronic resources will supplement rather than replace the more conventional, reasoned indexes of subjects and themes.

Advances of a different sort are coming from the distribution of digitized images of Greek and Latin inscriptions over the world wide web. Since it is always desirable to inspect at firsthand any epigraphic text one wishes to consult, and since direct access to the inscribed objects themselves is often impractical, the publication of legible photographs and facsimiles has always been an indispensable, though not infallible (see above, pages 53–5), aid to epigraphic research. Even before Mommsen produced the first fascicle of the *Corpus Inscriptionum Latinarum*, Friedrich Ritschl had published a magnificent *auctarium* of images, employing the most advanced technology of the day (lithographic reproduction), which remains an invaluable resource (*Priscae Latinitatis Monumenta Epigraphica*, Berlin 1862). The cost of producing plates in conventional print publications, however, has frequently deterred publishers from providing complete photographic documentation of all newly published inscriptions, with the result that many texts are today accessible to most scholars only through printed transcriptions. The possibility of disseminating clear images at low cost in electronic form via the Internet and on CD-ROM promises to make available in coming years visual representations of a far greater number of ancient Greek and Latin epigraphic texts than have been widely seen before. An important early initiative in this direction has been undertaken at Oxford University's Centre for the Study of Ancient Documents (CSAD), where digitized images of the Centre's extensive collection of paper squeezes (some 20,000 in all, mostly of Greek historical inscriptions) and of selected writing tablets from Vindolanda (see above, pages 64–6) are being mounted at the Centre's webpage (http://www.csad.ox.ac.uk).

Eventually, full scale electronic editions of Greek and Latin inscriptions, with hypertext links to digitized images and other electronic resources (such as maps, word indexes, and literary texts) stand to replace the traditional forms of epigraphic publication developed in the middle of the nineteenth century and little changed since then. Plans for an electronic "supercorpus" of all ancient Greek and Latin inscriptions are being formulated by a committee of experts under the auspices of the international organization of epigraphists (Association Internationale d'Épigraphie Grecque et Latine), but the project is as yet in its infancy (cf. Agnati 1998). A principal advantage of the electronic medium of the Internet, in addition to its widespread availability and comparatively low cost to individuals, is the possibility it provides of allowing continuous updating: new or corrected readings and interpretations can easily be mounted beside or in place of earlier versions of a text, so that an epigraphical edition becomes a truly dynamic and collaborative enterprise, whose utility is limited only by the limits of individual initiative rather than by the practical restrictions imposed by the costs of publishing pages of printed texts, each new edition of which renders its predecessor obsolete. A pioneering project in this area is the Programme d'Enregistrement, de Traitement, et de Recherches Automatiques en Épigraphie (PETRAE) directed by Alain Bresson at the University of Bordeaux, which is producing a number of epigraphic databases from different parts of Gaul (Aquitania), northern Spain, Sardinia, Tunisia, Greece, Cyprus, and Turkey and is mounting them, as they become available, at the project's webpage (http://silicon.montaigne.u-Bordeaux.FR:8001/).

For now, however, none of the new electronic tools seems likely to replace the best of the standard printed collections, which have an integrity and an autonomy not easily matched by the more ephemeral, if adaptable, electronic media. The following survey, arranged alphabetically by abbreviated title, covers only the works of greatest use to the ancient historian. Fuller publication information can be found at the relevant entries in the *Guide*, which are recorded in parentheses after each title. Where not otherwise indicated, the lemmata and accompanying notes of standard editions are written in Latin. Good narrative surveys in English of basic Greek and Roman epigraphical publications are provided by Woodhead 1981 or 1992: 94–107 (Greek) and Gordon 1983: 8–12 (Roman). For those large collections that have been entered, in whole or in large part, into electronically searchable databases, the URL (if available via the Internet) or publication information (if available only on CD-ROM) is included at the end of the entry. For more complete and up-to-date information on electronic tools for research in epigraphy, see the webpage of the American Society of Greek and Latin Epigraphy maintained by T. Elliott at the University of North Carolina in Chapel Hill (http://asgle.classics.unc.edu) or the *Fonti epigraphiche* produced by A. Cristofori at the University of Bologna (http://www.economia.unibo.it/dipartim/stoant/rassegna1/epigrafi.html).

For basic introductions to the study of Greek and Latin inscriptions, the most helpful guides are, for Greek inscriptions, the overview by Woodhead (1981, 1992) and the manuals of Larfeld (1914) (partly outdated but still useful) and Guarducci (1967–78) (comprehensive, in four volumes, with many examples) and (1987) (differently oriented from the multi-volume work); for Latin inscriptions, the introductory guides of Sandys (1927) and Keppie (1991) and the manuals of Cagnat (1914) (still basic), Gordon (1983) (focused on inscriptions on stone, with 100 examples, arranged chronologically), and Calabi-Limentani (1974, 1991) provide a basic orientation.[2]

AE L'Année épigraphique (Paris 1888–) (Guide³ 1142 = Guide² 821)

Designed to supplement the standard *Corpus Inscriptionum Latinarum*, *AE* provides an annual survey (in French) of epigraphic publications relating to Latin inscriptions and, since 1966, Greek inscriptions concerning the organization of the Roman empire, down to the end of the seventh century CE. From its foundation by R. Cagnat in 1888 until 1965 (covering the year 1964), *AE* appeared as an appendix in the annual volumes of *Revue archéologique*; since then it has been published separately each year. (The originally planned supplement to *CIL*, *Ephemeris Epigraphica*, produced nine volumes, in two phases [1872–9, 1903–13], before dying out at the start of World War I.) The early volumes of *AE*, as conceived by Cagnat, aimed only to register important new inscriptions without systematically reproducing their texts. Since 1968 (for the year 1966), when editorial policies were revised in four ways, coverage has been more comprehensive: the summaries of scholarly interpretations are now more substantial, and transcriptions of newly published texts (with the exception of fragments too small to contain a name or other term that can be registered in the indices) are given in lower case letters, with modern punctuation, supplements, and expanded abbreviations. In 1991 a new team under the direction of M. Corbier further expanded the range and improved the level of coverage, particularly of Greek texts.

Within each volume the material is arranged geographically, according to the plan of *CIL* (see below), with material originating outside the boundaries of the Roman empire assembled after that of the administrative region geographically closest to it. Each volume is equipped with a set of indices (skeletal and frequently lacunose during the early years, increasingly full and accurate since 1968), and consolidated indices at ten-year intervals are available for the years 1888–1960 (the first covers the years 1888–1900; all seven are gathered into a single volume published in 1968) and for 1961–80. Since 1961 each volume has concluded with a series of concordances and the following indices and lists: periodicals and works surveyed in the current volume and the names of modern authors cited; provenances; *nomina gentilicia; cognomina*; tribes; gods, goddesses, and heroes; priests and religious affairs (including priestly colleges, festivals and games, Jewish and Christian affairs, and *notabilia varia*); geographical names (ancient and modern French); kings, emperors, empresses, princes, and princesses; public offices and things related to Roman administration (including imperial and consular dates, provincial and local eras, and indictions); military affairs (including legions, cohorts, *alae*, Roman garrisons, *numeri* and *auxilia palatia, vexillationes*, fleets, and individual ranks); provincial and municipal administration; *collegia* and crafts; ancient authors; and *notabilia varia* (a potpourri, listed alphabetically but indiscriminately in French, Latin, and Greek, including grammatical peculiarities, types of inscription and materials, motifs, and individual words). A comprehensive concordance between *AE* and *CIL* is provided by R. Gruendel, *Addenda bibliographica praecipue ad CIL e periodico L'Année épigraphique nominato excerpta* (Berlin 1965).

Two electronic databases, which differ in character and scope, make much of this material available on the world wide web. The Epigraphische Datenbank Heidelberg, under the direction of G. Alföldy, provides revised and corrected versions of the texts published in *AE* between 1900 and 1990, with abbreviations expanded, fragmentary texts restored, and bibliographical references updated (http://www.uni-heidelberg.de/institute/sonst/adw/edh/; for inquiries write to epigraphische.datenbank@urz.uni-heidelberg.de). M. Clauss at the Goethe University in Frankfurt provides the texts of all the Latin inscriptions published in *AE* from the beginning to the present (currently up to 1993), along with selected texts from *CIL*, including the new fascicles of *CIL* II (Spain) and VI (Rome); currently they number some 107,000 (http://www.rz.uni-frankfurt.de/~clauss/).

Bull. ép. or *BE Bulletin épigraphique* (Paris 1888–) (*Guide*[3] 1146 = *Guide*[2] 825)

Published annually in *Revue des études grecques* and separately under its own title, *Bulletin épigraphique* reviews epigraphical publications and summarizes (and often evaluates and corrects) articles and reports from a wide variety of journals not generally available in many parts of the English-speaking world. The years 1938–84, when *Bull. ép.* was edited by Louis Robert and his wife Jeanne (issued separately in ten volumes, along with five volumes of consolidated indices of Greek words, publications, and topics, in French [Paris 1972–87]), are a treasure of information illuminated by vast erudition. Probably the most stimulating, and certainly the most humbling, way into the world of Greek epigraphy, especially of Asia Minor, is to peruse the pages of *Bull. ép.* written during the 1960s and 1970s, when Louis Robert's unparalleled ability to situate the least promising and most intractable texts within their broader cultural context was most sharply focused on the most interesting material.

Following Robert's death in 1985, the *Bulletin* was revived in 1987 by an international (predominantly French) team led by Philippe Gauthier and has regained vigor since then. Arranged according to a combination of geographical and thematic criteria and produced by various hands, the new *Bull. ép.* does not always make it easy to find discussion of particular texts; but it is admirably up-to-date, and the quality of the coverage is high. Though less comprehensive than its English-language counterpart, *SEG* (see below), *Bull. ép.* serves a valuable purpose in providing discussion, as well as reportage, of significant new texts (for important statements of its editorial principles, see *Revue des études grecques* 1986, 117–18; 1958, xv–xvi).

CIL Corpus Inscriptionum Latinarum (Berlin 1863–) (Guide³ 429 = Guide² 334)

The standard collection of Latin inscriptions from the earliest period (sixth century BCE) down to the early eighth century CE. Founded by Mommsen in 1853 on the model of August Boeckh's *Corpus Inscriptionum Graecarum* (see below, under *IG*), *CIL* is likewise arranged geographically, with the exception of volumes I (inscriptions up to the death of Caesar), IV (wall inscriptions of Pompeii, Herculaneum, and the other regions buried by Vesuvius), XV (*instrumentum domesticum* of Rome), XVI (military diplomas), XVII (milestones), and XVIII (*carmina epigraphica*). Most volumes of *CIL* were published between 1870 and 1890 and have since been updated by supplements, of which several (notably those for volumes III and VIII) incorporate substantial revisions of material published in the original volumes. Only volumes I and II have undergone second editions, of which the first is not yet complete, and the latter is in its early stages. For further details on the progress of *CIL*, consult the *CIL* webpage, http://www.bbaw.de/vh/cil/index.html.

In order to learn whether an inscription published in *CIL* has been improved by a new reading or republication, one must consult the indices of the supplements, a tedious process alleviated, in the case of the inscriptions of Rome (excluding *instrumentum*), by the concordance of U. Lehmann, *Quibus locis inveniantur additamenta titulorum voluminis VI Corporis Inscriptionum Latinarum* (1986). A similar aid for the remaining volumes of *CIL*, now under preparation, is eagerly awaited. In the meantime, for the Latin inscriptions of Italy outside of Rome, the new series of *Supplementa Italica* provides, town by town, bibliographical updates for the material published in *CIL* (volumes IV, V, IX, X, XI, XII, XIV), as well as full editions, with commentary, of new and subsequently published texts. For inscriptions from the Roman provinces and from Italian towns not yet covered by *Suppl. Ital.* n.s., several of the relevant volumes of *CIL* have been supplemented and in part superseded by various regional corpora, some superior to their models in execution and scope; for details see the *Guide²*, pages 76–127 or *Guide³*, pages 87–149 *passim*.

I Inscriptions down to the death of Caesar (Guide³ 435–6 = Guide² 342–3)

The first edition, edited by Mommsen (miscellaneous texts, calendars, and coins) and W. Henzen (*fasti consulares*), inaugurated the publication of *CIL* in 1863. With the most recent addenda to the second edition (pars II, fasc. iv), published in 1986, the number of Latin inscriptions known from the period of the Republic down to 44 BCE (only a handful belong to the pre-Republican era of Rome), amounts to some 3,700 (see further below, at *ILLRP*). Most of these are fully indexed; the index to the latest fascicle includes textual variants. Part one of the second edition, comprising the lists of consuls, *elogia*, and calendars, is superseded by A. Degrassi, *Inscriptiones Italiae XIII*, 1. *Fasti consulares et triumphales* (Rome 1947), 2. *Fasti anni Numani et Iuliani* (1963), 3. *Elogia* (1937).

II Spain (Guide³ 448 = Guide² 351)

The first edition (1869) and supplement (1892), edited by E. Huebner, comprised 6,350 entries. A second edition currently being prepared by G. Alföldy, M. Mayer and A. U. Stylow, of which the first fascicles (covering the *conventus* of southeastern Tarraconensis, Cordoba, and

Astigitanus in Baetica, with indices and excellent photographs, in half-tone *ad loc.*, and on supplemental microfiches) began to appear in 1995, will eventually register some 22,000 texts. No other region of the Roman empire has experienced such an exponential growth of its epigraphic patrimony over the past hundred years.

III Northern and eastern provinces (Noricum and Raetia, Pannonia and Moesia, Dacia, Thrace, Greece, Crete, Asia Minor, Syria, Judaea, Arabia, Cyrenaica and Egypt) (Guide³ 488 = Guide² 379)

Mommsen edited the first two fascicles in 1873 but had not himself seen much of what he published. In 1902, along with O. Hirschfeld and A. Domaszewski, he produced a supplement, in two parts, with many improvements and corrections to the texts included in the original volumes. The index to part two of the supplement (pp. 2331–2622) supersedes that of the original edition (pp. 1065–1197). A second edition of the inscriptions of Noricum is being prepared by E. Weber, M. Hainzmann (*instrumentum domesticum*) and others. The texts on stone known as of 1984 have been equipped by Hainzmann and P. Schubert with a computerized word index and thesaurus: *Inscriptiones lapidariarum Latinarum provinciae Norici usque ad annum MCMLXXIV repertarum Indices* (1986) (*ILLPRON Indices*).

IV Pompeii, Herculaneum, Stabiae and the territories buried by Vesuvius: graffiti, waxed tablets, and painted inscriptions (Guide³ 536 = Guide² 418)

R. Schoene and C. Zangemeister edited the first harvest of painted inscriptions and graffiti on walls and clayware in 1871, and Zangemeister added a supplement on the waxed tablets from Pompeii in 1898. A. Mau contributed a supplement of new material in 1909. M. Della Corte produced three fascicles of a third supplement in 1952, 1955, and 1963, to which F. Weber and P. Ciprotti added a fourth in 1970. None of the fascicles produced in the latter half of the twentieth century has an index. A fifth fascicle with addenda and corrigenda to all the previously published texts and indices to those in the third supplement is currently under preparation. A fourth supplement being prepared by A. Varone will comprise computerized word indexes to all the inscriptions in *CIL* IV.

V Northern Italy (Cisalpine Gaul) (Guide³ 545 = Guide² 426)

Mommsen produced two excellent volumes, covering the Tenth (1872), Eleventh, and Ninth (1877) Augustan regions of Italy, to which E. Pais added an equally valuable supplement in 1888 (*Suppl. Ital.*).

VI Rome (Guide³ 576 = Guide² 443)

By far the largest collection of Latin inscriptions anywhere, some 54,000 in number, not counting *instrumentum domesticum*, which is registered in *CIL* XV. The sacral texts and inscriptions of emperors and magistrates were published by E. Bormann and W. Henzen in 1876. Beginning in 1882, Bormann, Henzen, and C. Hülsen began publishing the huge quantity of sepulchral stones then known and increasing daily from the unearthing of the extensive burial grounds (particulary north of the ancient city, outside the Porta Salaria), then being uncovered during construction of the new suburban quarters of the modern city; twenty years later, when Hülsen published his final *auctarium*, they numbered some 35,000. M. Bang produced an *index nominum* in 1926 and a supplement in 1933. In 1974 and 1975 E. J. Jory and D. G. Moore compiled a computerized index of key words in context to all the texts, and L. Vidman added an *index cognominum* in 1980. In 1996 G. Alföldy produced the first fascicle (inscriptions of emperors) of a new three-part supplement, of which he will also edit a second fascicle on magistrates; S. Panciera will produce a third fascicle covering all other types of inscription except Christian texts, graffiti, and painted inscriptions.

A CD-ROM, *Epigraph, A Database of Roman Inscriptions*, published by E. J. Jory (Melbourne 1992) comprises two databases of the entire corpus published up to 1990—apparently based on those compiled by Jory and Moore for the printed keyword-in-context index—one of bare text (excluding lemmata and restorations), the other marked up with code tagging unusual letter-forms, ligatures, etc., and a search engine that supports Boolean searches by inscription number, full text, *cognomina*, numerals, ligatures, reversed letters, Greek text, Claudian letters, and short and tall letters.

VII Britain (Guide³ 618 = Guide² 471)

E. Hübner edited a volume in 1873 and produced three supplements in *Ephemeris Epigraphica*, the short-lived series intended to supplement *CIL* (see above, under *AE*); two others were added by F. Haverfield in 1892 and 1913. The inscriptions on stone were newly edited in 1965 in volume 1 of *The Roman Inscriptions of Britain* (an index was added in 1983); volume 2, in nine parts (1990–5), comprises the *instrumentum domesticum*. A computerized concordance, *Auxilia Epigraphica I. Roman Inscriptions of Britain*, was published on CD-ROM in 1999 by M. Hainzmann and P. Schubert (Berlin: De Gruyter).

VIII Africa (Guide³ 624 = Guide² 481)

The two volumes published by G. Willmanns in 1881 were quickly eclipsed by a series of supplements produced between 1891 and 1916 by R. Cagnat, J. Schmidt, and H. Dessau. A very full set of indices to the whole material appeared between 1942 and 1959; the last two fascicles of the indices (V, 2 and 3) incorporate the major regional corpora of Latin inscriptions of Africa produced after the publication of *CIL* VIII.

IX South-eastern Italy: Augustan regions II, IV, V (Calabria, Apulia, Samnium, Sabine country, Picenum) (Guide³ 674 = Guide² 531)

Mommsen's original volume (1883), supplemented by M. Ihm in *Ephemeris Epigraphica* in 1899, will be partially updated by M. Buonocore's forthcoming supplement to the inscriptions of the Fourth Augustan region (Samnium).

X South-western Italy: Augustan regions I and III (Bruttium, Lucania, Campania), Sicily, Sardinia (Guide³ 703 = Guide² 550)

Mommsen published *CIL* X in two volumes (part one on Bruttium, Lucania, and Campania, part two on Sicily and Sardinia), based in large part on his earlier edition of the inscriptions of the Bourbon kingdom of Naples (1852), at the same time that he produced *CIL* IX (1883). M. Ihm provided a supplement in *Ephemeris Epigraphica* in 1899. A second edition, including more than 20,000 inscriptions, is currently being prepared by a team of scholars working under the direction of H. Solin.

XI Central and Northern Italy: Augustan regions VI, VII, VIII (Aemilia, Etruria, Umbria) (Guide³ 732 = Guide² 567)

E. Bormann published the volume in two parts in 1888 (Aemilia and Etruria: regions VII, VIII) and 1901 (Umbria: region VI); a list of addenda and three indices (only)—of *nomina*, *cognomina*, and emperors—were published in 1926. Supplementary indices have subsequently been compiled by various scholars: of consuls (H.-G. Pflaum, *Studi Romagnoli* 20 [1969] 421–45); of military affairs, geographical terms, and monuments, buildings, and topographical indications of Regio VIII (A. Donati, *Studi Romagnoli* 20 [1969] 447–79); of provinces, towns, *pagi*, and *vici* (B. Galsterer-Kroll, *Epigraphica* 37 [1975] 224–52); of attendants (*apparitores*) of magistrates, emperors, and revenues (G. W. Houston, *Epigraphica* 45 [1983] 158–62); of military affairs of Regiones VI and VII (A. M. Rossi Aldrovandi, *Epigraphica* 45 [1983] 162–93); of matters relating to water (R. Vattuone, *Epigraphica* 46 [1984] 198–200); of *collegia* and professions (A. M. Rossi Aldrovandi, *Epigraphica* 47 [1985] 110–31); of *res sacrae* (D. Rigato, *Cultura epigrafica dell'Appennino* 1985: 233–78); and of *divisiones* (donations and distributions) (J. Donahue, *Epigraphica* 58 [1996] 197–200). W. Eck and E. Pack are currently preparing a supplement on the inscriptions of Etruria.

XII Narbonese Gaul (Guide³ 753 = Guide² 580)

O. Hirschfeld published the volume in 1888.

XIII Gaul and Germany (Guide³ 775 = Guide² 598)

Between 1899 and 1906 O. Hirschfeld and C. Zangemeister produced three fascicles of inscriptions on stone and bronze and O. Bohn added two others of *instrumentum domesticum*. A supplement covering the two Germanies, of which a first fascicle on Lower Germany is well advanced, is currently being prepared by R. Wiegels and colleagues at Osnabrück.

XIV Latium (Guide³ 815 = Guide² 637)

H. Dessau published the Latin inscriptions of old Latium in a single volume, with indices, in 1887. In 1930 L. Wickert added a supplement for the inscriptions of Ostia and Portus (excluding those on *instrumentum domes-ticum*, which are gathered in *CIL* XV), which he followed in 1933 with a set of topographical indices registering their findspots. M. G. Granino Cecere is currently preparing a supplement covering the rest of Latium.

XV Instrumentum domesticum of Rome and its environs (Guide³ 821 = Guide² 644)

H. Dressel collected in part one (1891) the stamps on bricks and tiles and large clay objects (*dolia, mortaria*, which he called *pelves*, terracotta pipes and sarcophagi, antefixes, and Campana reliefs) produced at Roman brick manufactories and, in the first fascicle of part two (1899), the stamps and other writing on amphorae, lamps, vases, and other glass and metal objects. The first part of a projected second fascicle devoted to seals, gems, and rings, comprising the bronze stamps gathered by Dressel, was published posthumously in 1975. None of these was provided with indices. Only the brickstamps of Rome have subsequently been equipped with these essential tools, in exemplary fashion, by H. Bloch (1948) and E. M. Steinby (1987).

XVI Military diplomas (Guide³ 836 = Guide² 656)

H. Nesselhauf gathered the Roman military diplomas in a single volume (1936) and a supplement (1955), each with its own indices. Since 1954 new finds and improvements to earlier editions are registered in an ongoing series of supplements by M. M. Roxan (1978, 1985, 1994 = *RMD* 1–3).

XVII Milestones (Guide³ 838)

G. Walser published a first fascicle (part II), on the material from the Gauls and Germany, in 1986 and, along with A. Kolb and G. Winkler, has a second fascicle (part IV,1), covering Raetia and Noricum in an advanced stage of preparation.

XVIII Carmina Latina Epigraphica

Three parts are under preparation, comprising the verse inscriptions of Rome (under the editorship of B. E. Thomasson), Spain (J. Gómez Pallarès), and Roman Africa (M. G. Schmidt).

GHI M. N. Tod, *A Selection of Greek Historical Inscriptions*, vol. 1² (Oxford 1951); vol. 2 (1948); and R. Meiggs and D. Lewis, *A Selection of Greek Historical Inscriptions* (Oxford 1969, 2nd ed. 1988) (*Guide³* 41, 42 = *Guide²* 34, 35)

Texts with bibliography and commentary, arranged chronologically. Volume 1² of Tod's anthology is now superseded by the selection of Meiggs and Lewis, which presents 95 texts from the eighth century down to 405 BCE. The second volume of Tod's collection, which has never been revised and is badly in need of a replacement, covers the period down to the death of Alexander. Whereas Tod "normalized" the spelling of his texts so that they appear in standard Attic Greek, Meiggs and Lewis preserve the original orthography (which is mostly Attic in any case). The second edition of Meiggs–Lewis, which displaced many inscriptions from Tod's collection (of which the most important are published in the second volume of B. D. Merrit, H. T. Wade-Gery, and M. F. MacGregor, *The Athenian Tribute Lists* [Cambridge, Mass. 1939]), adds more than twenty new texts and includes addenda and a concordance with *IG* I³, *CEG*, *SEG*, and a useful volume of English translations: C. Fornara, *Translated Documents of Greece and Rome* I: *Archaic Times to the End of the Peloponnesian War* (Cambridge 1983).

IG Inscriptiones Graecae (Berlin 1903–) (*Guide³* 61–2 = *Guide²* 57–8)

The successor to A. Boeckh's grand enterprise, the *Corpus Inscriptionum Graecarum*, which was out of date already by the time its indices were published in 1877, *IG* is, and is likely to remain, incomplete, inasmuch as other editions published since its inception have filled some gaps sufficiently well that not all the originally projected volumes are needed (for example, *IG* XIII has been rendered superfluous by *Inscriptiones Creticae*). By design the series omits *instrumentum domesticum*. Arranged geographically, like its predecessor, the series began with Attica; volumes covering the rest of Greece, Italy, and the western provinces followed. Beginning in 1913 several of these have since undergone second editions—notably those devoted to Attica (*IG* I² and II² replace *IG* I–III), Epidaurus (*IG* IV²,1), and Aetolia, Acarnania, and western Locris (*IG* IX²,1). (These second editions are sometimes referred to as "minores," in reference to the size of their pages rather than to the scale of their

coverage. The original editions must still be consulted for older bibliography and critical readings and conjectures.) The inscriptions of Attica
down through the fourth century BCE are available in a third edition
and have recently been equipped with a full set of indices registering
the names of men and women; towns, peoples, clans, and places; tax
and tribute sums; tribes and trittyes; demes and demotics; sacred buildings; gods, heroes, festivals, phratries, clubs, and statues; months; ships;
words; the first lines of poems; and (uniquely) poetic words and expressions (*IG* I^3,3 [1998]).

For the rest of the Greek-speaking world outside Europe, the relevant volumes of *IG* are badly out of date, and for this reason a detailed
enumeration of their contents (as above, with *CIL*) would not be helpful. In order to consult up-to-date versions of most texts, one must resort
to the regional corpora, such as *Tituli Asiae Minoris* (*TAM: Guide*^{3} 226 =
Guide^2 1801) or *Inscriptions grecques et latines de la Syrie* (*IGLS: Guide*^{3} 366 =
Guide^2 289) or to the individual volumes of the series *Inschriften griechis-
cher Städte aus Kleinasien* (*IK: Guide*^{3} 227 = *Guide*^{2} 1803), and to thematic
collections, such as F. Sokolowski's *Lois sacrées des cités grecques* (Paris 1969)
and its complements (Sokolowski 1955, 1962: *Guide*^{3} 993–5 = *Guide*^{2}
728–30). The *Guide* (*Guide*^{3} 55–428 = *Guide*^{2} 60–333) and Woodhead (1981:
103–7) provide more detailed overviews of the published volumes of *IG*,
their replacements, and supplements. Horsley–Lee (1994) presents a
useful checklist of abbreviations of Greek epigraphic corpora, with a
valuable Appendix (161–4), alphabetically arranged by place-name, of
texts published in journals and not registered in *SEG*.

The Packard Humanities Institute CD-ROM #7, "Greek
Documentary Texts" (Los Altos 1997), contains, along with the Duke
Databank of Documentary Papyri, a large assemblage of Greek epigraphic
corpora, including *IG* volumes I–II; IV (and IV,1^2); V; VII; IX,2;
XI,2,4; and XII,9, as well as the standard corpora for Crete, Delos, Delphi,
Ionia, and Caria and a large selection of Christian inscriptions (see below,
s.v. *ILCV; Guide*^{3} 428). The version currently under preparation will include
what amounts to an electronic corpus for certain areas of Greece
(notably Thrace and Macedonia) not covered in *IG*. A complete list of
contents can be found at the webpage of the Greek Epigraphy Project
at Cornell University, http://132.236.125.30/content.html. For the
Greek inscriptions of Asia Minor, J. Malitz at the Catholic University
in Eichstätt has published on CD-ROM (for IBM PC or compatible
machines) and on the world wide web (at http://www.gnomon.
ku-eichstaett.de/LAG/IGEyst.html) an extensive database of texts from

Bithynia and Pontus with a search engine that allows individual word searches and serves as a concordance (*IG Eystetenses*).

IGRR R. Cagnat et al., *Inscriptiones Graecae ad Res Romanas Pertinentes* (Paris 1906–27), three volumes (1, 3, and 4: volume 2 was never published) (*Guide*[3] 885 = *Guide*[2] 673)

Transcriptions in lower case letters, with supplements and brief critical notes, of Greek inscriptions pertaining to Roman affairs (narrowly conceived of in the eastern Mediterranean, much more broadly interpreted for Italy and the western provinces, especially Rome itself). The first volume, devoted to Italy and the western provinces, and the third, devoted to the eastern provinces (as demarcated in the early second century CE) excepting Asia Proconsularis, appeared in 1906; the fourth, devoted to the Roman province of Asia was published in 1927. All three volumes are equipped with full and useful indices (including, in addition to the standard registers, indexes of provincial offices and liturgies, games, calendrical and chronological systems, acclamatory formulae, and first lines of poems) but must be used with caution, owing to numerous errors and lacunae, especially in volume four (left incomplete at the death of its author, George Lafaye), which omits altogether the inscriptions of Ephesus, Miletus, and Caria. A bibliographical supplement for the inscriptions of Egypt is provided by E. Bernand, *Inscriptions grecques d'Egypte et de Nubie: Répertoire bibliographique des "IGRR"* (Paris 1983).

ILCV E. Diehl, *Inscriptiones Latinae Christianae Veteres*, vols 1–3 (Berlin, Dublin, Zürich 1925–31); vol. 4: Supplement, by J. Moreau and H. I. Marrou (Zürich 1967) (*Guide*[3] 51 = *Guide*[2] 48)

Volume one comprises some 3,000 texts pertaining to Roman (part I) and Christian (part II) affairs and involving members of the upper classes, the military, the imperial government, the church hierarchy, and persons whose rank or occupation is mentioned on their tombstones. Volume two (part II, continued) gathers some 3,500 Christian epitaphs arranged according to the commemorative formulae employed. The third volume contains a full set of indices. In addition to the standard lists of names (Christian and Jewish), places, emperors, kings, religious affairs

(Christian, Jewish, and pagan), *res Romanae*, and *notabilia varia*, volume three includes an index of consuls and other chronological indicators that amounts to a register of virtually all dated Christian inscriptions. The fourth volume constitutes a supplement, with corrections and concordances to the earlier material, and adds an index of first lines of poems. A. Ferrua, *Nuove correzioni alla Silloge del Diehl, Inscriptiones Latinae Christianae Veteres* (Vatican City 1981) provides an important repertoire of corrections to all this material.

The Packard Humanities Institute CD-ROM #7, "Greek Documentary Texts" (Los Altos 1997) contains a large selection of Christian and Jewish inscriptions in Latin as well as in Greek, including those registered in *ILCV* volumes one and two and in J. B. Frey, *Corpus Inscriptionum Iudaicarum* (Rome 1936–52: *Guide*³ 1026 = *Guide*² 750) (see above, under *IG*).

ILLRP A. Degrassi, *Inscriptiones Latinae Liberae Rei Publicae* (Florence) vol. I² (1965), vol. 2 (1963) (*Guide*³ 437 = *Guide*² 344)

A wide selection of some 1,300 Latin texts from the earliest period down to 31 BCE, transcribed in minuscule, with supplements and expanded abbreviations, modern punctuation, and incisive critical notes by the leading Latin epigraphist of the twentieth century. With the exception of the major public laws (for which see Crawford 1996, vol. 1), most important public documents, as well as a representative selection of epitaphs and *instrumentum*, are included. Photographs of many of the texts were published by Degrassi in a valuable companion volume, *Inscriptiones Latinae Liberae Rei Publicae. Imagines* (Berlin 1965) (an *auctarium* to *CIL*). Though largely superseded for scholarly purposes by the latest fascicle of volume I² of *CIL* (likewise edited by Degrassi and published posthumously with additions by H. Krummrey), which, however, closes with the death of Caesar in 44 BCE and so excludes the triumviral period, the two compact volumes of *ILLRP* retain their value for the purpose for which they were intended, *in usum scholarum*, and for Degrassi's critical comments, which are not always reproduced in full in *CIL*.

After a brief (but at the time of publication comprehensive) presentation of the oldest inscriptions down to the fourth century BCE and of the only surviving consular list and calendar from the Republic, the *fasti Antiates maiores*, the material is arranged by theme, with the first volume comprising inscriptions of gods and priests, Roman magistrates and their families, soldiers, milestones, and boundary stones, as well as (in its second edition) additions and corrections to material in the first edition of both volumes. The second volume includes *leges sacrae*, decrees of the senate, edicts of magistrates and other public documents, inscriptions of magistrates and local priests, of urban, suburban, and municipal associations, of craftsmen and public slaves, and of private individuals, money-changers' tags (*tesserae nummulariae*), hospitality tokens (*tesserae hospitales*), lots (*sortes*), sling bullets (*glandes*), painted texts (including Pompeian electoral posters) and graffiti, curse tablets, and *instrumentum domesticum*. The volume concludes with an exemplary set of indices (including, exceptionally, a brief register of noteworthy palaeographic features) and a concordance with earlier publications.

An extensive and valuable supplement, comprising 154 new entries, with photographs and a list of publications from which they are culled, edited by S. Panciera, with contributions by various authors, was published in *Epigrafia. Actes du colloque en mémoire de Attilio Degrassi* (Rome 1991) 241–491.

ILS H. Dessau, *Inscriptiones Latinae Selectae*, 3 volumes in 5 parts (Berlin 1892–1916) (*Guide*³ 48 = *Guide*² 43)

The most comprehensive *florilegium* of Latin inscriptions and the best general introduction into the historical world illuminated by Latin epigraphy. Three volumes, in five fascicles, compiled over forty years, at first by W. Henzen (one of the main editors for *CIL* of the inscriptions of Rome), and following his death in 1887, by his colleague H. Dessau (editor for *CIL* of the inscriptions of Latium and North Africa), who imposed his stamp on the entire collection. The selection comprises more than 9,400 Latin texts (and some 150 Greek inscriptions relevant to Roman affairs), arranged by theme, and includes almost all the Latin inscriptions of note known at the time. Only some well known texts published elsewhere, such as the *monumentum Ancyranum* (containing the *Res Gestae Divi Augusti*), and inscriptions remarkable only for palaeographic features were excluded by design; representative excerpts of some long and repetitive texts, such as the lists of magistrates (*fasti consulares*) and the civil calendar, are provided *exempli gratia*. The third volume, in two parts, presents a superb set of indices, modeled on the best of those in *CIL* and elaborated over 950 pages, which embrace all the texts except those registered in a *mantissa* in volume II part 2 (nos. 9482–9522); the reprinted editions now most widely used include a concordance with

CIL that was originally published separately as a supplement to the *Dizionario epigrafico di antichità romane* (*Diz. epigr.*) (Rome 1950).

Unlike its predecessor, G. Wilmanns' *Exempla Inscriptionum Latinarum in usum praecipue academicum* (Berlin 1873), Dessau's collection was intended for scholars as well as for students. It nonetheless caters for the latter in providing transcriptions in minuscule with modern punctuation (though normally with only the more cryptic abbreviations expanded) and brief critical notes and especially in its internal arrangement, which presents the texts within each section in an order (sometimes chronological, sometimes of increasing complexity or obscurity) designed to allow earlier examples to facilitate comprehension of later ones.

The first volume contains individual chapters on inscriptions of historical moment from the period of the Republic; inscriptions illustrating the careers of emperors and members of the imperial house; foreign kings and princes; men and women of the senatorial order; Roman knights; imperial procurators and agents of freed and servile status; magistrates' attendants (*apparitores*) and public slaves; texts illustrating the rules of citizenship; inscriptions of soldiers and the military; and men famous from literature. Volume two, part one, comprises chapters on religious texts and inscriptions of priests; inscriptions pertaining to public games and shows; inscriptions of public works and places, boundary stones, and private buildings; and texts illustrating municipal life, including the so-called municipal charters from Heraclea, Tarentum, and Spain, local *fasti* and *tabulae patronatus* from Italy and the western provinces, and honorific texts of municipal officials from individual Italian towns and provinces. The second part of volume two presents chapters on professional and private associations (*collegia*); inscriptions of artisans, craftsmen, and domestic servants; epitaphs and a variety of funerary texts (imprecations, declarations of burial rights, inscribed wills, etc.); a wide selection of *instrumentum domesticum*; miscellaneous inscriptions, including calendars and curse tablets; an appendix of Greek texts; and a lengthy section (192 pages) of additions, corrections, and supplements to the earlier volumes. The two fascicles of indices (volume three, parts one and two) are exemplary not only for their accuracy but for the rationale of their organization and the precision of their articulation. The index of abbreviations, geminated letters indicating plurals, and numerical notations provides an excellent introduction to basic Latin epigraphic notation. The register of grammatical and orthographical peculiarities is an invaluable, if unsystematic (see vol. III,2, p. iv), guide to colloquial Latin.

J. Malitz at the Catholic University in Eichstätt has published on CD-ROM and on the world wide web (at http://www.gnomon.

ku-eichstaett.de/Gnomon/ILS.html), a large database (in capital letters without expansions or supplements) of all the texts in *ILS*, along with selected texts from *AE* and *CIL* (to date more than 110,000).

OGIS W. Dittenberger, *Orientis Graeci Inscriptiones Selectae*, two vols (Leipzig 1903–5) (*Guide*³ 33 = *Guide*² 26)

Conceived as a supplement to the second edition of Dittenberger's *Sylloge Inscriptionum Graecarum* (*Syll.*³ below), *OGIS* presents a selection of some 775 Greek inscriptions from the eastern Mediterranean after the time of Alexander, in the same format as *Syll.*³, with copious historical notes. Volume one covers the Hellenistic kingdoms generously; volume two surveys the eastern Roman provinces more selectively and includes additions and corrections to both volumes; a concordance with earlier publications (including *IGRR*); and indexes of personal names, places (including ethnics and demotics), gods, heroes, priests and shrines, holidays and festivals, months, kings, queens, and their families, emperors and their families, *notabilia varia*, grammar and orthography, and findspots.

E. Bernand, *Inscriptions grecques d'Égypte et de Nubie. Répertoire bibliographique des "OGIS"* (Paris 1982) provides updated bibliography for the inscriptions from Egypt. See also below, under *Syll.*³

SEG *Supplementum Epigraphicum Graecum*, vols 1–25 (Leiden 1923–71), vols 26– (Amsterdam 1979–) (*Guide*³ 1141 = *Guide*² 820)

Intended to supplement *IG* by providing summaries (in English) of epigraphical publications of Greek inscriptions, the original volumes of *SEG*, issued annually under the editorship of J. J. E. Hondius (up to volume 11) and A. G. Woodhead (up to volume 25), were devoted, individually, to particular geographical areas of the Greek-speaking world and covered the publications relevant to each area over several years. Volume eight, for example, is devoted entirely to Palestine, volume nine to Cyrenaica, and so on. Indexes of proper names and of provenances of the material covered in volumes 11–20 (for the years 1950–64) were published by G. Pfohl.

Interrupted in 1972, the series resumed in 1979 (with a volume covering the years 1976 and 1977; for 1971–5 a lacuna remains) with renewed vigor and a new design, under the editorship of R. S. Stroud, who covers Attica and the Peloponnese, and H. W. Pleket, who covers the rest of the Hellenic world; in 1995 J. H. M. Strubbe joined Pleket as editor in Leiden, and in 1998 A. Chaniotis assumed editorial responsibility for Greece and the islands other than Attica and the Peloponnese. Arranged geographically, according to the design of *IG*, the new *SEG* provides wider coverage than previously (articles and books making extensive use of inscriptions are summarized in a section of *Varia*), and each volume is now equipped with a concordance with earlier publications and a full set of indices—of names (of men, women, animals, and objects); of kings, dynasts, and their families; of Roman emperors and their families; of geographical names, tribes, and demes; of religious and military terms (with Latin entries following the Greek in each of these categories); of important Greek words; and of selected topics.

Better indexed and more comprehensive than *Bull. ép.*, *SEG* lags a couple of years behind its French counterpart and, unlike *Bull. ép.*, generally eschews critical evaluation and proposed emendation of the works it registers. Although there is inevitably some overlap between the two series, they tend to complement rather than to duplicate each other, and each serves a valuable purpose (see the editors' defense of their editorial principles in the preface to *SEG* 37 [1987] vi, with reference to earlier policy statements in *SEG* 34 [1984] and 26 [1976–7]). Current plans call for the production of future volumes of *SEG* on CD-ROM as well as in book form, with the former medium helping to support (and perhaps eventually replacing) the latter. For further information, consult the *SEG* webpage at http://www.let.leidenuniv.nl/history/seg/seg.html.

*Syll.*³ or *SIG*³ W. Dittenberger, *Sylloge Inscriptionum Graecarum*, 3rd edition, vols 1–3 (Leipzig 1915–20); vol. 4, index, by F. Hiller von Gaertringen (Leipzig 1924) (*Guide*³ 32 = *Guide*² 25)

Modelled on G. Wilmanns' anthology of Latin inscriptions (the precursor of Dessau's *ILS*, q.v.), with texts transcribed in lower case letters, modern punctuation, and brief critical notes, Dittenberger's original collection (published in 1883) was designed to illustrate the classical Greek world (and so restricted itself to the regions where Greek was spoken before Alexander) but did so generously by equipping each text with rather full historical notes; verse inscriptions were omitted on the grounds that

G. Kaibel's *Epigrammata Graeca ex lapidibus collecta* (Berlin 1878) made them readily accessible, and texts of purely linguistic or dialectal interest were likewise excluded. In the second edition Dittenberger removed a number of inscriptions attesting relations between the states of classical Greece and the territories added by Alexander that had found a place in the first edition and announced his intention to provide a separate collection for the Hellenistic kingdoms (*OGIS*, above).

The third edition, produced after Dittenberger's death by a team led by F. Hiller von Gaertringen, credits individual entries to their principal authors, J. Kirchner (Attica), J. Pomtow (Delphi), H. Ziebarth (Euboea and legal texts), H. Diels, O. Weinreich (religious texts) and Hiller von Gaertringen. Entries new to the third edition are preceded by a small triangle (Δ); Dittenberger's original contributions are signalled by an absence of attribution or notation. The first two volumes, comprising some 900 entries, divide the material chronologically according to six periods, each ending with a major historical event: the end of the Peloponnesian War (405/4 BCE); the death of Alexander (324/3 BCE); the peace of Naupactus (217/16 BCE) (volume one); the destruction of Corinth (146 BCE); the Battle of Actium (31 BCE); and the death of Justinian and the closing of Plato's Academy (565 CE) (volume two). The third volume presents another 360 entries distributed into three broad categories of public affairs, religious matters, and private life, each subdivided into more specific categories which are helpfully preceded by summary listings of the entries in the first two volumes that might have been included beneath the same headings; a concordance of entry numbers between the second and third editions is appended at the end of the volume. Volume four, in two fascicles compiled by Hiller von Gaertringen, contains, in part one, indexes of kings and emperors, of *nomina sacra*, and of the names of men (arranged geographically)—by far the largest section—and of places, peoples, tribes, phratries and the like; part two presents what remains the best general guide to Greek epigraphic usage—a lexicon of most Greek words in the inscriptions in the first three volumes, judiciously excerpted to illustrate their grammatical functions.

W. Gawantka, *Aktualisierende Konkordanzen zu Dittenbergers Orientis Graeci Inscriptiones Selectae und zur dritten Auflage der von ihn begründeten Sylloge Inscriptionum Graecarum* (Hildesheim 1977) provides not only a concordance (in both directions) between Dittenberger's two anthologies but a concordance with earlier publications, a comprehensive index of provenances, and updated bibliographies, with an indication of published photographs and translations of inscriptions in both collections.

Larger reproductions of selected illustrations

The following four pages show selected illustrations in a larger format. For the full caption and further details of Figure 1.7, see page 53. For the full caption and further details of Figure 1.8, see page 54. For the full caption and further details of Figure 1.9, see page 55. For the full caption and further details of Figure 5.1, see page 120.

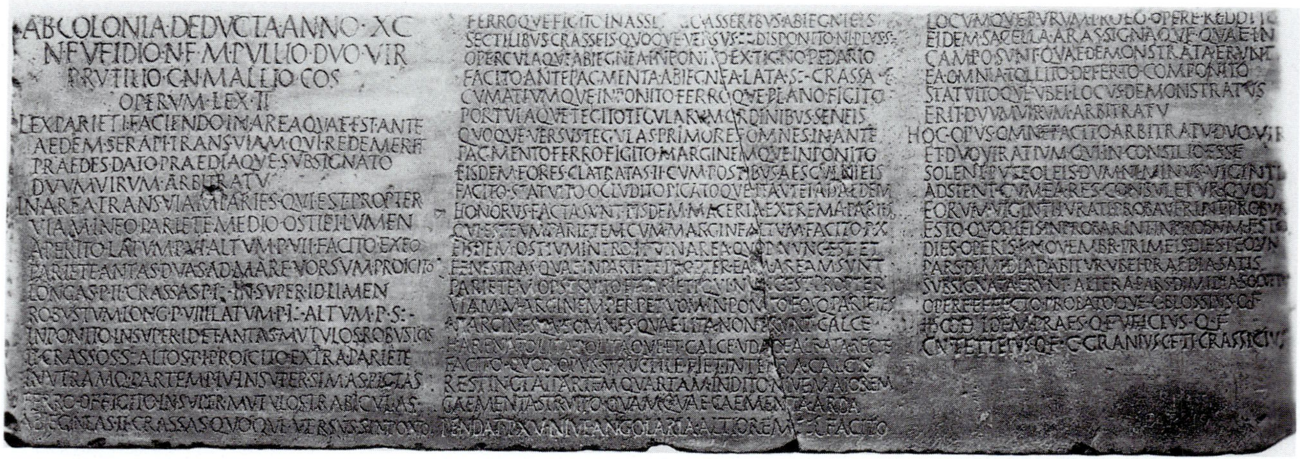
AB·COLONIA·DEDVCTA·ANNO·XC
N·FVFIDIO·N·F·M·PVLLIO·DVO·VIR
P·RVTILIO·CN·MALLIO·COS
OPERVM·LEX·II

Figure 1.7

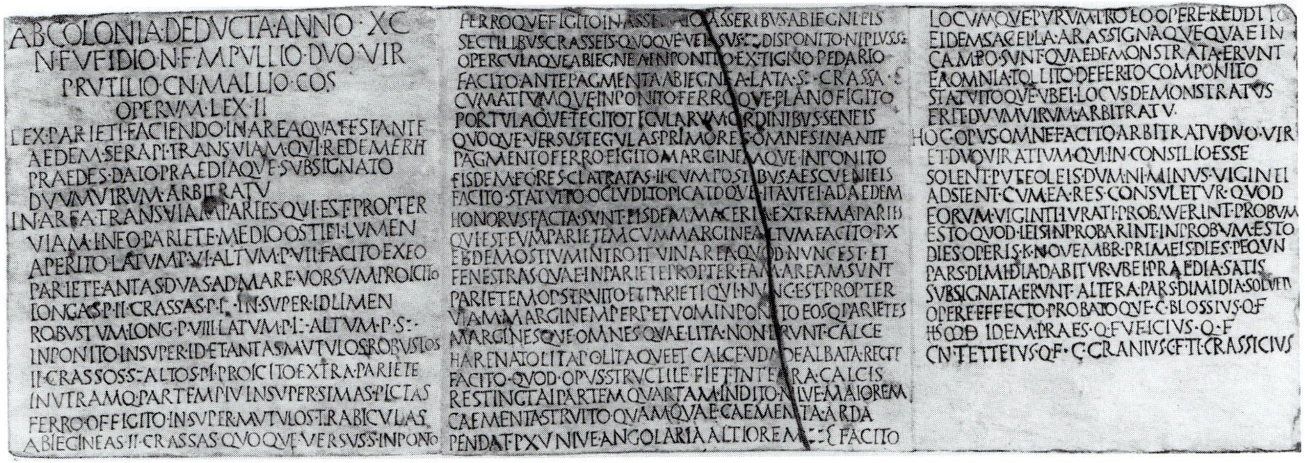

Figure 1.8

AB COLONIA DEDVCTA ANNO XC
M VEIDIO NE M PVLLIO DVO VIR
PRVTILIO CN MALLIO COS
OPERVM LEX II

LEX PARIETI FACIENDO IN AREA QVAE EST ANTE
AEDEM SERAPI TRANS VIAM QVI REDEMERIT
PRAEDES DATO R AEDIA QVE SVBSIGNATO
DVVMVIRVM ARBITRATV
IN AR FA TRANS VIA MVRI ARIES QVI EST PROPTER
VIA M INFRA PARIETE MEDIO OSTIEI LVMEN
APERITO LATVM P V ALTVM P VI FACITO EXPO
PARIETE ANTAS DVAS AD MARE VORSVM PROICITO
LONGAS P II CRASSAS P S INSVPER ID LIMEN
ROBVST VM LONG P VIII LATVM P I ALTVM P S
IN PONITO IONS VPER ID DE ANTAS MVTVLOS QVOS VLOS
II CRASSOS S ALTOS M PROICITO EXTRA PARIETE
IN VTRA M Q PARTEM P IV INS VPER IMA ASPICVLAS
FERRO OFFIGITO IN SVTRA VT MOX TRABICVLAS
A BIE CINE AS II CRASSAS QVOQ VERSVS IN PONO

PER ROQVE FICITO IN ASSE TOT AS SERIBVS ABIEGNEIS
SECTILIEVS CRASSES QVOQVE VOSE DISPONTO IN IVSE
OPER VLA QVAE ABIEGNE MINTONITO EXTIGNO PEDARIO
FACITO ANTE PAGMENTA ABIEGN A A LATAS CRASSA S
CVMAT VAQVE IN TO LITO FERRO QVE PLANO FIGITO
PORTVLA QVAE FICIOT SCVLARV QVORINIBVS SENEIS
QVOQVE NVI RE GVL A SPI A MORE ROMANES IN ANT
PAGMENIO FER RO FIGITOM ARGINE QVE IN FONITO
FISDE MECRES CVLTRA QVHIC QVA POSI DVSA LESCV SNEIS
FACITO STAT VTO OCCV DEI OCATO DI VRA VTEI ADA EDIM
HONO RO VS FACTAS SVNTEISDE M MACER EXTREMA PARIETH
QVI ESTE VT A PARIETE TE A CVMMA ARGINE V MATA FICITO X
E DEA MOS TI VM IN TRO IT VINAR FAQ DENVM EST ET
FENESTRAS QVAE IN DAR IE TE IN ROITREFA RAREA MAS VNT
PARIETEM OPS TEN ITO IT TRIE TEI QVI VIN INGES PROPTER
VIA M A RGINE V M PERPET VO MAIN DO TO TEO Q PARIETES
MARGINES QVO M NES VE LIIT A NONT SVNT CALCE
HAR ENA OLIT AP OLITA QVET CALCEN DA REAL BAT ARECIT
FACITO QVOD OPVS STRV CILIE FIET IN TE RA CALCIS
RESTINGTA IP ARTEM QVART A MON DITO LVMEA LORENA
CAE MENTA STRVTO QVA MOQ AE CAE MEN TA RDA
PENDA FP X VNI VEA NGOLARIA ALTIORE A S T FACITO

LOC VM QVE VT VRVM VIRO LOCO PER E REDDI TO
EIDE M SA KE LLA A RASIGNA QVE QVAE IN
CAM POS VN FO QVAE DE M ANOST RAE RVNT
EA M ONIATO LITO DE FERITO COMPONITO
STAT VITO QVE VBEI LOC VS DE MONSTRAT VS
ERIT DVVM VIRVM ARBITRAT V

HO C OPVS OM NE FACITO ARBITR ATV DVO VIR
ET DVO VIR ATI VM QVI IN CONSIL IO ESSE
SOLENT IPVE FOLEIS DVA MIN V MIN VS VICIN EI
ADSENT CVM A RES CON SV LET V R Q VOD
EOR VM VIGINTI VIRA TE VRO SE VE R INT PROBA VA
ESTO QVOD HE IS IN PROBA RIN FINI PROBV MA ESTO
DIES OPE RIS IS NOVE M ABR PRI MA EIS DIES TIRO QVN
PAR SDI M HD AD ABIT VR V SE FER RA EDIA SATIS
SVBSIGNATA E RVNT A LITE RA PAR SDI MIDIA SO Vm
OPER E FFECTO RO PROBATO QVE F C BLOSSIVS Q F
HOOD IDE MIPRA ES Q F VEICI VS Q F
CN TEITEI VS Q F C CRANI VS C F TI CRASSICIVS

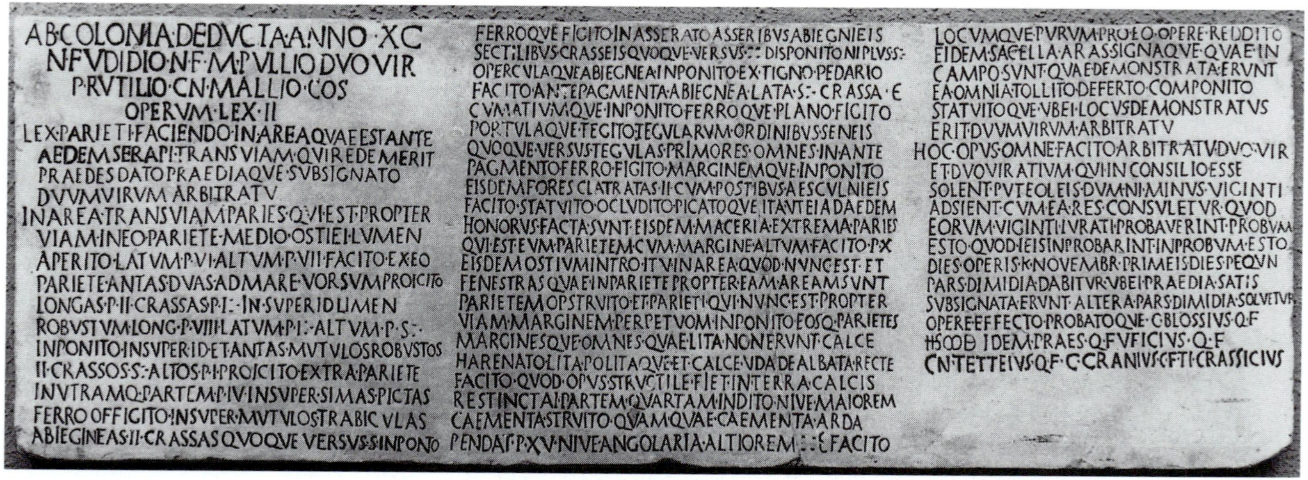

Figure 1.9

Figure 5.1

Notes

I Epigraphy and the ancient historian

1 Susini (1973: 1–8, 59–65) provides an excellent introduction to the topic and proposes a functional definition of epigraphy as "the historical study of the manner in which certain ideas were chosen to be displayed for public and permanent information" (64). For the palaeography of Greek inscriptions, see Jeffery–Johnston (1990), on the development of the Greek alphabet from the eighth to the fifth centuries BCE; Woodard (1997), on the linguistic background and the place of the Cypriot syllabary in this development; Immerwahr (1990), setting Greek vase-inscriptions, *ostraka*, and graffiti into this context; Tracy (1990, 1995), identifying the hands of individual Attic letter-cutters of the periods 340–290 and 229–86 BCE. For Latin lettering, see Mallon (1952, 1982), especially on the genesis of errors in Latin inscriptions (cf. Solin 1995); Gordon–Gordon (1957, 1958–65), on Latin letters in stone; and, briefly, Ireland (1983), on the artistic qualities of Roman lettering.

2 The last two are among the latest inscriptions included in the *Corpus Inscriptionum Latinarum*, for which Mommsen originally set an approximate chronological *terminus* at the end of the sixth century CE (*CIL* III.1, p. v) and which the editors of the new second edition of the inscriptions from the Iberian peninsula have now extended down to the early eighth century CE (e.g. *CIL* II²/5, p. xiii, citing a dated text of 711 CE). The origin of writing (an area of controversy)—sometime probably before the end of the fourth millennium BCE—is of course closely tied to epigraphy: Schmandt–Besserat 1990. The earliest alphabetic writing now seems (on the evidence of newly discovered inscriptions carved on a limestone cliff beside the road from Abydos to Thebes at Wadi el-Hol) to have been the invention of a Semitic-speaking people living deep in the heart of Egypt around 1900–1800 BCE. Excluding the Mycenaean scripts of the second millennium (Linear A and B), the earliest Greek inscriptions thus far known are all roughly datable around 800 BCE (Jeffery–Johnston 1990: 424–8; cf. Powell 1991: 5–67), but new early texts, which continue to come to light (recently near Ragusa in Sicily), may change this picture. For more systematic surveys of the types of inscriptions that have survived, see Guarducci 1967–78, vols 2–4 (Greek) and Di Stefano Manzella 1987: 75–108 (Latin texts on stone).

3 Similar arguments once widely invoked to explain a broad change in Roman burial customs, from cremation to inhumation, over roughly the same period by an appeal to "oriental," particularly Christian, religious beliefs were challenged nearly 70 years ago by A. D. Nock (Nock 1932).

4 I owe this estimate to Silvio Panciera, who reports *per litteras*, in addition to the 39,600 texts published in the existing fascicles of *CIL* VI, another 15,000 inscriptions destined for inclusion in the new series, as well as 45,000 Christian texts. According to E. M. Steinby (*per litteras*), the number of surviving examples of Roman brickstamps (many of which originated at brickyards outside Rome, throughout the Tiber valley) surpasses 30,000, representing nearly 5,000 different types.

5 For the relevance of the Cypriot syllabary in the development of Greek writing and its importance to the question of Greek literacy, see Woodard 1997.

6 At Sparta, as at Athens (and in contrast to Crete), most inscriptions of the archaic age were personal, concerned with the commemoration of individuals, but in other respects (*pace* Whitley 1997) the epigraphic profiles of the two communities are very different.

7 The linguistic dividing line between the Greek-speaking East and the Latin West has always been defined by the findspots of inscriptions and has never been precisely drawn. Mommsen and the other editors of *CIL* III (covering the Greek provinces of the Roman empire) implicitly drew it along the northern border of Macedonia, Lower Moesia, and Thrace, but Latin maintained its dominance, in epigraphy at least, in a number of Roman enclaves south of that border along the Via Egnatia in Epirus and the Peloponnese. For a recent survey of the question, see Rizakis 1995.

8 See Audollent 1904: 207–12 no. 155 for a transcription, Gager 1992: 67–71 no. 14 for a translation, both with commentary. Some 600 such "binding spells" have been published; another 500 have been found and await further investigation: see Faraone 1991: 22 n. 4 and, for the related category of "judicial prayers" (appeals to a divinity for justice), of which some 300 are known from Britain alone, Versnel 1991 and Gager 1992: 175–99.

9 Whereas "nonsense inscriptions"—series of letters in no intelligible sequence—were in vogue in early Greek culture during the sixth century BCE and became more rare beginning in the early fifth century, as literacy spread (Harris 1989: 52), cryptic "nonsense" letters and characters in curse tablets and binding spells grew notably more common over the first four centuries CE. At the same time, curse tablets recording only the name of the victim (presumably because the curse was delivered orally), common in the early period, fell out of use completely by the first century CE, as the written formulae grew increasingly complex: Faraone 1991: 4–5.

10 I borrow for this section the title of John Sparrow's stimulating book (1969), derived from his Sandars Lectures in Bibliography at Cambridge in 1964, about the history since the Renaissance of inscriptions in and as works of art and architecture and in printed books. Petrucci (1993) traces the history of public lettering in urban contexts in Italy from the eleventh century down to the present day. The early Middle Ages marked the nadir in western history for monumental, and especially urban, epigraphy (but note Mitchell [1990] for a remarkable exception in the early ninth century at the

monastery of San Vincenzo al Volturno, north of Venafro). Its zenith was reached in Rome of the early imperial period: see Corbier (1987).

11 The two most famous word squares (below) have both been found at Pompeii and therefore originated long before the time of their greatest popularity in late antiquity, when the second became widely associated with Christianity: see Guarducci 1965: 256–70; 1978: 1743–5.

R O M A
O L I M
M I L O
A M O R

R O T A S
O P E R A
T E N E T
A R E P O
S A T O R

12 The genealogical inscription of Licinnia Flavilla from Oenoanda mentioned above is one of the latest examples of the style. A comparable, though less common, technique of carving a text in vertical columns (*kionedon*) likewise seems designed to attract attention rather than to aid comprehension as, e.g. in a bilingual metrical epitaph of the late first or early second century CE from Dion in northern Greece (Horsley 1994).

13 Saller–Shaw 1984: 124 n. 1 estimate that epitaphs constitute about three-quarters of the surviving Latin inscriptions (170,000–190,000 of some 250,000 or more published). Epitaphs represent a smaller portion of extant epigraphic texts in Greek (probably somewhat more than half) but are nonetheless very numerous: see Guarducci 1967–78: 1.8–11. For a useful bibliographical survey of the vast amount written about Greek and Latin epitaphs, see Pfohl–Pietri (1983).

14 Though not precisely paralleled, the form *patronabus* (like the more common *libertabus*, on the model of *duabus*), indicating a plurality of female patrons, is a type of formation found commonly in private inscriptions, particularly epitaphs (cf. *ILS* 3.2, p. 844). Not so much errors as linguistic experiments, these feminine forms point to a popular desire not revealed by our upper-class literary authorities to distinguish social roles by gender. Not the least value of reading inscriptions is the opportunity it affords to experience the dialectal, orthographic, and grammatical flexibility of ancient Greek and Latin as living languages: see, e.g. Threatte 1980; Väänänen 1966; below, Ch. 2.

15 Meritt–Wade-Gery (1962) argued for the adoption of the four-barred sigma around 446 BC, but doubts were raised already by Pritchett (1965: 425–7). More recently, Chambers–Gallucci–Spanos (1990) have made a convincing case for a three-barred sigma in an inscription of 418/17 BCE, and the Athenian Standards Decree (also known as the Coinage Decree), of which a copy from Cos written in Attic exhibits the three-barred sigma, has now been brought down from the early 440s to 425/4 BCE (Mattingly 1993). The possibility of a later date, on palaeographical grounds, for any particular inscription exhibiting a three-barred sigma does not, however, amount to an historical probability of a later date, which must of course depend upon a variety of

considerations: see Figueira 1998: 442–8, urging caution in the case of the Athenian Standards Decree; Mattingly 1999, defending his redating of the copy from Cos.

16 The Gordons' *Album of Dated Latin Inscriptions* (1958, 1964, 1965), in seven fascicles, copiously indexed (in volume 4) and covering three periods (Augustus to Nerva, 100–199 CE, 200–525 CE), with two fascicles, of text and plates, devoted to each, provides legible photographs of 365 dated or approximately datable stones (or squeezes) from the time of Augustus (with half a dozen examples from earlier in the first century BCE) to that of Valentinian III (525 CE). Along with the companion volume of palaeographical commentary, based mainly on the material in volume 1 (Augustus to Nerva) (Gordon–Gordon 1957), the *Album* presents an indispensable guide to the subject.

2 Local languages and native cultures

1 See also the recent demonstration that a broad comparative study of writing and of its uses can play a substantial part in the deconstruction of "the myth of the unity of Greco-Roman culture" (Bowman–Woolf 1994: 14).

2 "As redefined and reconstituted by [Emmanuel] Levinas, alterity has come to mean in particular the condition of difference and exclusion suffered by an 'out' group against which a dominant group and its individual members define themselves negatively in ideally polarized opposition" (Cartledge 1993: 2). The polarization of Hellene and barbarian seems to have been "invented" in Athens in the wake of the Persian wars (Hall 1989: 3–13).

3 The following are but a few items in an ample field: Meid 1980, Neumann–Untermann 1980, Polomé 1983, MacMullen 1990, Millar 1993 and 1995.

4 In light of recent anthropological research which suggests that language is often a secondary *indicium* in the construction of ethnic identity, Hall 1995 argues "that while language could play an important role within Greek ethnicities, those ethnicities were not themselves primarily defined by linguistic criteria" (85). Rather, "if an Athenian considered the speech of a Megarian to be related to that of a Laconian or a Cretan this would not be on purely linguistic grounds, but rather because he/she knew that Megarians, Laconians, and Cretans all proclaimed a shared Dorian ancestry" (88). Language, however, could occasionally be used to reinforce ethnic boundaries, and the deliberate retention of archaisms in Laconian can be viewed as a "policy designed to preserve Laconian distinctiveness and to mark out the Spartans as the true Dorians of the Peloponnese" (90). It is only in the wake of the Persian wars, when the basis for Greek self-definition became oppositional (that is, when the concept of "Greekness" emerged from the creation of an "out-group") that language may have played a role in the creation of a wider Greek identity. At a time when no standardized Greek language, either spoken or written, existed, the shared language posited by Herodotus in his famed definition of Greekness could only be "an abstraction which, like the dialect groups themselves, rested on no clearly defined linguistic basis" (Hall 1995: 93).

5 From the bibliography appended to Hainsworth 1982: 998–1000, one might profitably select Bechtel 1921–4, Coleman 1963, and Buck 1966.

6 So Thucydides of the Eurytanians, "who are the largest tribe in Aetolia, and, so it is said, speak a language which is almost unintelligible (ἀγνωστότατοι δὲ γλῶσσαν) and eat their meat raw" (3.94.5, trans. Rex Warner).

7 Of the Spartan dialect in *Lysistrata*, Henderson 1987: xlvi remarks that "possible distorting factors are caricature; modification in the interest of intelligibility (including the introduction of Attic words); errors in the transcription of the original script (which may have been written in the Old Attic alphabet); and the subsequent entry into the text of corruptions and intrusive dialect items. In the medieval tradition atticizing is the most common corruption." See, in general, Colvin 1999.

8 According to Sommerstein 1980: 199–200, "as appears by comparison with Boeotian inscriptions, the representation by Ar[istophanes] of the Theban dialect is much less accurate than that of the Megarian. This may well be in part intentional: Boeotian had many unique features, especially in its vowel system, and must have been considerably harder than Megarian for an Attic speaker to understand."

9 Cartledge 1978: 25–37; Boring 1979. Harris 1989: 112–13 pessimistically concludes that "the literate were probably a small minority."

10 Following an observation of Jeffery (in Jeffery–Johnston 1990: 187) that the neatness and competence shown in many late archaic Laconian inscriptions suggest that "the trade of stone-mason and letterer may have been confined to one particular family as an hereditary profession," Cartledge 1978: 32 posits a possible division of labor, according to which the formal inscriptions on stone commissioned by Spartiates were executed by *perioeci*, or "dwellers around," as the free inhabitants of Laconia without Spartan citizenship were called.

11 On graffiti, see Jeffery–Johnston 1990: 186, 194. No casual message of the type "Gone fishing" has been recovered at Sparta, while excavations of the Athenian agora have revealed thousands of informal inscriptions scratched or painted on potsherds and other domestic utensils. The one which reads ". . . put the saw under the threshold of the garden gate" was written by a Megarian in dialect and letter-forms different from those used in Attica: Lang 1974: no. 18 = Agora inventory P 17824.

12 The oft-quoted definition of epigraphy by Gabriel Sanders (1977: 62) bears repeating here: "it claims to invest the written text with everlasting life and undying influence and, above all, it purports to save the individual from the deadly fear of oblivion."

13 On the coexistence of Greek and Demotic in Ptolemaic Egypt, see principally Rémondon 1964: 126–46 (discussing a second-century BCE letter in which a Greek woman is delighted to hear that a male relative is learning Egyptian); Peremans 1982: 143–54, 1983: 253–80, and 1985: 246–62; Clarysse 1987: 9–33; Rochette 1994: 313–15; and Verhoogt–Vleeming 1998. On the coexistence of Greek and Latin in general, see Dubuisson 1981: 27–45 and Rochette 1996: 3–19, and for their particular "cohabitation" in Egypt, see Daris 1991a: 47–67 and 1991b; and Rochette 1994: 316–20.

14 Compare the papers of Dionysius, son of Kephalas, which reveal a man straddling the Egyptian and the Greek worlds in the second century BCE: Boswinkel–Pestman 1982. On archives see also Martin 1994. Similarly, six centuries later, "we find the poet and lawyer Dioscorus of Aphrodite writing

amateurish poems in Greek, compiling a Greek/Coptic literary glossary and operating in his legal activities in both languages": Bowman 1989: 122; further MacCoull 1988.

15 From the extensive bibliography on the Italic dialects one may wish to consult Ernout 1909, Vetter 1953, Palmer 1954, Pulgram 1978, and Vine 1993.

16 A fragmentary letter in which reference is made to clothing sent to Vindolanda confirms that socks and underpants (*subligaria*), rarely represented on monuments, were worn by soldiers posted in colder regions (*Tab. Vindol.* 2.346).

17 Adams 1977 is an exemplary linguistic study of letters written in Egypt around 115 CE in a military environment similar to that from which the Vindolanda letters derive.

18 In Gaul, too, Celtic texts were inscribed in Latin characters on sheets of lead and were thrown in sacred springs or buried in graves: Coromines 1975 and Lejeune 1985b.

19 This mark of the accusative—transliterated *yth*—appears several times in the comic renditions of Punic in Plautus' *Poenulus* (e.g. line 930: *ythalonimualonuth sicorathisymacomsyth*, with Sznycer 1967: 48–55).

3 Names and identities: onomastics and prosopography

1 Uses of prosopography: Devijver 1976–93: 1964–5; Dietz 1980: 286–340; Vogel-Weidemann 1982: 14–15. The classic study of the Roman nobility is Münzer 1920; an extreme example of Roman politics seen mainly as a struggle of personalities and parties is Scullard 1951 (in the preface to the second edition of 1973 Scullard answers criticisms of his analysis; cf. also below n. 3). Greeks in the Roman senate: Halfmann 1979 and 1982. There has been such rapid progress in the methods applied to the study of local origins (for a recent discussion see Birley 1993) that what is said, e.g. about the origins of Roman officials even in a book as recent as that of Pflaum 1960–1 (on the careers of equestrian procurators) in many cases now seems old-fashioned and out of date. Patterns of advancement in Rome: Eck 1974. Many studies on governors and other provincial officials (e.g. Alföldy 1969, on administrative personnel in Roman Spain, or Rémy 1988, on several provinces in Asia Minor) include detailed investigations of the career patterns of the same men; indeed, Pflaum 1972: 320 says explicitly that the essential aim of lists of governors is to find out what kind of men were promoted to certain posts.

2 *Legio IX Hispana*: Eck 1972. Sardinia: Eck 1971; Bithynia–Pontus: Rémy 1986: 65, 87–92; Baetica: Alföldy 1995b.

3 Undue optimism is perhaps manifested by Dabrowa 1993 (on the officers of the *legio X Fretensis*—not at all a promising subject) or by Pflaum 1972: 320, assuring us that an analysis of 35 *iudices ex quinque decuriis* of African origin "permet de confirmer ce que l'on savait sur la romanisation de l'Afrique." Outsized: the more than 700 pages of Vogel-Weidemann 1982, though useful in many respects, are perhaps not entirely justified by the results. Excellent books with a prosopographical approach, such as Alföldy's illuminating analyses of Roman governors in Spain (1969) or of the Roman

consuls of the Antonine period (1977)—to say nothing of Syme's classic, *The Roman Revolution* (1939)—are, of course, much more than mere "prosopographical" studies. Serious discussion: *contra*, e.g. Den Boer 1969, Carney 1973, Graham 1974; *pro* Briscoe 1992, arguing for the validity of prosopography for the study of Republican politics. For balanced assessments of both points of view, Gruen 1974: 49 and Maurin 1982. Raepsaet-Charlier 1987: v, nn. 3–8 provides a selection of published opinions of scholars working with prosopographical material of the Empire. Much of Eck 1993 is relevant to the whole question.

4 For the basic elements of the Roman *tria nomina* of male citizens (*praenomen, nomen gentilicium, cognomen*, and tribe), see below. Many onomastic details are discussed in Salomies 1987 (e.g. 150–60, on the geographical distribution of Roman *praenomina*; 229–41, on the names of freedmen; 241–9, on those of new citizens; 277–313, on the evolution of the use and on the nature of the *cognomen*; 390–413, on the disappearance of the *praenomen*); for the interpretation of polyonymous names see Salomies 1992. The basic books on Roman names, written from a philological rather than an historical viewpoint, are those of Schulze (1904) on family names and Kajanto (1965) on *cognomina* (with information useful to the social historian on the geographical distribution of some of the *cognomina*); for additions to both Schulze and Kajanto see Solin–Salomies 1988. The distribution of family names must in most cases be studied with the help of the indexes to the major corpora of inscriptions. A most rewarding paper on some aspects of the interpretation of Roman names is E. Birley 1951; other useful studies of names from a more historical viewpoint are Mommsen 1864 (mainly Republican names), Schulze 1904: 487–521 (on the evolution between Republic and Empire), Kunkel 1967: 84–113 (on the problematic interpretation of names, especially during the Empire), Salway 1994 (more generally on the development of Roman nomenclature, from beginning to end). Doer 1937 and Thylander 1952 are not recommended: cf. Salomies 1987: 14 and 1992: 1. It is significant that all manuals on Latin epigraphy include sections, often substantial sections, on names (e.g. Gordon 1983: 17–30), whereas introductions to Greek epigraphy discuss personal names only in passing, if at all.

5 For nomenclature as a clue to local origin, cf. n. 1 and the reference there to Birley 1993; also, e.g. Syme 1939: 361 (with n. 3) on the origin, emerging from the names Sotidius and Libuscidianus, of the senator Sex. Sotidius Strabo Libuscidianus. Some *nomina* appear practically in only one city (e.g. Digitius in Paestum: relevant for the senator L. Digitius Bassus, *PIR*[2] B 87). For names typical of one city or area in the Greek world, see Robert in *Bull. ép*. 1972: 166–7.

6 For the Roman "epigraphic habit" see above, Ch. 1, pages 6–10; the phrase "epigraphic culture" was first suggested by R. Gordon in Gordon–Beard–Reynolds–Roueché 1993: 155 n. 402. The "epigraphic revolution" in Augustan Rome is described by Alföldy 1991. For the dramatic rise in the numbers of Athenian epitaphs in the first half of the fourth century BCE, see Meyer 1993: 99–100. Occasionally inscriptions can be used also in studies of earlier periods: see, e.g. McGregor 1974 on the epigraphic evidence of Solon's archonship; for an exceptional inscription shedding light on early Roman prosopography, observe the *lapis Satricanus* (*CIL* I[2] 2832a), mentioning the

suodales of a P. Valerius of the early fifth century BCE, who must be a patrician Valerius, perhaps the famous Publicola who was consul during the first year of the Republic.

7 Athenian archons are regularly referred to in dates by a single name alone—"Eukleides" for instance, the archon of 403/2 BCE who introduced the mention of the deme into the official nomenclature, for whom neither patronymic nor demotic is known (*PA* 5674; Develin 1989: 199). Name types can vary even within a single inscription according to the status of the person named; for instance, in decrees at Athens after 403 BCE, the archon and the proposer are normally referred to by name alone (later the practice with proposers changed, cf. Meyer 1993: 110 n. 26, citing Osborne 1985: 66), whereas the *epistates* often has also the demotic and the *grammateus* has both patronymic and demotic (cf. the summary in Larfeld 1898: 71–149).

8 Inscriptions giving the full nomenclature of persons otherwise known only by the *nomen* and *cognomen* include also, e.g. *ILS* 983 (Dillius Vocula; cf. *PIR²* D 90), 986 (Plautius Aelianus; cf. *PIR²* P 480), 1328 (Fulvius Plautianus; cf. *PIR²* F 553). For inscriptions disclosing additional names, cf. also, e.g. *ILS* 972 (Ummidius Quadratus, known from Tacitus, who acquires a *praenomen* and an additional *nomen* "Durmius"); *ILS* 989 (Valerius Festus; cf. Salomies 1992: 40); *ILS* 1117 (Bruttius Praesens; cf. Salomies 1992: 35–6; for further instances, cf. Salomies 1992: 37, 41–2, 91, 93, 95, 104, 114, 116, 119, etc.).

9 Observe also the many useful studies by H.-G. Pflaum on the historic persons mentioned (or omitted) in the lives of second-century emperors in the *Historia Augusta* (e.g. Pflaum 1970: 173–232, on the lives of Hadrian and Marcus Aurelius, especially 194–5 on people known from inscriptions but omitted in the life of Hadrian; for a list of Pflaum's other articles on this subject, see the bibliography in Raepsaet-Charlier 1987: 731–2).

4 The family and society

1 It is true that Fustel's argument was primarily concerned with the early Greek family, but since he used fourth-century literary evidence to support his case, it is reasonable to test his case with fourth-century epigraphic evidence.

2 Meyer 1990 overstates the connection between inheritance and commemoration: the fathers who disproportionately commemorated their teenage sons and daughters are unlikely to have inherited from these children, who would probably have been *in potestate* and hence unable to own property or to make a will.

5 Civic and religious life

1 Urso: *FIRA* 1² no. 21 = *CIL* II 5439 = I² 594 = *ILS* 6087 = *RS* no. 25; for English translations, see Hardy 1913: 23–60 and Crawford 1996: 421–32. The three municipal charters are the *lex Salpensana*: *FIRA* 1² no. 23 = *CIL* II 1963 = *ILS* 6088, with translations in Hardy 1913: 83–97 and Sherk 1988: no. 97; the *lex Malacitana*: *FIRA* 1² no. 24 = *CIL* II 1964 = *ILS* 6089, with a translation in Hardy 1913: 98–118; the *lex Irnitana*: González 1986, which includes a translation; for a recent and concise discussion of their contents and significance, see Lintott 1993: 137–43.

2　See especially *IG* II–III² 1696–1739 (archons and councilors), 1740–1834 (*prytaneis*), 1933–50 (priests), and 1960–2291 (ephebes).

3　For *prytaneis* inscriptions, the most recent and important work is Meritt–Traill 1974; the earlier ephebic inscriptions are collected and discussed by Pélékidis 1962.

4　The standard edition is now Degrassi 1947: no. 1, but the edition of T. Mommsen, W. Henzen, and C. Huelsen in *CIL* I²,1 is still worth consulting; for a brief but useful introduction, see Sandys 1927: 167–72. The *fasti Capitolini* take their name from their installation by Michelangelo in the Sala della Lupa of the Palazzo dei Conservatori on the Capitoline Hill in Rome, where they are preserved today. Their original location is disputed: many now think that they were engraved on an arch of Augustus, but Simpson 1993 argues in favor of an earlier theory that they were carved instead on the walls of the Regia.

5　The campaign material from Pompeii is collected in *CIL* IV, especially 7129–975 *passim*; a good selection is provided in *ILS* 6398–438. See the analysis of Franklin 1980.

6　*SIG*³ 951 = *IG* XII,9 8; cf. *IG* XII,9 9. For literary sources, see Herodotus 6.99 and 8.66, 112, and 121; Thucydides 1.98, 4.42–3, and 7.57; Livy 31.45 and 32.16–17; full references are provided by H. von Geisau, *RE* 10 (1919) 2256–9.

7　Prott–Ziehen 1906 remains a fundamental collection; it is supplemented by Sokolowski 1955 for Asia Minor (not covered by Prott–Ziehen) and Sokolowski 1962 for mainland Greece and the islands. Sokolowski 1969 is an updated version of the original collection of Prott–Ziehen but does not completely replace it.

8　Richter 1911 is little more than a pamphlet. Several of the most interesting Latin *leges sacrae* are gathered in *ILS* 4906–16.

9　The standard edition of all calendars and related texts is now Degrassi 1963, with a lengthy commentary; but, again, the earlier edition and commentary of Mommsen, Henzen, and Huelsen in *CIL* I² is not wholly superseded. Michels 1967 is an important study in English. Scullard 1981 is a brief but useful discussion of sacrifices and festivals organized around the framework of the calendars.

10　See Pritchett–Neugebauer 1947, Meritt 1961, and Pritchett 1963 and 1999. An annual calendar of sacrifices was inscribed in the Royal Stoa at the very end of the fifth century BCE, but only small fragments survive: see especially Oliver 1935, and Dow 1960 and 1961; note also the calendar of the Marathonian Tetrapolis (*LSCG* 20 = *IG* II² 1358) and the sacrificial accounts of the deme Erchia (*LSCG* 18). Mikalson 1975 attempts to synthesize the religious and civil material into a comprehensive account of the Athenian calendar.

11　See in general the discussion of Price 1984: 107–14, which deals specifically with the imperial cult but can equally be applied to others.

12　Scheid 1990a: 42. For the inscriptions, see *CIL* VI 2023–119, 32338–98, and 37164–5, with a selection in *ILS* 5026–49; all the inscriptions, together with recently discovered fragments have been re-edited by Scheid–Tassini–Rüpke 1998, now the standard edition. For detailed analyses see Scheid 1990a and 1990b.

13 The best editions are Devoto 1954, with a Latin translation; Poultney 1959, with an English translation; and Prosdocimi 1984; all three include extensive discussions.

14 Other examples are collected in *IG* XII,1, e.g. nos. 155–65; see further Pugliese Carratelli 1939–40.

6 Inscribed *instrumentum* and the ancient economy

1 Dressel undertook the task of publishing the inscribed *instrumentum* of Rome and its environs in 1878 for the Berlin Academy of Sciences at the instigation of Mommsen. Fascicle I, 1 of *CIL* XV, comprising all the *latericia* (brickwork), was published in 1891; fascicle II, 1, on amphorae, terracotta and glass vessels, lamps, and metal objects, appeared in 1899; fascicle II, 2, devoted to bronze seals, gems, and rings, was published posthumously in 1975.

2 Some thoughts on the relationship between archaeology and history are traced in Pucci 1993b, especially pp. 87–102. See also Pucci 1999.

3 A similar analysis, based on new evidence, was conducted by Pucci 1973. Pucci 1999 reconsiders the figure of Gummerus beside that of Rostovtzeff.

4 For material culture, see Carandini 1975. A great effort to insert archaeological evidence into the theoretical analysis of the ancient Roman economy was made in the 1970s and 1980s. The work of Moses I. Finley was an important stimulus for many students (see Garnsey–Hopkins–Whittaker 1983); in Italy the work of the team assembled at the Gramsci Institute in Rome (see Giardina–Schiavone 1981, Giardina 1986) was especially significant.

5 *Gezeichnetes Instrumentum* 1991, Harris 1993, *Epigrafia della distribuzione e della produzione* 1994.

6 Doubts about the authenticity of the text persist: Guarducci 1967–78 3: 418.

7 A vase with a fragmentary signature (—]ινος μ'ἐποίεσε) belonging to the end of the eighth century BCE has been found at Pithecusae (Ischia). The first complete signature (Καλ(λ)λικλέας ποίασε) is on a proto-Corinthian vase datable to between 680 and 660. Slightly later is the crater (whether produced in Greece or in the East is unknown) signed by Aristonothos (Ἀριστόνοθος ἐποίεσεν). The first signed Attic vase is that of Sophilos (580 BCE); the last were signed around 470. Outside of Athens the practice was much rarer: see Guarducci 1967–78 3: 471–95, Siebert 1978b.

8 The oldest example is a crater from Naxos of the mid-seventh century BCE (Guarducci 1967–78 3: 473). The first vase on which two different names appear, one associated with the verb ποιεῖν, the other with γράφειν, is the François Vase made at Athens around 570 (Ἐργότιμος μ'ἐποίεσεν/Κλιτίας μ'ἔγραφσεν).

9 See most recently the discussion between Cook 1971 and Robertson 1972 and, for a recapitulation of the problem, Rosati 1977.

10 Sometimes stamps were applied even to products destined to be consumed, like bread (Manacorda 1993: 45), or transformed, like ingots of lead or other minerals (e.g. sulfur).

11 On the epigraphy of Greek amphorae, especially those of Thasos, much has been written in recent years by Y. Garlan (1982, 1983, 1985a, 1985b, 1986, 1987, 1990, 1993a, 1993b).

12 See Morel 1988. The anonymity of the producers has been seen in connection with the contemporary development of the slave mode of production in Italy (Carandini 1979: 193). According to others (Pedroni 1988), the stamps disappeared because of the *plebiscitum Claudianum* of 218 BCE, because they represented proof of the involvement of the *nobilitas* in an activity regarded as dishonorable. But this hypothesis is untenable, since neither before nor after 218 do we know of prominent persons—and certainly not senators, to whom alone the prohibition against *quaestus* applied—involved in the production of black-glazed ware (Pucci 1993a).

13 The investigations of Manacorda (1989, 1990, 1993, 1994) have given concrete substance to the theoretical elaborations of students of Roman law (Di Porto 1984a, 1984b). See also Carandini 1989: 506–9.

14 Aubert (1993), aligning himself with Steinby, has confirmed in this regard the more traditional point of view (see Priuli 1986 and Bruun 1991) concerning the interpretation of brickstamps.

Appendix

1 From 1938 to 1980 the *Bulletin épigraphique* was authored by Louis Robert (from 1978–80 with his wife Jeanne); see further below, under *Bull. ép*. Since 1966 Joyce Reynolds has been the guiding inspiration of the surveys in the *Journal of Roman Studies*, as sole author for the years 1961–75 (*JRS* 56 [1966] 116–21; 61 [1971] 136–52; 66 [1976] 174–99) and subsequently, for the years 1976–95, with the collaboration principally of Mary Beard, Charlotte Roueché, and, since 1993, Richard Gordon (*JRS* 71 [1981] 121–43, with R. Duncan-Jones; 76 [1986] 124–46; 83 [1993] 131–58; 87 [1997] 203–40).

2 For Greek inscriptions, Reinach (1885) remains useful. For Latin inscriptions, Almar (1990) and Walser (1988) provide introductions similar to Gordon's (1983). Di Stefano Manzella (1987) is a practical (and technical) guide to the cataloging of inscriptions on stone; Susini (1982) (without index) focuses on inscriptions as monuments. For Christian epigraphy, the introductions by Grossi Gondi (1928) (a manual) and Marucchi (1912) (primarily a selection of texts, with commentary, focused on the city of Rome) are out of date and must be used with caution. The series of archaeological introductions published by the Wissenschaftliche Buchgesellschaft includes volumes on Latin epigraphy by E. Meyer (1973) and on the epigraphy of the Middle Ages and early modern period by Kloos (1980). For the early history of Latin epigraphy manuals, note also Calabi Limentani (1996).

Bibliography

Abbot, F. F. (1908) "Some Spurious Inscriptions and Their Authors," *Classical Philology* 3: 22–30.

Adams, J. N. (1977) *The Vulgar Latin of the Letters of Claudius Terentianus (P. Mich. VIII, 467–72)*, Manchester: Manchester University Press.

—— (1992) "British Latin: The Text, Interpretation and Language of the Bath Curse Tablets," *Britannia* 23: 1–26.

—— (1994) "Latin and Punic in Contact? The Case of the Bu Njem Ostraca," *Journal of Roman Studies* 84: 87–112.

—— (1995) "The Latin of the Vindolanda Writing Tablets," *Journal of Roman Studies* 85: 86–134.

Agnati, U. (1998) "A Computerized Epigraphical Database," *Epigraphica* 60: 207–22; cf. 316–17.

Agostiniani, L. (1982) *Le "iscrizioni parlanti" dell'Italia antica* (Lingue e iscrizioni dell'Italia antica 3), Florence: L. S. Olschki.

Alföldy, G. (1969) *Fasti Hispanienses. Senatorische Reichsbeamte und Offiziere in den spanischen Provinzen des römischen Reiches von Augustus bis Diocletian*, Wiesbaden: F. Steiner Verlag.

—— (1977) *Konsulat und Senatorenstand unter den Antoninen. Prosopographische Untersuchungen zur senatorischen Führungsschicht* (Antiquitas 1: 27), Bonn: Habelt.

—— (1987) *Römische Heeresgeschichte. Beiträge 1962–1985* (Mavors. Roman Army Researches 3), Amsterdam: Gieben.

—— (1990) *Der Obelisk auf dem Petersplatz in Rom. Ein historisches Monument der Antike* (Sitzungsberichte der Heidelberger Akademie der Wissenschaften, Philosophisch-Historische Klasse, Jahrg. 1990, Bericht 2), Heidelberg: C. Winter.

—— (1991) "Augustus und die Inschriften: Tradition und Innovation. Die Geburt der imperialen Epigraphik," *Gymnasium* 98: 289–324.

—— (1992) *Studi sull'epigrafia augustea e tiberiana di Roma* (Vetera 8), Rome: Edizioni Quasar.

—— (1995a) "Eine Bauinschrift aus dem Colosseum," *Zeitschrift für Papyrologie und Epigraphik* 109: 195–226.

—— (1995b) "Der Status der Provinz Baetica um die Mitte des 3. Jahrhunderts," in R. Frei-Stolba and M. A. Speidel (eds) *Römische Inschriften: Neufunde, Neulesungen und Neuinterpretationen. Festschrift für Hans Lieb* (Arbeiten zur römischen Epigraphik und Altertumskunde 2), Basel: F. Reinhardt.

Alföldy, G. and Halfmann, H. (1973) "M. Cornelius Nigrinus Curiatius Maternus, General Domitians und Rivale Trajans," *Chiron* 3: 331–73; reprinted with important addenda by G. Alföldy, in Alföldy 1987: 153–201.

Almar, K. P. (1990) *Inscriptiones Latinae. Eine illustrierte Einführung in die lateinische Epigraphik* (Odense University Classical Studies 14), Odense: Odense University Press.

Amphores romaines et histoire économique (1989) = *Amphores romaines et histoire économique. Dix ans de recherche: Actes du colloque de Siemme (22–24 mai 1986)* (Collection de l'École française de Rome 114), Rome: École française de Rome.

Amyx, D. A. (1958) "The Attic Stelai, Part III, Vases and Other Containers," *Hesperia* 27: 275–80, 287–307.

Aubert, J.-J. (1993) "Workshop Managers," in Harris 1993: 171–82.

Audollent, A. (1904) *Defixionum Tabellae*, Paris: Albert Fontemoing.

Ausbüttel, F. M. (1982) *Untersuchungen zu den Vereinen im Westen des römischen Reiches* (Frankfurter Althistorische Studien, Heft 11), Kallmunz: M. Lassleben.

Austin, R. P. (1938) *The Stoichedon Style in Greek Inscriptions*, London: Oxford University Press.

Badian, E. (1968) Review of Degrassi 1966 (*Imagines*), *Journal of Roman Studies* 58: 240–9.

—— (1989) "History from Square Brackets," *Zeitschrift für Papyrologie und Epigraphik* 79: 59–70.

—— (1993) "Alexander and Philippi," *Zeitschrift für Papyrologie und Epigraphik* 95: 131–9.

Bagnall, R. S. and Frier, B. W. (1994) *The Demography of Roman Egypt*, Cambridge: Cambridge University Press.

Baratta, G. (1994) "Bolli su botti," in *Epigrafia della produzione e della distribuzione*: 555–65.

Barbieri, G. (1975) "Une nuova epigrafe d'Ostia e ricerche sugli acrostici," *Quarta miscellanea greca e romana*: 301–403.

—— (1977) "Ancora sugli acrostici," *Quinta miscellanea greca e romana*: 339–42.

Beard, M. (1985) "Writing and Ritual: A Study of Diversity and Expansion in the Arval Acta," *Papers of the British School at Rome* 53: 114–62.

—— (1991) "Writing and Religion: Ancient Literacy and the Function of the Written Word in Roman Religion," in M. Beard, A. K. Bowman, M. Corbier, et al., *Literacy in the Roman World* (Journal of Roman Archaeology, Supplementary Series 3), Ann Arbor: Journal of Roman Archaeology: 35–58.

—— (1998) "*Vita Inscripta*," in *La Biographie Antique* (Entretiens sur L'Antiquité Classique 44), Vandoeuvres and Geneva: Fondation Hardt: 83–114.

Bechtel, F. (1917) *Die historischen Personennamen des Griechischen bis zur Kaiserzeit*, Halle: Niemeyer.

—— (1921–4) *Die griechischen Dialekte*, 3 vols, Berlin: Weidmann.

Bellen, H. (1971) *Studien zur Sklavenflucht im römischen Kaiserreich* (Forschungen zur antiken Sklaverei 4), Wiesbaden: Franz Steiner Verlag.

Beltrán Lloris, F. (1995) *Roma y el nacimiento de la cultura epigráfica en occidente*, Zaragoza: Institución "Fernando el Católico".

Bengtson, H. (1975) *Einführung in die alte Geschichte*, 7th ed., Munich: Beck.

Bérard, F., Feissel, D., Petitmengin, P., et al. (1989) *Guide de l'épigraphiste. Bibliographie des épigraphies antiques et médiévales*, 2nd ed., Paris: Presses de l'École Normale Supérieure, with supplements in 1990. [= *Guide²*]

—— (2000) *Guide de l'épigraphiste. Bibliographie des épigraphies antiques et médiévales*, 3rd ed., Paris: Presses de l'École Normale Supérieure. [= *Guide³*]

Berger, A. (1953) *Encyclopedic Dictionary of Roman Law* (Transactions of the American Philosophical Society, New Series 43.2), Philadelphia: American Philosophical Society.

Bernand, A. and Bernand, E. (1960) *Les inscriptions grecques et latines du Colosse de Memnon*, Cairo: Institut français d'archéologie orientale.

—— (1969) *Les inscriptions grecques de Philae* volume 1. *Époque ptolémaïque* (A. Bernand); *Les inscriptions grecques et latines de Philae* volume 2. *Haut et Bas Empire* (E. Bernand), Paris: Centre National de la Recherche Scientifique. [= *IPhilae*]

Berve, H. (1926) *Das Alexanderreich auf prosopographischer Grundlage*, 2 vols, Munich: Beck.

Bettini, M. (1991) *Anthropology and Roman Culture: Kinship, Time, Images of the Soul*, Baltimore: Johns Hopkins University Press.

Billanovich, M. P. (1967) "Falsi epigrafici," *Italia Medioevale e Umanistica* 10: 25–110.

Bingen, J. (1989) "Normalité et spécificité de l'épigraphie grecque et romaine de l'Égypte," *Egitto e storia antica dall'ellenismo all'età araba*, Bologna: Cooperativa Libraria Universitaria Editrice: 15–35.

Birley, A. (1981) *The Fasti of Roman Britain*, Oxford: Clarendon Press.

—— (1993) "Nomenclature as a Guide to Origin," in Eck 1993: 35–50.

Birley, E. (1951) "The Origins of Equestrian Officers: Prosopographical Method," *Durham University Journal* (June 1951): 86–95; reprinted in id., *Roman Britain and the Roman Army* (Kendal: T. Wilson 1953) 154–71.

Biró, M. (1975) "The Inscriptions of Roman Britain," *Acta Archaeologica Academiae Scientiarum Hungaricae* 27: 13–58.

Blech, M. (1980) "Heinrich Dressel," in J. M. Blazquez Martinez (ed.) *Producción y comercio del aceite en la antigüedad: primer congreso internacional bajo el patronato de Ministerio de Cultura*, Madrid: Universidad Complutense: 13–18.

Bloch, H. (1947) *I bolli laterizi e la storia edilizia romana*, Rome: Comune di Roma, Ripartizione Antichità e Belle Arti.

—— (1948) *Supplement to Volume XV, 1 of the Corpus Inscriptionum Latinarum, Including Complete Indices to the Roman Brick-stamps*, Cambridge, Mass.: Harvard University Press; reprint of *Harvard Studies in Classical Philology* 56–57 (1947) 1–128 and 58–59 (1948) 1–104.

—— (1959) "The Serapeum of Ostia and the Brick-Stamps of 123 AD," *American Journal of Archaeology* 63: 225–40.

Boatwright, M. T. (1991) "Plancia Magna of Perge: Women's Roles and Status in Roman Asia Minor," in S. B. Pomeroy (ed.) *Women's History and Ancient History*, Chapel Hill: University of North Carolina Press: 249–72.

Bodel, J. (1983) *Roman Brick Stamps in the Kelsey Museum*, Ann Arbor: University of Michigan Press.

—— (1994) *Graveyards and Groves. A Study of the* Lex Lucerina (American Journal of Ancient History 11), Cambridge, Mass.: E. Badian.

—— (1997) "Monumental Villas and Villa Monuments," *Journal of Roman Archaeology* 10: 5–35.

Boethius, A. (1941) "La datazione dei mattoni," *Eranos* 39: 152–6.

Boring, T. A. (1979) *Literacy in Ancient Sparta*, Leiden: E. J. Brill.

Boswinkel, E. and Pestman, P. W. (eds) (1982) *Les archives privées de Dionysius, fils de Kephalas*, Leiden: E. J. Brill.

Bowman, A. K. (1989) *Egypt after the Pharaohs*, Berkeley: University of California Press.

—— (1994) *Life and Letters on the Roman Frontier: Vindolanda and its People*, London: British Museum Press.

Bowman, A. K. and Thomas, J. D. (1983) *Vindolanda: the Latin Writing-Tablets*, with contributions by J. N. Adams and R. Tapper (Britannia Monograph Series 4), Gloucester: A. Sutton. [= *Tab. Vindol.* 1]

—— (1987) "New Texts from Vindolanda," *Britannia* 18: 125–41.

—— (1994) *The Vindolanda Writing-Tablets (Tabulae Vindolandenses II)*, with contributions by J. N. Adams, London: British Museum Press. [= *Tab. Vindol.* 2]

Bowman, A. K. and Woolf, G. (eds) (1994) *Literacy and Power in the Ancient World*, Cambridge: Cambridge University Press.

Bradford, A. S. (1977) *A Prosopography of Lacedaemonians from the Death of Alexander the Great, 323 BC, to the Sack of Sparta by Alaric, AD 396* (Vestigia 27), Munich: Beck.

Bradley, K. R. (1991) *Discovering the Roman Family*, New York: Oxford University Press.

Breslin, J. (1977) *A Greek Prayer*, Pasadena: The J. Paul Getty Museum.

Briscoe, J. (1992) "Political Groupings in the Middle Republic: A Restatement," in C. Deroux (ed.) *Studies in Latin Literature and Roman History* 6 (Collection Latomus 217), Brussels: Latomus: 70–83.

Bruun, C. (1991) *The Water Supply of Ancient Rome. A Study of Roman Imperial Administration* (Commentationes Humanarum Litterarum, Societatis Scientiarum Fennicae 93), Helsinki: Societas Scientiarum Fennica.

Bua, M. T. (1971) *I giuochi alfabetici delle tavole Iliache* (Memorie dell'Accademia nazionale dei Lincei, Ser. 8.16.1), Rome: Accademia nazionale dei Lincei.

Buchner, E. (1996) "Horologium Augusti," in E. M. Steinby (ed.) *Lexicon Topographicum Urbis Romae*, volume terzo: *H–O*, Rome: Edizioni Quasar: 35–7.

Buck, C. D. (1966) *The Greek Dialects*, 2nd ed., Chicago: University of Chicago Press.

Burnyeat, M. F. (1997) "Postcript on Silent Reading," *Classical Quarterly* 47: 74–6.

Burzachechi, M. (1962) "Oggetti parlanti nelle epigrafi greche," *Epigraphica* 24: 3–54.

Caballos, A., Eck, W., and Fernández, F. (1996) *El senadoconsulto de Cneo Pisón padre*, Seville: Universidad de Sevilla.

Cagnat, R. (1914) *Cours d'épigraphie latine*, 4th ed., Paris; reprinted 1964, Rome: "l'Erma" di Bretschneider.

Calabi Limentani, I. (1974) *Epigrafia latina*, 3rd ed., Milan: Cisalpino–La Goliardica.

—— (1991) *Epigrafia latina*, 4th ed., Milan: Cisalpino–La Goliardica.

—— (1996) "Linee per una storia del manuale di epigraphia Latina (dall'Agustin al Cagnat)," *Epigraphica* 58: 9–35.

Camodeca, G. (1999) *Tabulae Pompeianae Sulpiciorum (TPSulp.). Edizione critica dell'archivio puteolano dei Sulpicii* (Vetera 12), Rome: Edizioni Quasar.

Carandini, A. (1975) *Archeologia e cultura materiale*, Bari: De Donato.

—— (1979) *L'anatomia della scimmia. La formazione economica della società prima del Capitale*, Turin: Einaudi.

—— (1989) "L'economia italica fra tarda repubblica e medio impero considerata dal punto di vista di una merce: il vino," in *Amphores romaines et histoire économique*: 505–21.

Carney, T. F. (1973) "Prosopography: Payoffs and Pitfalls," *Phoenix* 27: 156–79.

Cartledge, P. (1976) "A New 5th-century Spartan Treaty," *Liverpool Classical Monthly* 1: 87–92.

—— (1978) "Literacy in the Spartan Oligarchy," *Journal of Hellenic Studies* 98: 25–37.

—— (1993) *The Greeks. A Portrait of Self and Others*, Oxford: Oxford University Press.

Castner, C. J. (1988) *Prosopography of Roman Epicureans from the Second Century BC to the Second Century AD* (Studien zur klassischen Philologie 34), Frankfurt an Mainz: Lang.

Cels Saint-Hilaire, J. (1986) "Numen Augusti et Diane de l'Aventin. Le Témoignage de l'Ara Narbonensis," in P. Lévêque and M.-M. Mactoux (eds) *Les grandes figures religieuses. Fonctionnement pratique et symbolique dans l'antiquité*, Paris: Les Belles Lettres: 455–89.

Chambers, M. H., Gallucci, R. and Spanos, P. (1990) "Athens' Alliance with Egesta in the Year of Antiphon," *Zeitschrift für Papyrologie und Epigraphik* 83: 38–63.

Chaniotis, A. (1988) *Historie und Historiker in den griechischen Inschriften: epigraphische Beiträge zur griechischen Historiographie* (Heidelberger Althistorische Beiträge und Epigraphische Studien 4), Wiesbaden: Franz Steiner Verlag.

Chastagnol, A. (1978) *L'Album municipal de Timgad*, Bonn: Habelt.

Chelotti, M. et al. (1985) *Le epigrafi romane di Canosa* I, Bari: Regione Puglia.

Cherry, D. (1995) "Re-Figuring the Roman Epigraphic Habit," *Ancient History Bulletin* 9: 143–56.

Chevallier, R. (1972) *Épigraphie et littérature à Rome* (Epigrafia e Antichità 3), Faenza: Fratelli Lega Editori.

Clarysse, W. (1987) "Greek Loan Words in Demotic," in S. P. Vleeming (ed.) *Aspects of Demotic Lexicography. Acts of the Second International Conference for Demotic Studies*, Leuven: Peeters: 9–33.

Clemente, G. (1972) "Il patronato nei collegia dell'imperio romano," *Studi Classici e Orientali* 21: 142–229.

Clinton, K. (1974) *The Sacred Officials of the Eleusinian Mysteries* (Transactions of the American Philosophical Society, New Series 64.2), Philadelphia: American Philosophical Society.

—— (1996) "A New *Lex Sacra* from Selinus: Kindly Zeuses, Eumenides, Impure and Pure Tritopatores, and Elasteroi," *Classical Philology* 91: 159–79.

Coarelli, F. (ed.) (1980) *Artisti e artigiani in Grecia. Guida storica e critica*, Rome: Laterza.

Coleman, R. (1963) "The Dialect Geography of Ancient Greece," *Transactions of the Philological Society* 61: 58–126.

Colonna, G. (1983) "Identità come appartenenza nelle iscrizioni di possesso dell'Italia preromana," *Epigraphica* 45: 49–64.

Colvin, S. (1999) *Dialect in Aristophanes and the Politics of Language in Ancient Greek Literature*, Oxford: Clarendon Press.

Cook, R. M. (1971) " 'Epoiesen' on Greek Vases," *Journal of Hellenic Studies* 91: 137–8.

Corbier, M. (1987) "L'écriture dans l'espace public romain," in *L'Urbs. Espace urbain et histoire (Ier siècle av. J.-C.–IIIe siècle ap. J.-C.* (Collection de l'École française de Rome 98), Rome: École française de Rome: 27–60.

—— (1995) "L'écriture dans l'image," in Solin–Salomies–Liertz (1995), 113–62.

Coromines, J. (1975) "Les plombs sorothaptiques d'Arles," *Zeitschrift für romanische Philologie* 91: 1–53.

Cotton, H. M., Cockle, W. E. H. and Millar, F. G. B. (1995) "The Papyrology of the Near East: A Survey," *Journal of Roman Studies* 85: 214–35.

Courby, F. (1922) *Les vases grecs à reliefs*, Paris: de Boccard.

Courtney, E. (1995) *Musa Lapidaria. A Selection of Latin Verse Inscriptions*, Atlanta: Scholars Press.

Cox, C. A. (1995) "The Names of Adoptees: Some Prosopographical After-thoughts," *Zeitschrift für Papyrologie und Epigraphik* 107: 249–54.

Crawford, M. H. (ed.) (1996) *Roman Statutes* volume I: *Epigraphically Attested Leges* (Bulletin of the Institute of Classical Studies Supplement 64), London: Institute of Classical Studies, University of London. [= *RS*]

Cugusi, P. (1985) *Aspetti letterari dei Carmina Latina Epigraphica*, Bologna: Pàtron.

Cunliffe, B. (1988) *The Temple of Sulis Minerva at Bath*, II. *The Finds from the Sacred Spring* (Oxford University Committee for Archaeology Monograph 16), Oxford, 59–277.

Curchin, L. A. (1982) "Familial Epithets in the Epigraphy of Roman Spain," in *Mélanges offerts en hommage au révérend père Etienne Gareau*, Ottawa: Editions de l'Université d'Ottawa: 179–82.

Dabrowa, A. (1993) *Legio X Fretensis. A Prosopographical Study of its Officers (I–III c. AD)* (Historia Einzelschriften 66), Stuttgart: F. Steiner Verlag.

Damon, C. and Takács, S. (1999) *The Senatus Consultum de Cn. Pisone Patre: Text, Translation, Discussion* (American Journal of Philology 120.1), Baltimore: Johns Hopkins University Press.

Daris, S. (1991a) "Latino ed Egitto romano," in *Il bilinguismo degli antichi: XVIII Giornate filologiche genovesi*, Genoa: Università di Genova, Facoltà di lettere: 47–67.

—— (1991b) *Il lessico latino nel greco d'Egitto*, 2nd ed., Barcelona: Institut de Teologia fonamental, Seminari de Papirologia.

D'Arms, J. H. (1973) "Eighteen Unedited Latin Inscriptions from Puteoli and Vicinity," *American Journal of Archaeology* 77: 151–67 and plates 27–30.

—— (1981) *Commerce and Social Standing in Ancient Rome*, Cambridge, Mass.: Harvard University Press.

Daux, G. (1936) *Delphes au IIème et du Ier siècles depuis l'abaissement de l'Etolie jusqu'à la paix romaine, 191–31 av. J. C.* (Bibliothèque des Écoles françaises d'Athènes et de Rome 140), Paris: de Boccard.

—— (1983) "Le calendrier de Thorikos au Musée J. Paul Getty," *L'Antiquité classique* 52: 150–74.

Den Boer, W. (1969) "Die prosopographische Methode in der modernen Historiographie der Kaiserzeit," *Mnemosyne* 22: 268–80; reprinted in id. (1979) *Syngrammata. Studies in Graeco-Roman History*, edited by H. W. Pleket et al. Leiden: E. J. Brill: 264–75.

Degrassi, A. (1947) *Inscriptiones Italiae* XIII. 1: *Fasti Consulares et Triumphales*, Rome: La Libreria dello Stato.

—— (1963) *Inscriptiones Italiae* XIII. 2: *Fasti anni Numani et Iuliani*, Rome: La Libreria dello Stato.

—— (1966) *Corpus Inscriptionum Latinarum. Auctarium. Inscriptiones Latinae Liberae Rei Publicae: Imagines*, Berlin: De Gruyter.

Derks, T. (1998) *Gods, Temples, and Ritual Practices. The Transformation of Religious Ideas and Values in Roman Gaul* (Amsterdam Archaeological Studies 2), Amsterdam: Amsterdam University Press.

Detienne, M. (1988) "L'espace de la publicité: ses opérateurs intellectuels dans la cité," in M. Detienne (ed.) *Savoirs de l'écriture en Grèce ancienne*, Villeneuve-d'Ascq: Presses universitaires de Lille: 56–64.

Develin, R. (1989) *Athenian Officials 684–321 BC*, Cambridge: Cambridge University Press.

Devijver, H. (1976–93) *Prosopographia militiarum equestrium quae fuerunt ab Augusto ad Gallienum*, 5 vols, Leuven: Universitaire Pers.

Devoto, G. (1954) *Tabulae Iguvinae*, 2nd ed., Rome: Publica Officina Polygraphica.

Dietz, K. (1980) *Senatus contra Principem. Untersuchungen zur senatorischen Opposition gegen Kaiser Maximinus Thrax* (Vestigia 29), Munich: Beck.

Di Porto, A. (1984a) "Impresa agricola e attività collegate nell'economia della villa," *Sodalitas. Studi in onore di A. Guarino*, Naples: Jovene 7: 3235–77.

—— (1984b) *Impresa collettiva e schiavo manager in Roma antica (II sec. a.C.–II sec. d.C.)*, Milan: A. Giuffre.

Di Stefano Manzella, I. (1987) *Mestiere di epigrafista. Guida alla schedatura del materiale epigrafico lapideo*, Rome: Edizioni Quasar.

Doer, B. (1937) *Die römische Namengebung. Ein historischer Versuch*, Stuttgart: Kohlhammer.

Dornseiff, F. (1925) *Das Alphabet in Mystik und Magie*, 2nd ed. (Stoicheia 7), Leipzig and Berlin: B. G. Teubner.

Dow, S. (1937) *Prytaneis: A Study of the Inscriptions Honoring the Athenian Councillors* (Hesperia Supplement 1), Athens: American School of Classical Studies at Athens.

—— (1960) "The Athenian Calendar of Sacrifices: The Chronology of Nikomakhos' Second Term," *Historia* 9: 270–93.

—— (1961) "The Walls Inscribed with Nikomakhos' Law Code," *Hesperia* 30: 58–73.

—— (1969) *Conventions in Editing* (Greek, Roman and Byzantine Scholarly Aids 2), Durham, North Carolina: Duke University Press.

Dubuisson, M. (1981) "Problèmes du bilinguisme romain," *Les études classiques* 49: 27–45.

Duncan-Jones, R. P. (1978) Review of P. Huttunen, *The Social Strata in the Imperial City of Rome* (Oulu: The University, 1974), *Journal of Roman Studies* 68: 195–7.

—— (1982) *The Economy of the Roman Empire. Quantitative Studies*, 2nd ed., Cambridge: Cambridge University Press.

—— (1990) *Structure and Scale in the Roman Economy*, Cambridge: Cambridge University Press.

Dušanić, S. (1984) *"Loci Constitutionum Fixarum," Epigraphica* 46: 91–115.

Duthoy, R. (1976) "Recherches sur la répartition géographique et chronologique des termes *sevir Augustalis, Augustalis* et *sevir* dans l'Empire romain," *Epigraphische Studien* 11: 143–214.

—— (1978) "Les *Augustales," in H. Temporini (ed.) (1972–) *Aufstieg und Niedergang der römischen Welt* II.16.2: Berlin and New York: De Gruyter: 254–309.

Eck, W. (1971) "Zum Rechtsstatus von Sardinien im 2. Jh. n. Chr.," *Historia* 20: 510–12.

—— (1972) "Zum Ende der legio IX Hispana," *Chiron* 2: 459–62.

—— (1973) "Sozialstruktur des römischen Senatorenstandes der hohen Kaiserzeit und statistische Methode," *Chiron* 3: 375–94; reprinted in Eck 1996: 11–26.

—— (1974) "Beförderungskriterien innerhalb der senatorischen Laufbahn, dargestellt an der Zeit von 69 *bis* 138 n.Chr.," in H. Temporini (ed.) (1972–)

Aufstieg und Niedergang der römischen Welt II.1: Berlin and New York: De Gruyter: 158–228; reprinted in Eck 1996: 27–83, with addenda, 84–93.

—— (1975) "Die Laufbahn eines Ritters aus Apri in Thrakien. Ein Beitrag zum Ausbau der kaiserlichen Administration in Italien," *Chiron* 5: 365–92.

—— (1982) "Senatoren aus Germanien, Raetien, Noricum?" in *Epigrafia e ordine senatorio: Atti del Colloquio internazionale AIEGL su epigrafia e ordine senatorio, Roma, 14–20 maggio 1981*, II (Tituli 5), Rome: Edizioni di Storia e Letteratura: 539–52.

—— (1984) "Senatorial Self-Representation: Developments in the Augustan Period," in F. Millar and E. Segal (eds) *Caesar Augustus: Seven Aspects*, Oxford: Oxford University Press: 129–67.

—— (1987) "Römische Grabinschriften. Aussageabsicht und Aussagefähigkeit im funerären Kontext," in H. von Hesberg and P. Zanker (eds) *Römische Gräberstrassen. Selbstdarstellung–Status–Standard* (Abh. Bayer. Akad. Wiss., Phil.-Hist. Kl. 96) Munich: C. H. Beck: 61–83; reprinted in Eck 1996: 227–49.

—— (1988) "Aussagefähigkeit epigraphischer Statistik und die Bestattung von Sklaven im kaiserzeitlichen Rom," in P. Kniessel and V. Losemann (eds) *Alte Geschichte und Wissenschaftsgeschichte, Festschrift für Karl Christ zum 65 Geburtstag*, Darmstadt: Wissenschaftliche Buchgesellschaft, 130–9.

—— (1989) "Die Einrichtung der Prokuratur der IIII publica Africae," in M. Taceva and D. Bojadziev (eds) *Studia in honorem B. Gerov*, Sofia: Sofia Press: 50–63; reprinted in Eck 1995a: 349–54.

—— (1992) "Ehrungen für Personen hohen soziopolitischen Ranges im öffentlichen und privaten Bereich," in H.-J. Schalles, F. von Hesberg, and P. Zanker (eds) *Die römische Stadt im 2 Jahrhundert n. Chr., der Funktionswandel des öffentlichen Raumes: Kolloquium in Xanten vom 2. bis 4. Mai 1990*, Cologne: Rheinland-Verlag in Kommission bei R. Habelt: 359–76; reprinted in Eck 1996: 299–318.

—— (ed.) (1993) *Prosopographie und Sozialgeschichte. Studien zur Methodik und Erkenntnismöglichkeit der kaiserzeitlichen Prosopographie*, Cologne, Vienna, Weimar: Böhlau.

—— (1995a) *Die Verwaltung der römischen Reiches in der hohen Kaiserzeit. 1. Band.* (Arbeiten zur römischen Epigraphik und Altertumskunde Band 1), Basel: F. Reinhardt.

—— (1995b) "'Tituli honorarii' curriculum vitae und Selbstdarstellung in der Hohen Kaiserzeit," in Solin–Salomies–Liertz (1995), 211–37; reprinted in Eck 1996: 319–40.

—— (1996) *Tra epigrafia prosopografia e archeologia. Scritti scelti, rielaborati ed aggiornati* (Vetera 10), Rome: Edizioni Quasar.

Eck, W., Caballos, A., and Fernández, F. (1996) *Das Senatus Consultum de Cn. Pisone Patre* (Vestigia 48), Munich: C. H. Beck. [= *SCPP*]

Eck, W. and Wolff, H. (1986) *Heer und Integrationspolitik: Die römischen Militärdiplome als historische Quelle* (Passauer Historische Forschungen 2), Cologne: Böhlau.

Egbert, J. C. (1896) *Introduction to the Study of Latin Inscriptions*, New York: American Book Company.

Elliott, R. T. (1914) *The Acharnians of Aristophanes*, Oxford: Clarendon Press.

Epigrafia della distribuzione e della produzione (1994) = *Epigrafia della distribuzione e della produzione. Actes de la VIIe rencontre franco-italienne sur l'épigraphie du monde romain* (Collection de l'École française de Rome 193), Rome: École française de Rome.

Ernout, A. E. (1909) *Les éléments dialectaux du vocabulaire latin*, Paris: H. Champion.

Éry, K. K. (1969) "Investigations on the Demographic Source Value of Tombstones Originating from the Roman Period," *Alba Regia* 10: 51–68.

Etienne, A. and O'Meara, D. (1996) *La philosophe épicurienne sur pierre: les fragments de Diogène d'Oenoanda* (Vestigia 20), Paris: Cerf.

Fantham, E., Foley, H. P., Kampen, N. B., Pomeroy, S. B., and Shapiro, H. (1994) *Women in the Classical World: Image and Text*, New York: Oxford University Press.

Faraone, C. A. (1991) "The Agonistic Context of Early Greek Binding Spells," in Faraone–Obbink 1991: 3–32.

—— (1996) "Taking the 'Nestor's Cup Inscription' Seriously: Erotic Magic and Conditional Curses in the Earliest Inscribed Hexameters," *Classical Antiquity* 15: 77–112.

Faraone, C. A. and Obbink, D. (eds) (1991) *Magika Hiera: Ancient Greek Magic and Religion*, New York: Oxford University Press.

Ferguson, J. (1987) *A Prosopography to the Poems of Juvenal* (Collection Latomus 200), Brussels: Latomus.

Figueira, T. (1998) *The Power of Money: Coinage and Politics in the Athenian Empire*, Philadelphia: University of Pennsylvania Press.

Finley, M. I. (1952) *Studies in Land and Credit in Ancient Athens, 500–200 BC*, New Brunswick: Rutgers University Press.

—— (1981) "Between Slavery and Freedom," in B. D. Shaw and R. P. Saller (eds) *Economy and Society in Ancient Greece*, New York: Viking Press: 116–32.

Flach, D. (1991) *Die sogennante Laudatio Turiae: Einleitung, Text, Ubersetzung und Kommentar*, Darmstadt: Wissenschaftliche Buchgesellschaft.

Flaig, E. (1992) *Den Kaiser herausfordern: die Usurpation im römischen Reich*, Frankfurt and New York: Campus.

Les Flavii de Cillium (1993) = *Les Flavii de Cillium. Étude du mausolée de Kasserine* (Collection de l'École française de Rome 169), Rome: École française de Rome.

Flory, M. (1978) "Family in *Familia*: Kinship and Community in Slavery," *American Journal of Ancient History* 3: 78–95.

Follet, S. (1976) *Athènes au IIe et au IIIe siècle. Études chronologiques et proso-pographiques*, Paris: Les Belles Lettres.

Forbis, E. P. (1996) *Municipal Virtues in the Roman Empire: The Evidence of Roman Honorary Inscriptions* (Beiträge zur Altertumskunde 79), Stuttgart and Leipzig: B. G. Teubner.

Fossey, J. M. (1991) *Epigraphica Boeotica* 1: *Studies in Boiotian Inscriptions*, Amsterdam: Gieben.

Foucault, M. (1986) *The Care of the Self*, trans. R. Hurley, New York: Random House.

Fouilles de Delphes (1929–) *Fouilles de Delphes*. III. *Épigraphie*, Paris: de Boccard.

Franchi De Bellis, A. (1981) *Le iovile capuane* (Lingue e iscrizioni dell'Italia antica 2), Florence: L. S. Olschki.

Frank, T. (1916) "Race Mixture in the Roman Empire," *American Historical Review* 21: 689–708.

—— (1920) *An Economic History of Rome*, Baltimore: Johns Hopkins University Press.

Franklin, J. L., Jr. (1980) *Pompeii: The Electoral Programmata, Campaigns and Politics AD 71–79* (Papers and Monographs of the American Academy in Rome 28), Rome: The American Academy in Rome.

Fraser, P. M. and Matthews, E. (eds) (1987, 1997) *A Lexicon of Greek Personal Names* volume I: *The Aegean Islands, Cyprus, Cyrenaica*; volume IIIA: *The Peloponnese, Western Greece, Sicily, and Magna Graecia*, Oxford: Clarendon Press (see Osborne–Byrne 1994).

Fustel de Coulanges, N. D. (1980) *The Ancient City*, Baltimore: Johns Hopkins University Press; trans. of *La Cité Antique*, Paris, 1864.

Gagé, J. (1977) *Res Gestae Divi Augusti ex Monumentis Ancyrano et Antiocheno Latinis, Ancyrano et Apolloniensi Graecis*, 3rd ed., Paris: Les Belles Lettres.

Gager, J. E. (1992) *Curse Tablets and Binding Spells from the Ancient World*, Oxford: Oxford University Press.

Galletier, E. (1922) *Étude sur la poésie funéraire romaine d'après les inscriptions*, Paris: Librairie Hachette.

Galvao-Sobrinho, C. R. (1995) "Funerary Epigraphy and the Spread of Christianity in the West," *Athenaeum* 83: 431–62.

Garlan, Y. (1982) "Les timbres amphoriques thasiens. Bilan et perspectives de recherche," *Annales. économies, societés, civilisations* 37: 837–46.

—— (1983) "Greek amphorae and trade," in Garnsey–Hopkins–Whittaker 1983: 27–35.

—— (1985a) "De l'usage par les historiens du matériel amphorique grec," *Dialogues d'histoire ancienne* 11: 239–55.

—— (1985b) "Un remblai thasien du IVe siècle avant notre ère. Amphores et timbres amphoriques," *Bulletin de correspondence hellénique* 109: 727–46.

—— (1986) "Quelques nouveaux ateliers amphoriques à Thasos," in J.-Y. Empereur and Y. Garlan (eds) *Recherches sur les amphores grecques*, Paris: de Boccard: 200–76.

—— (1987) "Prolégomènes à un nouveau corpus des timbres amphoriques thasiens," in *Céramiques hellénistiques et romaines* (Annales littéraires de l'Université de Besançon 331), Paris: Les Belles Lettres: 73–86.

—— (1990) "L'interprétation du timbrage amphorique grec," *Revue archéologique*: 211–13.

—— (1993a) "Nouvelles remarques sur la chronologie des timbres amphoriques thasiens," *Journal des Savants*: 149–81.

—— (1993b) "A qui étaient destinés les timbres amphoriques grecs?" *Comptes rendus de l'Académie des Inscriptions*: 181–90.

Garnsey, P., Hopkins, K., Whittaker, C. R. (eds) (1983) *Trade in the Ancient Economy*, Berkeley and Los Angeles: University of California Press.

Gauthier, P. (1985) *Les Cités grecques et leurs bienfateurs (IVe–Ier siècles avant J.C.)* (Bulletin de correspondance héllenique Supplement 12) Athens: École française d'Athènes; Paris: de Boccard.

Gavrilov, A. K. (1997) "Techniques of Reading in Classical Antiquity," *Classical Quarterly* 47: 56–73.

Geraci, G. (1971) "Ricerche sul Proskynema," *Aegyptus* 51: 3–211.

Gezeichnetes Instrumentum (1991) *Gezeichnetes Instrumentum und Sozial- und Wirtschaftgeschichte* (Specimina Nova Dissertationum ex Instituto Historico Universitatis Quincqueecclesiensis de Iano Pannonio Nominatae), Peč.

Ghiron-Bistagne, P. (1976) *Recherches sur les acteurs dans la Grèce antique*, Paris: Les Belles Lettres.

Giangiulio, M. (1994) "Le laminette auree nella cultura religiosa della Calabria greca: continuità e innovazione," in S. Settis (ed.) *La Calabria antica. Età italica e romana*, Rome and Reggio Calabria: Gangemi: 11–53.

Giardina, A. (ed.) (1986) *Società romana e impero tardoantico*, 4 vols, Rome: Laterza.

Giardina, A. and Schiavone, A. (eds) (1981) *Società romana e produzione schiavistica*, 3 vols, Rome: Laterza.

Gigante, M. (1979) *Civiltà delle forme litterarie nell'antica Pompei*, Naples: Bibliopolis.

Gómez Pallarès, J. (1997) *Edición y comentario de las inscripciones sobre mosaico de Hispania. Inscripciones no cristianas* (Studia Archeologica 87), Rome: "l'Erma" di Bretschneider.

González, J. (1986) "The Lex Irnitana: A New Copy of the Flavian Municipal Law," *Journal of Roman Studies* 76: 147–243.

Gordon, A. E. (1983) *Illustrated Introduction to Latin Epigraphy*, Berkeley: University of California Press.

Gordon, A. E. with Gordon, J. S. (1958, 1964, 1965) *Album of Dated Latin Inscriptions, Rome and the Neighborhood*, 4 parts in 7 vols, Berkeley: University of California Press.

Gordon, J. S. and Gordon, A. E. (1957) *Contributions to the Palaeography of Latin Inscriptions* (University of California Publications in Classical Archaeology 3.3), Berkeley: University of California Press.

Gordon, M. L. (1931) "The Freedman's Son in Municipal Life," *Journal of Roman Studies* 21: 65–77.

Gordon, R., Beard, M., Reynolds, J., and Roueché, C. (1993) "Roman Inscriptions 1986–90," *Journal of Roman Studies* 83: 131–58.

Graf, F. (1997) *Magic in the Ancient World*, Cambridge, Mass.: Harvard University Press; trans. by F. Philip of *Idéologie et pratique de la magie dans l'antiquité gréco-romaine*, Paris: Les Belles Lettres, 1994.

Graham, A. J. (1974) "The Limitations of Prosopography in Roman Imperial History (With Special Reference to the Severan Period)," in H. Temporini (ed.) *Aufstieg und Niedergang der römischen Welt* II.1: Berlin and New York: De Gruyter: 136–57.

Griffin, M. T. (1982) "The Lyons Tablet and Tacitean Hindsight," *Classical Quarterly* 32: 404–18.

Grossi Gondi, F. (1928) *Tratato di epigrafia cristiana latina e greca del mondo romano occidentale*, Rome: Università Gregoriana.

Gruen, E. S. (1974) *The Last Generation of the Roman Republic*, Berkeley: University of California Press.

—— (1990) *Studies in Greek Culture and Roman Policy* (Cincinnati Classical Studies, n.s. 7), Leiden: E. J. Brill.

Guarducci, M. (1965) "Il misterioso 'quadrato magico': L'interpretazione di Jérome Carcopino e documenti nuovi," *Archeologia Classica* 17: 219–70.

—— (1967–78) *Epigrafia greca*, 4 vols, Rome: Istituto Poligrafico dello Stato.

—— (1974) "Laminette auree orfiche: alcuni problemi," *Epigraphica* 36: 7–31.

—— (1978) "Dal gioco letterale alla crittografia mistica," in H. Temporini (ed.) (1972–) *Aufstieg und Niedergang der römischen Welt* II.16.2: Berlin and New York: De Gruyter:1736–73.

—— (1981) "La cosiddetta Fibula Prenestina. Antiquari, eruditi, e falsari nella Roma dell'ottocento," *Memorie dell'Accademia nazionale dei Lincei*, Ser. 8.24.4: 413–574.

—— (1984–6) "La cosiddetta Fibula Praenestina: elementi nuovi," *Memorie dell'Accademia nazionale dei Lincei*, Ser. 8.28: 125–77.

—— (1987) *L'Epigrafia greca dalle origini al tardo impero*, Rome: Libreria dello Stato.

Gummerus, H. (1916) "Industrie und Handel," *RE* 9: 1381–1535.

Habicht, C. (1969) *Die Inschriften von Pergamon 3. Die Inschriften des Asklepieions*, Berlin: De Gruyter.

—— (1972) "Beiträge zur Prosopographie der altgriechischen Welt," *Chiron* 2: 102–34 (cf. *Bull. ép.* 1972: 382–3).

—— (1994) *Athen in hellenistischer Zeit. Gesammelte Aufsätze*, Munich: Beck.

Hahn, J. and Leunissen, P. M. M. (1990) "Statistical Method and Inheritance of the Consulate under the Early Roman Empire," *Phoenix* 44: 60–81.

Hainsworth, J. B. (1982) "The Greek Language and the Historical Dialects," in J. Boardman, I. E. S. Edwards, N. G. L. Hammond, and E. Sollberger (eds) *Cambridge Ancient History* 3.1, 2nd ed., Cambridge: Cambridge University Press: 850–65.

Halfmann, H. (1979) *Die Senatoren aus dem östlichen Teil des Imperium Romanum bis zum Ende des 2. Jh. n. Chr.* (Hypomnemata 58), Göttingen: Vandenhoeck and Ruprecht.

—— (1982) "Die Senatoren aus den kleinasiatischen Provinzen des römischen Reiches vom 1. bis 3. Jahrhundert," in *Epigrafia e ordine senatorio: Atti del Colloquio internazionale AIEGL su epigrafia e ordine senatorio, Roma, 14–20 maggio 1981*, II (Tituli 5), Rome: Edizioni di Storia e Letteratura: 603–50.

Hall, A. S.†, Milner, N. P., and Coulton, J. J. (1996) "The Mausoleum of Licinnia Flavilla and Flavianus Diogenes of Oinoanda: Epigraphy and Architecture," *Anatolian Studies* 46: 111–44.

Hall, E. (1989) *Inventing the Barbarian. Greek Self-Definition through Tragedy*, Oxford: Clarendon Press.

Hall, J. M. (1995) "The Role of Language in Greek Ethnicities," *Proceedings of the Cambridge Philological Society* 40: 83–100.

Hallett, J. P. (1977) "*Perusinae Glandes* and the Changing Image of Augustus," *American Journal of Ancient History* 2: 151–71.

Hälvä-Nyberg, U. (1988) *Die Kontraktionen auf den lateinischen Inschriften Roms und Afrikas bis zum 8. Jh. n. Chr.* (Annales Academiae Scientiarum Fennicae, Dissertationes Humanarum Litterarum 49), Helsinki: Suomalainen Tiedeakatemia.

Hansen, M. H., Bjerstrup, L., Nielsen, T. H., Rubinstein, L., and Vestergaard, T. (1990) "The Demography of the Attic Demes: The Evidence of Sepulchral Inscriptions," *Analecta Romana Instituti Danici* 30: 25–44.

Hardy, E. G. (1913) *Roman Laws and Charters*, Oxford: Clarendon Press.

Harris, W. V. (1983) "Literacy and Epigraphy, I," *Zeitschrift für Papyrologie und Epigraphik* 52: 87–111.

—— (1989) *Ancient Literacy*, Cambridge, Mass.: Harvard University Press.

—— (ed.) (1993) *The Inscribed Economy. Production and Distribution in the Roman Empire in the Light of* instrumentum domesticum (Journal of Roman Archaeology, Supplementary Series 6), Ann Arbor: Journal of Roman Archaeology.

—— (1995) "*Instrumentum domesticum* and Roman Literacy," in Solin–Salomies–Liertz 1995: 18–27.

—— (1996) "Writing and Literacy in the Archaic Greek City," in J. H. M. Strubbe, R. A. Tybout, and H. S. Versnel (eds) *ENEPΓEIA: Studies on Ancient History and Epigraphy Presented to H. W. Pleket*, Amsterdam: J. C. Gieben: 57–77.

Hatzfeld, J. (1912) "Les Italiens résidant à Délos," *Bulletin de correspondance hellénique* 36: 1–213.

Häusle, H. (1980) *Das Denkmal als Garant des Nachrums: Beiträge zur Geschichte und Thematik eines Motivs in lateinischen Inschriften* (Zetemeta 75), Munich: C. H. Beck.

Hedrick, C. W., Jr (1999) "Democracy and the Athenian Epigraphical Habit," *Hesperia* 68: 387–439.

Heintz, F. (1998) "Circus Curses and their Archaeological Contexts," *Journal of Roman Archaeology* 11: 337–42.

Helen, T. (1975) *The Organization of Roman Brick Production in the First and Second Century AD. An Interpretation of Roman Brick Stamps* (Annales Academiae Scientiarum Fennicae, Dissertationes Humanarum Litterarum 5), Helsinki: Suomalainen Tiedeakatemia.

Henderson, J. (ed.) (1987) *Aristophanes, Lysistrata*, Oxford: Clarendon Press.

Hendrickson, G. L. (1929) "Ancient Reading," *Classical Journal* 25: 182–96.

Henry, A. S. (1977) *The Prescripts of Athenian Decrees* (Mnemosyne Supplement 49), Leiden: E. J. Brill.

Henzen, W. (1874) *Acta Fratrum Arvalium quae supersunt*, Berlin: G. Reimer.

Herlihy, D. and Klapisch-Zuber, C. (1985) *Tuscans and their Families. A Study of the Florentine Catasto of 1427*, New Haven: Yale University Press.

Hesberg, H. von and Zanker, P. (1987) *Römische Gräberstraßen. Selbstdarstellung–Status–Standard* (Bayerische Akademie der Wissenschaften, philosophisch-historische Klasse Abhandlungen, neue Folge 96), Munich: Beck.

Hesnard, A. and Gianfrotta, P. A. (1989) "Les bouchons d'amphore en pouzzolane," in *Amphores romaines et histoire économique*: 393–441.

Higbie, C. (1999) "Craterus and the Use of Inscriptions in Ancient Scholarship," *Transactions of the American Philological Association* 129: 43–83.

Hiller von Gaertringen, F. (1906) *Inschriften von Priene*, Berlin: G. Reimer.

Hitchner, R. B. (1995) "The Culture of Death and the Invention of Culture in Roman Africa," *Journal of Roman Archaeology* 8: 493–8.

Hölkeskamp, K.-J. (1992) "Written Law in Archaic Greece," *Proceedings of the Cambridge Philological Society* 38: 87–117.

—— (1994) "Tempel, Agora und Alphabet," in H.-J. Gehrke (ed.) *Rechtskodifizierung und soziale Normen im interkulturellen Vergleich*, Tübingen: G. Narr: 135–64.

Hondius, J. J. E. (1938) *Saxa Loquuntur*, Leiden: A. W. Sijthoff; reprinted 1976, Chicago: Ares.

Hoogma, R. P. (1969) *Der Einfluss Vergils auf die Carmina latina Epigraphica. Eine Studie mit besonderer Berücksichtigung der metrisch-technischen Grundsätze der Entlehnung*, Amsterdam: North-Holland.

Hope, V. M. (1997) "Words and Pictures: the Interpretation of Romano-British Tombstones," *Britannia* 28: 245–58.

Hopkins, K. (1966) "On the Probable Age Structure of the Roman Population," *Population Studies* 20: 245–64.

—— (1978) *Conquerors and Slaves*, Cambridge: Cambridge University Press.

—— (1983) *Death and Renewal*, Cambridge: Cambridge University Press.

—— (1987) "Graveyards for Historians," in F. Hinard (ed.) *La mort, les morts, et l'au-delà dans le monde romain. Actes du colloque de Caen*, Caen: Université de Caen: 113–26.

Horbury, W. and Noy, D. (1992) *Jewish Inscriptions of Graeco-Roman Egypt*. Cambridge: Cambridge University Press.

Horrocks, G. (1997) *Greek: A History of the Language and its Speakers*, London and New York: Longman.

Horsfall, N. (1979) "Stesichorus at Bovillae?" *Journal of Hellenic Studies* 99: 26–48.

—— (1982) "Allia Potestas and Murdia, Two Roman Women," *Ancient Society, Resources for Teachers* 12, 2: 27–33.

—— (1983a) "Some Problems in the 'Laudatio Turiae,'" *Bulletin of the Institute of Classical Studies* 30: 85–98.

—— (1983b) "*Tabulae Iliacae* in the Collection Froehner, Paris," *Journal of Hellenic Studies* 103: 144–7.

——— (1985) "*CIL* VI 37965 = *CLE* 1988 (Epitaph of Allia Potestas): A Commentary," *Zeitschrift für Papyrologie und Epigraphik* 61: 251–72.

Horsley, G. H. R. (1994) "A Bilingual Funerary Monument in κιονηδόν Form from Dion in Northern Greece," *Chiron* 24: 209–19.

Horsley, G. H. R. and Lee, J. A. L. (1994) "A Preliminary Checklist of Abbreviations of Greek Epigraphic Volumes," *Epigraphica* 56: 129–69.

Horstkotte, H. (1984) "Magistratur und Dekurionat im Lichte des Albums von Canusium," *Zeitschrift für Papyrologie und Epigraphik* 57: 211–24.

Humbert, M. (1972) *Le remariage à Rome: Etude d'histoire juridique et sociale*, Milan: A. Giuffrè.

Humphreys, S. C. (1980) "Family Tomb Cult in Ancient Athens: Tradition or Traditionalism?" *Journal of Hellenic Studies* 100: 96–126.

Hunt, P. (1998) *Slaves, Warfare, and Ideology in the Greek Historians*, Cambridge: Cambridge University Press.

Immerwahr, H. R. (1990) *Attic Script. A Survey*, Oxford: Oxford University Press.

Ireland, R. (1983) "Epigraphy," in M. Henig (ed.) *A Handbook of Roman Art*, Ithaca: Cornell University Press: 220–33.

Isager, S. (1998) "The Pride of Halicarnassos. Editio Princeps of an Inscription from Salmakis," *Zeitschrift für Papyrologie und Epigraphik* 122: 1–23.

Iverson, E. (1965) "The Date of the so-called Inscription of Caligula on the Vatican Obelisk," *Journal of Egyptian Archaeology* 51: 149–54.

Jaczynowska, M. (1978) *Les Associations de la jeunesse romaine sous le Haut-Empire* (Archiwum Filologiczne 36), Wroclaw: Zaktad Narodowy.

Jameson, M. H., Jordan, D. R., and Kotansky, R. D. (1993) *A Lex Sacra from Selinous* (Greek, Roman, and Byzantine Monographs 11), Durham, North Carolina: Duke University Press.

Jeffery, L. H. with Johnston, A. W. (1990) *The Local Scripts of Archaic Greece: A Study of the Origin of the Greek Alphabet and its Development from the Eighth to the Fifth Centuries BC*, revised edition with a supplement by A. W. Johnston, Oxford: Clarendon Press. [= *LSAG*]

Johnston, A. W. (1979) *Trademarks on Greek Vases*, Warminster: Arris and Phillips.

Jones, A. H. M., Martindale, J. R., and Morris, J. (1971) *The Prosopography of the Later Roman Empire* I, Cambridge: Cambridge University Press.

Jordan, D. R. (1985) "A Survey of Greek Defixiones Not Included in the Special Corpora," *Greek, Roman, and Byzantine Studies* 26: 151–97.

Joshel, S. R. (1992) *Work, Identity, and Legal Status at Rome. A Study of the Occupational Inscriptions*, Norman: University of Oklahoma Press.

Judge, E. A. (1997) "The Rhetoric of Inscriptions," in S. E. Porter (ed.) *Handbook of Classical Rhetoric in the Hellenistic Period 330 BC–AD 400*, Leiden: E. J. Brill: 807–28.

Kajanto, I. (1963) *Onomastic Studies in the Early Christian Inscriptions of Rome and Carthage* (Acta Instituti Romani Finlandiae 2.1), Rome: Institutum Romanum Finlandiae.

—— (1965) *The Latin Cognomina* (Societas Scientiarum Fennica, Commentationes Humanarum Litterarum 36.2), Helsinki: Societas Scientiarum Fennica.

—— (1966) *Supernomina. A Study in Latin Epigraphy* (Societas Scientiarum Fennica, Commentationes Humanarum Litterarum 40.1), Helsinki: Societas Scientiarum Fennica.

Kajava, M. (1995a) *Roman Female Praenomina. Studies in the Nomenclature of Roman Women* (Acta Instituti Romani Finlandiae 14), Rome: Institutum Romanum Finlandiae.

—— (1995b) "Some Remarks on the Erasure of Inscriptions in the Roman World (with Special Reference to the Case of Cn. Piso, cos. 7 BC)," in Solin–Salomies–Liertz 1995: 201–10.

Kampen, N. (1981) *Image and Status: Roman Working Women in Ostia*, Berlin: Mann.

Kehoe, D. P. (1988) *The Economics of Agriculture on Roman Imperial Estates in North Africa* (Hypomnemata 89), Göttingen: Vandenhoeck and Ruprecht.

Keppie, L. (1991) *Understanding Roman Inscriptions*, Baltimore and London: Johns Hopkins University Press.

Kirchner, J. (1901–3) *Prosopographia Attica*, Berlin: G. Reimer. [= *PA*]

Kleiner, D. E. E. (1977) *Roman Group Portraiture: The Funerary Reliefs of the Late Republic and Early Empire*, New York: Garland.

Kloos, R. M. (1980) *Einführung in die Epigraphik des Mittelalters und der frühen Neuzeit*, Darmstadt: Wissenschaftliche Buchgesellschaft.

Kolendo, J. (1989) *Nomenclator, "memoria" del suo padrone o del suo patrono* (Epigrafia e Antichità 10), Faenza: Fratelli Lega Editori.

Koortbojian, M. (1996) "*In commemorationem mortuorum*: Text and Image Along the 'Street of Tombs'," in J. Elsner (ed.) *Art and Text in Roman Culture*, Cambridge: Cambridge University Press: 210–33.

Krummrey, H. and Panciera, S. (1980) "Criteri di edizione e segni diacritici," *Tituli* 2, Rome: Edizioni di Storia e Letteratura: 205–15.

Kubitschek, J. W. (1889) *Imperium Romanum Tributim Discriptum*, Vienna: F. Tempsky.

Kunkel, W. (1967) *Herkunft und soziale Stellung der römischen Juristen*, 2nd ed. (Forschungen zum römischen Recht 4), Graz, Vienna, Cologne: Böhlau.

Ladage, D. (1979) "*Collegia iuvenum*: Ausbildung einer municipalen Elite?" *Chiron* 9: 319–46.

Laffi, U. (1978) "La *lex aedis Furfensis*," in *La cultura Italica: atti del Convegno della Società italiana di glottologia, Pisa, 19 e 20 dicembre 1977* (Orientamenti linguistici 5), Pisa: Giardini: 121–44.

Lalonde, G. V., Langdon, M. K. and Walbank, M. B. (1991) *The Athenian Agora* volume XIX: *Inscriptions: Horoi, Poletai Records, and Leases of Public Lands*, Princeton: American School of Classical Studies at Athens.

Lane Fox, R. (1986) *Pagans and Christians*, London and New York: Harper and Row.

Lang, M. L. (1974) *Graffiti in the Athenian Agora*, Princeton: American School of Classical Studies at Athens.

—— (1975) *The Athenian Agora* volume XXI: *Graffiti and Dipinti*. Princeton: American School of Classical Studies at Athens.

—— (1990) *The Athenian Agora* volume XV: *Ostraka*. Princeton: American School of Classical Studies at Athens.

Larfeld, W. (1898) *Handbuch der griechischen Epigraphik*. 2. Band. *Die attischen Inschriften*, Leipzig: Reisland.

—— (1914) *Griechische Epigraphik*, 3rd ed. (Handbuch der klassischen Altertumswissenschaft 1,5) Munich: Beck.

Lattimore, R. (1942) *Themes in Greek and Latin Epitaphs* (Illinois Studies in Language and Literature 28.1–2), Urbana: The University of Illinois Press.

Lazzarini, M. L. (1976) *Le formule delle dediche votive nella Grecia antica* (Memorie dell'Accademia nazionale dei Lincei, Ser. 8.19.2), Rome: Accademia nazionale dei Lincei.

Lehmann, H. (1989) "Wolfgang Helbig (1839–1915)," *Mitteilungen des Deutschen Archäologischen Instituts, Römische Abteilung* 96: 7–86.

Lejeune, M. (ed.) (1985a) *Receuil des inscriptions gauloises (R.I.G.)* volume I: *Textes gallo-grecs* (Gallia Supplement 45), Paris: Editions du Centre National de la Recherche Scientifique.

—— (1985b) "Le plomb de Larzac," *Etudes Celtiques* 22: 95–177.

Leppin, H. (1992) *Histrionen: Untersuchungen zur sozialen Stellung von Bühnenkünstlern im Westen des römischen Reiches zur Zeit der Republik und des Principats* (Antiquitas 1.41), Bonn: Habelt.

Lewis, N. (1986) *Greeks in Ptolemaic Egypt*, Oxford: Clarendon Press.

Lewis, S. (1996) *News and Society in the Greek Polis*, London: Duckworth.

Linders, T. (1992) "Inscriptions and Orality," *Symbolae Osloenses* 67: 27–40.

Lintott, A. (1993) *Imperium Romanum: Politics and Administration*, London and New York: Routledge.

Lissarague, F. (1988) "La stèle avant la lettre," in *La parola, l'immagine, la tomba. Atti del Colloquio Internazionale di Capri* (Annali dell'Istituto Orientale di Napoli 10), 97–105.

Loomis, W. T. (1994) "Entella Tablets VI (254–241 BC) and VII (20th cent. AD?)," *Harvard Studies in Classical Philology* 96: 129–60.

Lorber, F. (1979) *Inschriften auf korinthischen Vasen: archäologisch-epigraphische Untersuchungen zur korinthischen Vasenmalerei im 7. und 6. Jh. v. Chr.* (Archäologische Forschungen 6), Berlin: Mann.

MacCoull, L. (1988) *Dioscorus of Aphrodito: His Work and His World*, Berkeley: University of California Press.

McGregor, M. F. (1974) "Solon's Archonship: The Epigraphic Evidence," in J. Evans (ed.) *Polis and Imperium. Studies in Honour of E. T. Salmon*, Toronto: Hakkert.

MacMullen, R. (1966) "Provincial Languages in the Roman Empire," *American Journal of Philology* 87: 1–14; reprinted in MacMullen 1990: 32–40.

—— (1982) "The Epigraphic Habit in the Roman Empire," *American Journal of Philology* 103: 233–46.

—— (1986) "Frequency of Inscriptions in Roman Lydia," *Zeitschrift für Papyrologie und Epigraphik* 65: 237–8.

—— (1987) "Late Roman Slavery," *Historia* 36: 359–82; reprinted in MacMullen 1990: 236–49.

—— (1990) *Changes in the Roman Empire. Essays in the Ordinary*, Princeton: Princeton University Press.

Magi, F. (1963) "Le iscrizioni recentamente scoperte sull'Obelisco Vaticano," *Studi Romani* 11: 50–6.

Mallon, J. (1952) *Paléographie romaine* (Scripturae Monumenta et Studia 3), Madrid: Consejo Superior de Investigaciones Científicas, Instituto Antonio de Nebrija, de Filologia.

—— (1982) *De l'écriture. Receuil d'études publiées de 1937 à 1981*, Paris: Editions du Centre national de la recherche scientifique.

Manacorda, D. (1989) "Le anfore dell'Italia repubblicana: aspetti economici e sociali," in *Amphores romaines et histoire économique*: 443–67.

—— (1990) "Le fornaci di Visellio a Brindisi. Primi risultati dello scavo," *Vetera Christianorum* 27: 375–415.

—— (1993) "Appunti sulla bollatura in età romana," in Harris 1993: 37–54.

—— (1994) "Produzione agricola, produzione ceramica e proprieta della terra nella Calabria romana tra Repubblica e Impero," in *Epigrafia della distribuzione e della produzione*, 3–59.

Manacorda, D. and Panella, C. (1993) "Anfore," in Harris 1993: 55–64.

Mandowsky, E. and Mitchell, C. (1963) *Pirro Ligorio's Roman Antiquities. The Drawings in MS. XIII B.7 in the National Library in Naples* (Studies of the Warburg Institute 28), London: Warburg Institute, University of London.

Mann, J. C. (1985) "Epigraphic Consciousness," *Journal of Roman Studies* 75: 204–6.

Marcillet-Jaubert, M. (1960) "Philologie et inscriptions," *Revue des études anciennes* 62: 362–82.

Marek, C. (1993) "Euboia und die Entstehung der Alphabetschrift bei den Griechen," *Klio* 75: 27–44.

Marichal, R. (1988) *Les graffites de la Graufesenque* (Gallia Supplement 47), Paris: Editions du Centre National de la Recherche Scientifique.

—— (1992) *Les ostraca de Bu Njem* (Libya Antiqua Supplement 7), Tripoli: Directorate-General of Antiquities, Museums, and Archives.

Marinetti, A. (1985) *Le iscrizioni sudpicene* (Lingue e iscrizioni dell'Italia antica 5), Florence: L. S. Olschki.

Martin, A. (1994) "Archives privées et cachettes documentaires," *Proceedings of the 20th International Congress of Papyrology*, Copenhagen: 569–77.

Martin, D. B. (1996) "The Construction of the Ancient Family: Methodological Considerations," *Journal of Roman Studies* 86: 40–60.

Martin, F. (1996) "The Importance of Honorific Statues: A Case Study," *Bulletin of the Institute of Classical Studies* 41: 53–70.

Martindale, J. R. (1980–92) *The Prosopography of the Later Roman Empire* II–III, Cambridge: Cambridge University Press.

Marucchi, O. (1912) *Christian Epigraphy. An Elementary Treatise*, trans. by J. A. Willis of *Epigrafia cristiana* (Milan 1910), Cambridge: Cambridge University Press; repr. Chicago: Ares, 1974.

Mason, H. J. (1974) *Greek Terms for Roman Institutions. A Lexicon and Analysis* (American Studies in Papyrology 13), Toronto: Hakkert.

Mattingly, D. J. and Hitchner, R. B. (1995) "Roman Africa: An Archaeological Review," *Journal of Roman Studies* 85: 165–213.

Mattingly, H. B. (1993) "New Light on the Athenian Standards Decree (*ATL* II, D 14)," *Klio* 75: 99–102.

—— (1999) "What are the Right Dating Criteria for Fifth-Century Attic Texts," *Zeitschrift für Papyrologie und Epigraphik* 126: 117–22.

Maurin, J. (1982) "La prosopographie romaine: pertes et profits," *Annales. économies, societés, civilisations* 37: 824–36.

Meid, W. (1980) *Gallisch oder lateinisch? Soziolinguistische und andere Bemerkungen zu populären gallo-lateinisch Inschriften*, Innsbruck: Institut für Sprachwissenschaft der Universität Innsbruck.

Meritt, B. D. (1940) *Epigraphica Attica*, Cambridge, Mass.: Harvard University Press.

—— (1961) *The Athenian Year* (Sather Classical Lectures 32), Berkeley: University of California Press.

Meritt, B. D. and Traill, J. S. (1974) *The Athenian Agora* volume XV: *Inscriptions: The Athenian Councillors*, Princeton: American School of Classical Studies at Athens.

Meritt, B. D. and Wade-Gery, H. T. (1962) "The Dating of Documents to the Mid-Fifth Century–I," *Journal of Hellenic Studies* 82: 67–74.

Meyer, E. (1973) *Einführung in die lateinische Epigraphik*, Darmstadt: Wissenschaftliche Buchgesellschaft.

Meyer, E. A. (1990) "Explaining the Epigraphic Habit in the Roman Empire: The Evidence of Epitaphs," *Journal of Roman Studies* 80: 74–96.

—— (1993) "Epitaphs and Citizenship in Classical Athens," *Journal of Hellenic Studies* 113: 99–121.

Meyer, M. W. (1987) *The Ancient Mysteries: A Sourcebook*, San Francisco: HarperCollins.

Michels, A. K. (1967) *The Calendar of the Roman Republic*, Princeton: Princeton University Press.

Migeotte, L. (1976) "Emprunts publics à Karystos," *Phoenix* 30: 26–41.

Mikalson, J. D. (1975) *The Sacred and Civil Calendar of the Athenian Year*, Princeton: Princeton University Press.

Millar, F. (1968) "Local Cultures in the Roman Empire: Libyan, Punic and Latin in Roman Africa," *Journal of Roman Studies*, 58: 126–34.

—— (1983) "Epigraphy," in M. Crawford (ed.) *Sources for Ancient History*, Cambridge: Cambridge University Press: 80–136.

—— (1987) "Empire, Community and Culture in the Roman Near East: Greeks, Syrians, Jews and Arabs," *Journal of Jewish Studies*, 38: 143–62.

—— (1993) *The Roman Near East 31 BC–AD 337*, Cambridge, Mass.: Harvard University Press.

—— (1995) "Latin Epigraphy of the Roman Near East," in Solin–Salomies–Liertz 1995: 403–19.

Mingazzini, P. (1958) "Tre brevi note sui laterizi antichi," *Bullettino della Commissione Archeologica Comunale di Roma* 76 (1956) [1958]: 77–93.

Mitchell, J. (1990) "Literacy Displayed: The Use of Inscriptions at the Monastery of San Vincenzo al Volturno in the early Ninth Century," in R. McKitterick (ed.) *The Uses of Literacy in Early Mediaeval Europe*, Cambridge: Cambridge University Press: 186–225.

Mócsy, A. (1966) "Die Unkenntnis des Lebensalters im römischen Reich," *Acta Antiqua* 14: 387–421.

Momigliano, A. (1953) "In memoria di Michele Rostovtzeff 1870–1952," *Rivista storica italiana* 66: 67–106.

—— (1954) "M. I. Rostovtzeff," *The Cambridge Journal*, 7: 334–46; reprinted in id. (1955) *Contributo alla storia degli studi classici*. Rome: Edizioni di Storia e Letteratura.

Mommsen, T. (1852) *Inscriptiones Regni Neapolitani Latinae*, Naples: G. Wigand and A. Detken.

—— (1864) "Die römischen Eigennamen der republikanischen und augustischen Zeit," in id., *Römische Forschungen* I, Berlin: Weidmann: 1–68.

—— (1887) *Römisches Staatsrecht*, volume 3, Leipzig: S. Hirzel.

Mora, F. (1990) *Prosopografia Isiaca* (Etudes préliminaires aux religions orientales dans l'empire romain 113), Leiden: E. J. Brill.

Morel, J.-P. (1988) "Artisanat et colonisation dans l'Italie romaine aux IV et III siècles av. J.C.," in *Dialoghi di Archeologia*, 3rd ser., 6.2: 49–63.

Moretti, L. (1967, 1976) *Iscrizioni storiche ellenistiche*, 2 vols (Biblioteca di studi superiori 53), Florence: La nuova Italia.

Morris, I. (1992) *Death-Ritual and Social Structure in Classical Antiquity*, Cambridge: Cambridge University Press.

Mrozek, St. (1973) "À propos de la répartition chronologique des inscriptions latines dans le Haut-Empire," *Epigraphica* 35: 113–18.

—— (1988) "À propos de la répartition chronologique des inscriptions latines dans le Haut-Empire," *Epigraphica* 50: 61–4.

Münzer, F. (1920) *Römische Adelsparteien und Adelsfamilien*, Stuttgart: Metzler; English transl. by T. Ridley, *Roman Aristocratic Parties and Families*, Baltimore: Johns Hopkins University Press, 1999.

Neumann, G. and Untermann, J. (eds) (1980) *Die Sprachen im römischen Reich der Kaiserzeit* (Bonner Jahrbücher Beiheft 40), Cologne and Bonn: Rheinland Verlag and Habelt.

Niebuhr, B. G. (1815) "Dass Inschriften für die alte Geschichte den Urkunden für die neuere entsprechen," in A. Harnack, *Geschichte der Königlich Preussischen Akademie der Wissenschaften zu Berlin*, Berlin: Reichsdruckerei, 1900, volume 2: 379–82.

Nielsen, H. Sigismund (1996) "The Physical Context of Roman Epitaphs and the Structure of the Roman Family," *Analecta Romana Instituti Danici* 23: 7–27.

—— (1997) "Interpreting Epithets in Roman Epitaphs," in B. Rawson and P. Weaver (eds) *The Roman Family in Italy: Status, Sentiment, Space*, Oxford: Oxford University Press: 169–204.

Nielsen, T. H., Bjerstrup, L., Hansen, M. H., Rubinstein, L., and Vestergaard, T. (1989) "Athenian Grave Monuments and Social Class," *Greek, Roman, and Byzantine Studies* 30: 411–20.

Nock, A. D. (1932) "Cremation and Burial in the Roman Empire," *Harvard Theological Review* 25: 321–59; reprinted in Z. Stewart (ed.) *Essays on Religion and the Ancient World*, Oxford: Clarendon Press, 1972: 277–307.

North, J. A. (1979) "Religious Toleration in Republican Rome," *Proceedings of the Cambridge Philological Society* 25: 85–103.

—— (1996) "Pollution and Purification at Selinous," *Scripta Classica Israelica* 15: 293–301.

Noy, D. (1993) *Jewish Inscriptions of Western Europe* volume 1: *Italy (excluding the City of Rome), Spain and Gaul*, Cambridge: Cambridge University Press.

—— (1995) *Jewish Inscriptions of Western Europe* volume 2: *The City of Rome*, Cambridge: Cambridge University Press.

Oliver, J. H. (1935) "Greek Inscriptions: Laws," *Hesperia* 4: 5–32.

—— (1970) *Marcus Aurelius. Aspects of Civic and Cultural Policy in the East* (Hesperia Supplement 13), Princeton: American School of Classical Studies at Athens.

—— (1989) *Greek Constitutions of Early Roman Emperors from Inscriptions and Papyri* (Memoirs of the American Philosophical Society 178), Philadelphia: American Philosophical Society.

Olshausen, E. (1974) *Prosopographie der hellenistischen Königsgesandten.* Teil I: *Von Triparadeisos bis Pydna* (Studia Hellenistica 19), Louvain: Nauwelaerts.

L'Onomastique latine (1977) = *L'Onomastique latine. Colloque de Paris, 13–15 Octobre, 1975* (Colloques internationaux du Centre National de la Recherche Scientifique 564), Paris: Centre Nationale de la Recherche Scientifique.

Orlandos, A. K. (1966) *Les matériaux de construction et la technique architecturale des anciens Grecs*, translated from the Greek by V. Hadjimichali and K. Laumonier, Paris: de Boccard.

Osborne, M. J. and Byrne, S. G. (eds) (1994) *A Lexicon of Greek Personal Names* volume II: *Attica*, Oxford: Clarendon Press (see Fraser–Matthews 1987, 1997).

Osborne, R. (1985) *Demos: The Discovery of Classical Attika*, Cambridge: Cambridge University Press.

Pailler, J.-M. (1988) *Bacchanalia: La répression de 186 av. J-C. à Rome et en Italie* (Bibliothèque des Écoles françaises d'Athènes et de Rome 270), Rome: École française de Rome.

Palmer, L. R. P. (1954) *The Latin Language*, London: Faber and Faber; reprinted 1988, Norman, Oklahoma: University of Oklahoma Press.

Panciera, S. (1970) *Un falsario del primo ottocento: Girolamo Asquini e l'epigrafia antica delle Venezie* (Note e discussioni erudite 13), Rome: Edizioni di Storia e Letteratura.

—— (ed.) (1991a) "Inscriptiones Latinae Liberae Rei Publicae," in *Epigrafia. Actes du colloque en mémoire de Attilio Degrassi*, Rome: École française de Rome: 241–491.

—— (1991b) "Struttura dei supplementi e segni diacritici dieci anni dopo," *Supplementa Italica* n.s. 8: 9–21.

—— (1995) "La produzione epigrafica di Roma in età repubblicana. Le officine lapidarie," in Solin–Salomies–Liertz 1995: 319–42.

Pape, W. and Benseler, G. E. (1863–70) *Wörterbuch der griechischen Eigennamen*, 3rd ed., Braunschweig: F. Vieweg.

Parkin, T. (1992) *Demography and Roman Society*, Baltimore: Johns Hopkins University Press.

Patterson, J. R. (1994) "The Collegia and the Transformation of the Towns of Italy in the Second Century AD," in *L'Italie d'Auguste à Dioclétien* (Collection de l'École française de Rome 198), Rome: École française de Rome, 227–38.

Pavolini, C. (1980) "Heinrich Dressel e gli studi sulle lucerne romane," *Annali della Facoltà di Lettere e Filosofia dell'Università di Siena* 1: 175–9.

—— (1993) "I bolli sulle lucerne fittili delle officine centro-italiche," in Harris 1993: 65–71.

Peacock, D. P. S. and Williams, D. F. (1986) *Amphorae and the Roman Economy*, London and New York: Longman.

Pedroni, L. (1988) "La scomparsa dei bolli sulla ceramica a vernice nera," *Samnium* 61: 130–46.

Peek, W. (1969) *Inschriften aus dem Asklepion von Epidauros* (Abhandlungen der Sachsischen Akademie der Wissenschaften zu Leipzig, Philologisch-Historische Klasse 60.2), Berlin: Akademie-Verlag.

—— (1972) *Neue Inschriften aus Epidauros* (Abhandlungen der Sachsischen Akademie der Wissenschaften zu Leipzig, Philologisch-Historische Klasse 63.5), Berlin: Akademie-Verlag.

Pélékidis, C. (1962) *Histoire de l'éphébie attique des origines à 31 avant J.-C.* (École française d'Athènes, Travaux et Mémoires 13), Paris: de Boccard.

Peremans, W. (1982) "Le bilinguisme dans l'Égypte des Lagides," *Studia Paulo Naster oblata*, II: *Orientalia antiqua* (Orientalia Lovaniensia Analecta 13), Leuven: Departement Orientalistiek: Peeters: 143–54.

—— (1983) "Le bilinguisme dans les relations gréco-égyptiennes sous les Lagides," in E. van 't Dack, P. van Dessel, and W. van Gucht (eds) *Egypt and the Hellenistic World* (Studia Hellenistica 27), Leuven: Orientaliste: 253–80.

—— (1985) "Notes sur les traductions de textes non littéraires sous les Lagides," *Chronique d'Égypte* 60: 246–62.

Petrucci, A. (1993) *Public Lettering. Script, Power, and Culture*, trans. by L. Lappin of an updated edition of *La Scrittura. Ideologia e rappresentazione*, Rome (1980, 1986) Chicago: University of Chicago Press.

—— (1995) *Le scritture ultime. Ideologia della morte e strategie dello scrivere nella tradizione occidentale*, Torino: Einaudi.

Petzl, G. (1994) *Die Beichtinschriften Westkleinasiens* (Epigraphica Anatolica 22), Bonn: Habelt.

Pflaum, H.-G. (1948) *Le marbre de Thorigny* (Bibliothèque de l'École des Hautes Études 292), Paris: H. Champion.

—— (1950) *Les procurateurs équestres sous le Haut-Empire romain*, Paris: A.-Maisonneuve.

—— (1960–1) *Les carrières procuratoriennes équestres sous le Haut-Empire romain*, 3 vols, Paris: Paul Geuthner.

—— (1970) "La valeur de la source inspiratrice de la vita Hadriani et de la vita Marci Antonini à la lumière des personnalités contemporaines nommément citées," in A. Alföldi (ed.) *Bonner Historia–Augusta–Colloquium 1968/1969* (Antiquitas, Reihe 4, Beiträge zur H-A-Forschung, Band 7), Bonn: Habelt: 173–232.

—— (1972) "Quelques réflexions sur l'interprétation prosopographique de l'histoire romaine," *Rheinisches Museum* 115: 318–21.

—— (1978) *L'Afrique romaine. Scripta varia* I, Paris: l'Harmattan.

—— (1981) *La Gaule et l'empire romain. Scripta varia* II, Paris: l'Harmattan.

Pfohl, G. (1966) *Griechische Inschriften als Zeugnisse des privaten und öffentlichen Lebens*, Munich: Heimeran.

—— (1967) *Greek Poems on Stone.* volume I. *Epitaphs: From the Seventh to the Fifth Century BC*, Leiden: E. J. Brill.

Pfohl, G. and Pietri, C. (1983) "Grabinschrift I (griechisch)" [Pfohl] and "Grabinschrift II (lateinisch)" [Pietri], *Reallexicon für Antike und Christentum* 12, Stuttgart: Anton Hiersemann: 467–514, 514–90.

Piccaluga, G. (1983) "La scrittura coercitiva," *Cultura e Scuola* 85: 117–24.

Pighi, G. B. (1965) *De Ludis Saecularibus Populi Romani Quiritium Libri Sex*, 2nd ed., Amsterdam: E. Schippers.

Pikhaus, D. (1994) *Répertoire des inscriptions Latines versifiées de l'Afrique romaine (Ier–VIe siècles)* (Epigraphica Bruxellensia 2), Brussels: Epigraphica Bruxellensia.

Piso, I. (1993) *Fasti Provinciae Daciae.* I. *Die senatorischen Amtsträger* (Antiquitas 1.43), Bonn: Habelt.

Poland, F. (1909) *Geschichte des griechischen Vereinswesens*, Leipzig: B. G. Teubner.

Polomé, E. C. (1983) "The Linguistic Situation in the Western Provinces of the Roman Empire," in H. Temporini (ed.) (1972–) *Aufstieg und Niedergang der römischen Welt* II.29.2: Berlin and New York: De Gruyter: 509–53.

Poultney, J. W. (1959) *The Bronze Tablets of Iguvium* (American Philological Association Philological Monographs 18), Baltimore: American Philological Association.

Powell, B. P. (1991) *Homer and the Origin of the Greek Alphabet*, Cambridge: Cambridge University Press.

Preisendanz, K. (1972) "Fluchtafel (Defixio)," *Reallexicon für Antike und Christentum* 8: 1–24.

Price, S. R. F. (1984) *Rituals and Power: The Roman Imperial Cult in Asia Minor*, Cambridge: Cambridge University Press.

Pritchett, W. K. (1963) *Ancient Athenian Calendars on Stone*, Berkeley: University of California Press.

—— (1965) "The Koan Fragment of the Monetary Decree. Second Part," *Bulletin de correspondance hellénique* 89: 423–40.

—— (1999) "Postscript: The Athenian Calendar," *Zeitschrift für Papyrologie und Epigraphik* 128: 79–93.

Pritchett, W. K. and Neugebauer, O. (1947) *The Calendars of Athens*, Cambridge, Mass.: Harvard University Press.

Priuli, S. (1986) "Le iscrizioni sulle fistule," in *Il trionfo dell'acqua. Acque e acquedotti a Roma. IV sec. a.C.–XX sec.*, Rome: Paleani Editrice: 187–95.

Prosdocimi, A. (1984) *Le tavole Iguvine* (Lingue e iscrizioni dell'Italia antica 4), Florence: L. S. Olschki.

Prosopographia Imperii Romani (1897–8) E. Klebs, H. Dessau, and P. von Rohden (eds); 2nd ed. (now up to "P") (1933–), E. Groag, A. Stein, L. Petersen, et al. (eds) Berlin: De Gruyter. [= *PIR*]

Prott, J. von and Ziehen, L. (1896–1906) *Leges Graecorum sacrae e titulis collectae*, Leipzig: B. G. Teubner.

Pucci, G. (1973) "La produzione della ceramica aretina. Note sull' 'industria' nella prima età imperiale romana," *Dialoghi di Archeologia* 7: 255–93.

—— (1983) "Pottery and Trade in the Roman Period," in Garnsey–Hopkins–Whittaker 1983: 105–17.

—— (1985) "Terra sigillata italica," in *Enciclopedia dell'arte antica classica e orientale, Atlante delle forme ceramiche* II, Rome: Istituto dell'Enciclopedia Italiana: 372–406.

—— (1986) "Artigianato e territorio: le officine ceramiche galliche," in Giardina 1986: volume 3: 703–10.

—— (1993a) "I bolli sulla terra sigillata: fra epigrafia e storia economica," in Harris 1993: 73–80.

—— (1993b) *Il passato prossimo. La scienza dell'antichità alle origini della cultura moderna*, Rome: La Nuova Italia Scientifica.

—— (1999) "La documentazione archeologica nella storia economica e sociale prima di Rostovzev," *Annali della Facoltà di Lettere e Filosofia dell'Università di Siena* 20: 169–79.

Pugliese Carratelli, G. (1939–40) "Per le storia delle associazione in Rodi Antica," *Annuario della Regia Scuola Archeologica di Atene e delle Missioni Italiane in Oriente* n.s. 1–2: 147–200.

Pugliese Carratelli, G. and Garbini, G. (1964) *A Bilingual Graeco-Aramaic Edict by Asoka. The first Greek Inscription discovered in Afghanistan* (Serie Orientale Roma 29), Rome: Istituto italiano per il medio ed estremo Oriente.

Pulgram, E. (1978) *Italic, Latin, Italian: 600 BC to AD 1260 (Texts and Commentaries)* (Indogermanische Bibliothek: Reihe 1, Lehr- und Handbucher), Heidelberg: Winter.

Purcell, N. (1983) "The *Apparitores*: A Study in Social Mobility," *Papers of the British School at Rome* 51: 125–73.

—— (1995) "Literate Games: Roman Urban Society and the Game of *Alea*," *Past and Present* 147: 3–37.

Raepsaet-Charlier, M.-T. (1987) *Prosopographie des femmes de l'ordre sénatorial (Ier–IIe siècles)*, Louvain: Peeters.

Ramage, E. (1987) *The Nature and Purpose of Augustus' "Res Gestae"* (Historia Einzelschriften 54), Stuttgart: F. Steiner Verlag.

Raubitschek, A. E. (1964) "Die Inschrift als Denkmal. Bemerkungen zur Methodologie der Inschriftenkunde," *Studium Generale* 17: 219–28.

Rawson, B. M. (1966) "Family Life among the Lower Classes at Rome in the First Two Centuries of the Empire," *Classical Philology* 61: 71–83.

—— (1974) "Roman Concubinage and other De Facto Marriages," *Transactions of the American Philological Association* 104: 279–305.

—— (1986) "Children in the Roman *Familia*," in B. M. Rawson (ed.) *The Family in Ancient Rome: New Perspectives*, Ithaca, N.Y.: Cornell University Press: 170–200.

—— (1997) "'The Family' in the Ancient Mediterranean: Past, Present, Future," *Zeitschrift für Papyrologie und Epigraphik* 117: 294–6.

Reger, G. (1994) *Regionalism and Change in the Economy of Independent Delos, 314–167 BC* (Hellenistic Culture and Society 14), Berkeley: University of California Press.

Rehm, A. (1958) *Didyma* II. *Die Inschriften*, R. Harder (ed.), Berlin: Gebr. Mann.

Reinach, S. (1885) *Traité d'épigraphie grecque*, Paris: E. Leroux.

Remesal Rodríguez, J. (1989) "Cuestiones en torno a la epigrafía anfórica de la Bética," in *Amphores romaines et histoire économique*: 489–503.

Rémondon, R. (1964) "Problème du bilinguisme dans l'Égypte lagide (U.P.Z. I, 148)," *Chronique d'Égypte* 39: 126–46.

Rémy, B. (1986) *L'évolution administrative de l'Anatolie aux trois premiers siècles de notre ère* (Collection du Centre d'études romains et gallo-romains 5), Lyon: Centre d'études romains et gallo-romains.

—— (1988) *Les fastes sénatoriaux des provinces romaines d'Anatolie au Haut-Empire*, Paris: Éditions Recherche sur les Civilisations.

—— (1989) *Les carrières sénatoriales dans les provinces romaines d'Anatolie au Haut-Empire (31 av. J.-C.–284 ap. J.-C.)*, Istanbul and Paris: Institut français d'études anatoliennes.

Reynolds, J. (1971) "Roman Inscriptions 1966–1970," *Journal of Roman Studies* 61: 136–52.

—— (1976) "Roman Inscriptions 1971–5," *Journal of Roman Studies* 66: 174–99.

Reynolds, J. M. and Ward-Perkins, J. B. (1952) *The Inscriptions of Roman Tripolitania*, Rome: British School at Rome. [= *IRT*]

Rhodes, P. J., with Lewis, D. M. (1997) *The Decrees of the Greek States*, Oxford: Clarendon Press.

Richter, F. (1911) *Lateinische Sakralinschriften*, Bonn: A. Marcus and E. Weber.

Ritti, T. (1974–5) "L'uso di 'immagini onomastiche' nei monumenti sepolcrali di età greca," *Archeologia Classica* 25–26: 639–60.

—— (1977) "Immagini onomastiche sui monumenti sepolcrali di età imperiale," *Memorie dell'Accademia nazionale dei Lincei* 8.21: 257–396.

Rives, J. B. (1995) *Religion and Authority in Roman Carthage from Augustus to Constantine*, Oxford: Clarendon Press.

Rix, H. (1963) *Das etruskische Cognomen: Untersuchungen zu System, Morphologie und Verwendung der Personennamen auf den jungeren Inschriften Nordetruriens*, Wiesbaden: O. Harrassowitz.

Rizakis, A. (1995) "Le grec face au latin. Le paysage linguistique dans la péninsule balkanique sous l'empire," in Solin–Salomies–Liertz 1995: 373–92.

Robert, L. (1940–65) *Hellenica. Recueil d'épigraphie, de numismatique et d'antiquités grecques*, 13 vols, Limoges: Imprimerie A. Bontemps.

—— (1953) "Communication inaugurale," in *Actes du deuxième congrès international d'épigraphie grecque et latine*, Paris: Adrien Maisonneuve: 1–20.

—— (1968) "Les épigrammes satiriques de Lucilius sur les athlètes: parodie et réalités," in *L'épigramme grecque* (Entretiens sur L'Antiquité Classique 14), Vandoeuvres and Geneva: Fondation Hardt: 181–291.

—— (1971) "Un oracle gravé à Oenoanda," *Comptes rendus de l'Académie des Inscriptions et Belles-Lettres*: 597–619.

Robertson, M. (1972) "'Epoiesen' on Greek Vases: Other Considerations," *Journal of Hellenic Studies* 92: 180–3.

Robertson, N. (1987) "Government and Society at Miletus, 525–442 B.C.," *Phoenix* 41: 356–98.

Rochette, B. (1994) "Traducteurs et traductions dans l'Égypte gréco-romaine," *Chronique d'Égypte* 69: 313–15.

—— (1996) "Remarques sur le bilinguisme gréco-latin," *Les études classiques* 64: 3–19.

Rodríguez-Almeida, E. (1984) *Il Monte Testaccio. Ambiente, storia, materiali*, Rome: Edizioni Quasar.

Rosati, R. (1977) "La nozione di 'proprietà dell'officina' e l'*EPOIESEN* nei vasi attici," *Rendiconti dell'Accademia delle scienze dell'Istituto di Bologna* 65: 45–73.

Rostovtzeff, M. I. (1926, 1957) *The Social and Economic History of the Roman Empire*, 1926; 2nd ed., revised by P. M. Fraser, 1957, Oxford: Clarendon Press.

Roueché, C. (1989) *Aphrodisias in Late Antiquity* (Journal of Roman Studies Monographs 5), London: Society for the Promotion of Roman Studies.

Roxan, M. M. (1978) *Roman Military Diplomas 1954–1977* (University of London, Institute of Archaeology. Occasional Publication 2), London: University College London Institute of Archaeology. [= *RMD* 1]

—— (1985) *Roman Military Diplomas 1978–1984* (University of London, Institute of Archaeology. Occasional Publication 9), London: University College London Institute of Archaeology. [= *RMD* 2]

—— (1994) *Roman Military Diplomas 1985–1993* (University of London, Institute of Archaeology. Occasional Publication 14), London: University College London Institute of Archaeology. [= *RMD* 3]

Sabbatini Tumolesi, P. (1980) *Gladiatorum Paria: Annunci di spettacoli gladiatorii a Pompeii* (Tituli 1), Rome: Edizioni di Storia e Letteratura.

Sadurska, A. (1964) *Les tables Iliaques*, Warsaw: Panstwowe Wydawn: Naukowe.

Saller, R. P. (1982) *Personal Patronage under the Early Empire*, Cambridge: Cambridge University Press.

—— (1987a) "Men's Age at Marriage and its Consequences in the Roman Family," *Classical Philology* 82: 21–34.

—— (1987b) "Slavery and the Roman Family," *Slavery and Abolition* 8: 65–87.

—— (1994) *Patriarchy, Property, and Death in the Roman Family*, Cambridge: Cambridge University Press.

—— (1997) "Roman Kinship: Structure and Sentiment," in B. Rawson and P. Weaver (eds) *The Roman Family in Italy: Status, Sentiment, Space*, Oxford: Oxford University Press: 7–34.

Saller, R. P. and Shaw, B. D. (1984) "Tombstones and Roman Family Relations in the Principate: Civilians, Soldiers and Slaves," *Journal of Roman Studies* 74: 124–56.

Salomies, O. (1987) *Die römischen Vornamen. Studien zur römischen Namengebung* (Societas Scientiarum Fennica, Commentationes Humanarum Litterarum 82), Helsinki: Societas Scientiarum Fennica.

—— (1992) *Adoptive and Polyonymous Nomenclature in the Roman Empire* (Societas Scientiarum Fennica, Commentationes Humanarum Litterarum 97), Helsinki: Societas Scientiarum Fennica.

—— (1994) "Observations on the Development of the Style of Latin Honorific Inscriptions during the Empire," *Arctos* 28: 63–106.

Salway, B. (1994) "What's in a Name? A Survey of Roman Onomastic Practice from c. 700 BC to AD 700," *Journal of Roman Studies* 84: 124–45.

Samson, R. (1989) "Rural Slavery, Inscriptions, Archaeology and Marx," *Historia* 38: 99–110.

Sanders, G. (1970) "Les éléments figuratifs des *Carmina Latina Epigraphica*," in *Anamnèsis. Gedenkboek prof. dr. E. A. Leemans*, Brugge: 317–41; reprinted in Sanders 1991: 87–110.

—— (1977) "Les inscriptions latines païennes et chrétiennes: Symbiose ou métabolisme?" *Revue de l'Université Libre de Bruxelles* 1977: 44–64; reprinted in Sanders 1991: 155–77.

—— (1979) "L'Au-delà et les acrostiches des *Carmina Latina Epigraphica*," *Roczniki Humanistyczne*, Lublin, 27, 3: 57–75; reprinted in Sanders 1991: 183–205.

—— (1989) "Sauver le nom de l'oubli: le témoignage des *CLE* d'Afrique et aliunde," in A. Mastino (ed.) *L'Africa Romana. Atti del VI Convegno di Studio. Sassari 16–18 dicembre 1988* (Pubblicazioni del Dipartimento di storia dell'Università di Sassari 14), Sassari: Gallizzi: 43–79.

—— (1991) *Lapides Memores. Païens et Chrétiens face à la mort: le témoignage de l'épigraphie funéraire latine*, A. Donati, D. Pikhaus, M. van Uytfanghe (eds) (Epigrafia e Antichità 11), Faenza: Fratelli Lega Editori.

Sandys, J. E. (1927) *Latin Epigraphy. An Introduction to the Study of Latin Inscriptions*, 2nd ed. revised by S. G. Campbell, Cambridge: Cambridge University Press.

Sartori, A. (1995) "L'impaginazione delle iscrizioni," in Solin–Salomies–Liertz 1995: 183–200.

Šašel Kos, M. (1979) *Inscriptiones Latinae in Graecia repertae. Additamenta ad CIL III* (Epigrafia e Antichità 5), Faenza: Fratelli Lega Editori.

Scheid, J. (1990a) *Romulus et ses frères. Le collège des Frères Arvales, modèle du culte public dans la Rome des empereurs* (Bibliothèque des Écoles françaises d'Athènes et de Rome 275), Rome: École française de Rome.

—— (1990b) *Le collège des Frères Arvales. Étude prosopographique du recrutement (69–304)* (Saggi di storia antica 1), Rome: "l'Erma" di Bretschneider.

Scheid, J., Tassini, P., and Rüpke, J. (1998) *Recherches archéologiques à la Magliana: Commentarii Fratrum Arvalium qui supersunt: les copies épigraphiques des protocoles annuels de la confrérie arvale: 21 av.–304 ap. J.-C.*, Rome: École française de Rome; Soprintendenza archeologica di Roma.

Schmandt-Besserat, D. (1992) *Before Writing: From Counting to Cuneiform*, 2 vols, Austin: University of Texas Press.

Schmidt, K. H. (1983) "Keltisch-lateinische Sprachkontakte im römischen Gallien der Kaiserzeit," in H. Temporini (ed.) (1972–) *Aufstieg und Niedergang der römischen Welt* II. 29.2: Berlin and New York: De Gruyter: 988–1018.

Schulze, W. (1904) *Zur Geschichte lateinischer Eigennamen* (Abhandlungen der königlichen Gesellschaft der Wissenschaften zu Göttingen, Phil.–hist. Klasse V, 5), Berlin: Weidmann (numerous reprints, one of 1991 with some addenda by O. Salomies).

Schürer, E. (1979) *The History of the Jewish People in the Age of Jesus Christ (175 BC–AD 135)*, a new English version revised and edited by G. Vermes, F. Millar, and M. Black, volume 2, Edinburgh: T. and T. Clark.

Scullard, H. H. (1951) *Roman Politics 220–150 BC*, Oxford: Clarendon Press, 2nd ed. 1973, Oxford: Clarendon Press.

—— (1981) *Festivals and Ceremonies of the Roman Republic*, London: Thames and Hudson, and Ithaca: Cornell University Press.

Setälä, P. (1977) *Private Domini in Roman Brick Stamps of the Empire. A Historical and Prosopographical Study of Landowners in the District of Rome* (Annales Academiae Scientiarum Fennicae, Dissertationes Humanarum Litterarum 10), Helsinki: Suomalainen Tiedeakatemia.

Seyrig, H. (1970) "Sur l'usage de timbrer les amphores," *Syria* 47: 287–90.

Shaw, B. D. (1984) "Latin Funerary Epigraphy and Family Life in the Later Roman Empire," *Historia* 33: 547–97.

—— (1987) "The Age of Roman Girls at Marriage: Some Reconsiderations," *Journal of Roman Studies* 77: 30–46.

—— (1991) "The Cultural Meaning of Death: Age and Gender in the Roman Family," in D. I. Kertzer and R. P. Saller (eds) *The Family in Italy from Antiquity to the Present*, New Haven: Yale University Press, 66–90.

—— (1996) "Seasons of Death: Aspects of Mortality in Imperial Rome," *Journal of Roman Studies* 86: 100–38.

Sherk, R. K. (1988) *The Roman Empire: Augustus to Hadrian* (Translated Documents of Greece and Rome 6), Cambridge: Cambridge University Press.

Siebert, G. (1978a) *Recherches sur les ateliers de bols à reliefs du Péloponnèse à l'époque hellénistique* (Bibliothèque des Écoles françaises d'Athènes et de Rome 233), Paris: de Boccard.

—— (1978b) "Signatures d'artistes, d'artisans et de fabriquants dans l'antiquité classique," *Ktema* 3: 111–35.

Simpson, C. J. (1993) "The Original Site of the Fasti Capitolini," *Historia* 42: 61–81.

Smith, M. F. (1993) *Diogenes of Oenoanda: The Epicurean Inscription*, Naples.

—— (1994) "New Readings in the Demostheneia Inscription from Oinoanda," *Anatolian Studies* 44: 59–64.

Sokolowski, F. (1955) *Lois sacrées de l'Asie Mineure*, Paris: de Boccard. [= *LSAM*]

—— (1962) *Lois sacrées des cités grecques. Supplément*, Paris: de Boccard. [= *LSS*]

—— (1969) *Lois sacrées des cités grecques*, 2nd ed., Paris: de Boccard. [= *LSCG*]

Solin, H. (1970) *L'interpretazione delle iscrizioni parietali. Note e discussioni* (Epigrafia e Antichità 2), Faenza: Fratelli Lega Editori.

—— (1982) *Die griechischen Personennamen in Rom. Ein Namenbuch*, 3 vols, Berlin: De Gruyter.

—— (1995) "Zur Entstehung und Psychologie von Schreibfehlern in lateinischen Inschriften," in Solin–Salomies–Liertz 1995: 93–111.

—— (1996) *Die stadtrömischen Sklavennamen. Ein Namenbuch*, 3 vols (Forschungen zur Antiken Sklaverei, Beiheft 2), Stuttgart: F. Steiner Verlag.

—— (1998) *Analecta Epigraphica 1970–1997*, M. Kajava and K. Korhonen (eds) (Acta Instituti Romani Finlandiae 21), Rome: Institutum Romanum Finlandiae.

Solin, H. and Salomies, O. (1988) *Repertorium nominum gentilium et cognominum Latinorum* (Alpha–Omega 80), Hildesheim, Zürich, New York: Olms and Weidemann; reprinted 1994 with some addenda.

Solin, H., Salomies, O., and Liertz, U.-M. (eds) (1995) *Acta colloquii epigraphici Latini Helsingiae 3–6 sept. 1991 habiti* (Societas Scientiarum Fennica, Commentationes Humanarum Litterarum 104), Helsinki: Societas Scientiarum Fennica.

Sommerstein, A. H. (ed.) (1980) *The Comedies of Aristophanes.* volume 1. *Acharnians*, Warminster: Aris and Phillips.

Sparrow, J. (1969) *Visible Words: A Study of Inscriptions in and as Works of Art*, London: Cambridge University Press.

de Ste Croix, G. E. M. (1981) *The Class Struggle in the Ancient Greek World*, London: Duckworth.

Stein, A. (1931) *Römische Inschriften in der antiken Literatur*, Prague: Taussig and Taussig.

Steinby, E. M. (1982) "I senatori e l'industria laterizia urbana," in *Epigrafia e ordine senatorio* I (Tituli 4), Rome: Edizioni di Storia e Letteratura: 227–37.

—— (1987) *Indici complementari ai bolli doliari urbani (CIL XV, 1)* (Acta Instituti Romani Finlandiae 11), Rome: Institutum Romanum Finlandiae.

—— (1993) "L'organizzazione produttiva dei laterizi: un modello interpretativo per l'instrumentum in genere?" in Harris 1993: 139–44.

Sternini, M. (1993) "I vetri," in Harris 1993: 81–94.

—— (1995) *La fenice di sabbia. Storia e tecnologia del vetro nell'antichità*, Bari: Edipuglia.

Stoddart, S. and Whitley, J. (1988) "The Social Context of Literacy in Archaic Greece and Etruria," *Antiquity* 62: 761–72.

Stone, M. E. (1992) *Rock Inscriptions and Graffiti Project. Catalogue of Inscriptions* (Society of Biblical Literature, Resources for Biblical Study 29), 2 vols, Atlanta: Scholars Press.

Stroud, R. S. (1968) *Drakon's Law on Homicide*, Berkeley: University of California Press.

Susini, G. (1973) *The Roman Stonecutter: An Introduction to Latin Epigraphy*, English trans. by A. M. Dabrowski of *Il lapicida romano: introduzione all'epigrafia latina*, Rome: "L'Erma" di Bretschneider, 1966 (reprinted in Susini 1997: 7–69), E. Badian (ed.), Oxford: Basil Blackwell.

—— (1982) *Epigrafia romana* (Guide allo studio della civiltà romana X,1, Guide 9), Rome: Jouvence.

—— (1987–8) "Fabbrica del pensiero, grammatica della memoria," *Rivista storica dell'antichità* 17–18: 281–5; reprinted in Susini 1997: 199–205.

—— (1988) "Compitare per via: antropologia del lettore antico: meglio, del lettore romano / Spelling out along the road: Anthropology of the ancient reader, or rather, the Roman reader," *Alma Mater Studiorum* 1: 105–24; reprinted in Susini 1997: 157–80.

—— (1992) "Per una classificazione delle iscrizioni itinerarie," in L. Quilici and S. Quilici Gigli (eds) *Tecnica stradale romana*, Rome: "L'Erma" di Bretschneider, 119–21; reprinted in Susini 1997: 193–7.

—— (1997) *Epigraphica Dilapidata. Scritti scelti di Giancarlo Susini* (Epigrafia e Antichità 15), Faenza: Fratelli Lega Editori.

Svenbro, J. (1993) *Phrasikleia: The Anthropology of Reading in Ancient Greece*, English trans. by J. Lloyd of *Phrasikleia: Anthropologie de la lecture en Grèce ancienne*, Paris: La Découverte, 1988, Ithaca: Cornell University Press.

Syme, R. (1939) *The Roman Revolution*, Oxford: Clarendon Press.

—— (1958) "Imperator Caesar: A Study in Nomenclature," *Historia* 7: 172–88; reprinted in Syme 1979: 361–77.

—— (1979) *Roman Papers* I–II, E. Badian (ed.), Oxford: Clarendon Press.

—— (1984) *Roman Papers* III, A. Birley (ed.), Oxford: Clarendon Press.

—— (1988) *Roman Papers* IV, A. Birley (ed.), Oxford: Clarendon Press.

Szilagyi, J. (1961–7) "Beiträge zur Statistik der Sterblichkeit in den westeuropäischen Provinzen des römischen Imperiums," *Acta Archaeologica Academiae Scientiarum Hungaricae* 13 (1961): 125–55 and (under various titles) in vols 14 (1962) 297–396 (Illyria and northern Italy), 15 (1963) 129–224 (central and southern Italy and Spain), 17 (1965) 309–34, 18 (1966) 235–77, 19 (1967) 25–59 (North Africa).

Sznycer, M. (1967) *Les passages puniques en transcription latine dans le "Poenulus" de Plaute*, Paris: C. Klincksieck.

Tambiah, S. J. (1968) "The Magical Power of Words," *Man* 3: 175–208.

—— (1973) "Form and Meaning of Magical Acts: A Point of View," in R. Horton and R. Finnegan (eds) *Modes of Thought: Essays on Thinking in Western and non-Western Societies*, London: Faber: 199–229.

Taylor, L. R. (1960) *The Voting Districts of the Roman Republic. The Thirty-five Urban and Rural Tribes*, Rome: American Academy in Rome.

—— (1961) "Freedmen and Freeborn in the Epitaphs of Imperial Rome," *American Journal of Philology* 82: 113–32.

Tchernia, A. (1993) "Des timbres d'amphores à l'organisation du commerce," in Harris 1993: 183–5.

Thomas, E. and Witschel, C. (1992) "Constructing Reconstruction: Claim and Reality of Roman Rebuilding Inscriptions from the Latin West," *Papers of the British School at Rome* n.s. 60: 135–77.

Thomas, Rosalind (1992) *Literacy and Orality in Ancient Greece*, Cambridge: Cambridge University Press.

—— (1995) "Written in Stone? Liberty, Equality, Orality and the Codification of Law," *Bulletin of the Institute of Classical Studies* 40: 59–74.

Thompson Crawford, D. J. (1984) "The Idumaeans of Memphis and the Ptolemaic *politeumata*," *Atti del XVII Congresso Internazionale di Papirologia*, volume 3, Naples: Loffredo.

Threatte, L. (1980) *The Grammar of Attic Inscriptions*. 1. *Phonology*, Berlin and New York: De Gruyter.

Thylander, H. (1952) *Étude sur l'épigraphie latine*, Lund: Gleerup.

Tod, M. N. (1951) "Laudatory Epithets in Greek Epitaphs," *Annual of the British School at Athens* 46: 182–90.

Tomlin, R. S. O. (1998) "Roman Manuscripts from Carlisle: the Ink-Written Tablets," *Britannia* 29: 31–84.

Toynbee, J. and Ward-Perkins, J. (1956) *The Shrine of St. Peter and the Vatican Excavations*, London: Longman.

Tracy, S. V. (1990) *Attic Letter-Cutters of 229 to 86 BC*, Berkeley: University of California Press.

—— (1994) "Hands in Greek Epigraphy—Demetrios of Phaleron," in J. M. Fossey (ed.) *Boeotia Antiqua* IV, Amsterdam: J. C. Gieben: 151–61.

—— (1995) *Athenian Democracy in Transition: Attic Letter-Cutters of 340 to 290 BC*, Berkeley: University of California Press.

—— (1996) "Athenian Letter-Cutters and Lettering on Stone in Vth to Ist Centuries BC," in M. S. Macrakis (ed.) *Greek Letters From Tablets to Pixels*, New Castle, Delaware: Oak Knoll Press: 43–53.

Traill, J. S. (1994) *Persons of Ancient Athens* volume 1: *A to Alexandros*, Toronto: Athenians.

Treggiari, S. (1976) "Jobs for Women," *American Journal of Ancient History* 1: 76–104.

—— (1979) "Lower Class Women in the Roman Economy," *Florilegium* 1: 65–86.

—— (1981) "Concubinae," *Papers of the British School at Rome* 49: 59–81.

—— (1982) "Two Latin Inscriptions," *The J. Paul Getty Museum Journal* 10: 181–6.

Väänänen, V. (1966) *Le latin vulgaire des inscriptions pompéiennes*, 3rd ed., Berlin: Akademie-Verlag.

—— (1967) *Introduction au latin vulgaire*, 2nd ed., Paris: C. Klincksieck.

van Bremen, R. (1983) "Women and Wealth," in A. Cameron and A. Kuhrt (eds) *Images of Women in Antiquity*, Detroit: Wayne State University Press.

van Henten, J. W. and van der Horst, P. W. (eds) (1994) *Studies in Early Jewish Epigraphy*, Leiden: E. J. Brill.

Várhelyi, Z. (1996) "The Written Word in Archaic Attica," *Klio* 78: 28–52.

Verhoogt, A. M. F. W. and Vleeming, S. P. (eds) (1998) *The Two Faces of Graeco-Roman Egypt. Greek and Demotic and Greek-Demotic Texts and Studies Presented to P. W. Pestman* (Papyrologica Lugduno–Batava 30), Leiden, Boston, Cologne: E. J. Brill.

Versnel, H. (1991) "Beyond Cursing: The Appeal to Justice in Judicial Prayers," in Faraone–Obbink 1991: 60–106.

—— (1997) "IUN]IEI: A New Conjecture in the Satricum Inscription," *Mededelingen van het Nederlands Instituut te Rome* 56: 177–200.

Vetter, E. (1953) *Handbuch der italischen Dialekte*, Heidelberg: C. Winter.

Veyne, P. (1978) "La famille et l'amour sous le Haut Empire romain," *Annales. économies, societés, civilisations* 33: 35–63.

—— (1983) " 'Titulus Praelatus': Offrande, solennisation et publicité dans les ex-voto gréco-romains," *Revue archéologique* 1983: 281–300.

—— (1990) *Bread and Circuses: Historical Sociology and Political Pluralism*, English trans. by B. Pearce of *Le pain et le cirque: sociologie historique d'un pluralisme politique*, Paris: Seuil, 1976, London: Allen Lane.

Vidman, L. (1982a) *Fasti Ostienses*, 2nd ed., Prague: Academia Scientiarum Bohemoslovaca.

—— (1982b) "Osservazioni su i praefecti urbi nei primi due secoli," in *Epigrafia e ordine senatorio* I (Tituli 4), Rome: Edizioni di Storia e Letteratura: 289–303.

Vine, B. (1993) *Studies in Archaic Latin Inscriptions* (Innsbrucker Beiträge zur Sprachwissenschaft 75), Innsbruck: Institut für Sprachwissenschaft der Universität Innsbruck.

Vogel-Weidemann, U. (1982) *Die Statthalter von Africa und Asia in den Jahren 14–68 n. Chr.* (Antiquitas 1: 31), Bonn: Habelt.

Wachter, R. (1989) "Zur Vorgeschichte des griechischen Alphabets," *Kadmos* 28: 19–78.

Wagner, G. (1993) "L'épigraphie du village dans l'Égypte gréco-romaine," in A. Calbi, A. Donati, and G. Poma (eds) *L'epigrafia del villaggio* (Epigrafia e Antichità 12), Faenza: Fratelli Lega Editori: 101–15.

Wallace, W. P. (1962) "Loans to Karystos about 370 BC," *Phoenix* 16: 15–28.

Wallace-Hadrill, A. (1990) "Roman Arches and Greek Honours: The Language of Power at Rome," *Proceedings of the Cambridge Philological Society* n.s. 36: 143–81.

Walser, G. (1988) *Römische Inschrift-Kunst. Römische Inschriften für den akademischen Unterricht und als Einführung in die lateinische Epigraphik*, Stuttgart: F. Steiner Verlag.

Waltzing, J. P. (1895–96) *Étude historique sur les corporations professionelles chez les Romains*, Brussels: F. Hayez.

Warmington, E. H. (1940) *Remains of Old Latin* volume IV: *Archaic Inscriptions* (Loeb Classical Library 359), Cambridge, Mass.: Harvard University Press.

Weaver, P. R. C. (1974) "Social Mobility in the Early Roman Empire: The Evidence of the Imperial Freedmen and Slaves," in M. I. Finley (ed.) *Studies in Ancient Society*, Oxford: Routledge and Kegan Paul: 121–40.

—— (1986) "The Status of Children in Mixed Marriages," in B. Rawson (ed.) *The Family in Ancient Rome: New Perspectives*, Ithaca: Cornell University Press: 145–69.

—— (1990) "Where Have All the Junian Latins Gone? Nomenclature and Status in the Early Empire," *Chiron* 20: 275–305.

—— (1991) "Children of Freedmen (and Freedwomen)," in B. Rawson (ed.) *Marriage, Divorce, and Children in Ancient Rome*, Oxford: Clarendon Press: 166–90.

Webster, T. B. L. (1972) *Potter and Patron in Classical Athens*, London: Methuen.

Welles, C. B. (1934) *Royal Correspondence in the Hellenistic Period. A Study in Greek Epigraphy*, New Haven: Yale University Press.

West, S. (1985) "Herodotus' Epigraphical Interests," *Classical Quarterly* 35: 278–305.

—— (1994) "Nestor's Bewitching Cup," *Zeitschrift für Papyrologie und Epigraphik* 101: 9–15.

Whitley, J. (1997) "Cretan Laws and Cretan Literacy," *American Journal of Archaeology* 101: 635–61.

Wigtil, D. N. (1982a) "The Translator of the Greek *Res Gestae* of Augustus," *American Journal of Philology* 103: 189–94.

—— (1982b) "The Ideology of the Greek *Res Gestae*," in H. Temporini (ed.) (1972–) *Aufstieg und Niedergang der römischen Welt* II.30.1: Berlin and New York: De Gruyter: 624–38.

Wilkes, J. J. (1977) "The Population of Roman Dalmatia," in H. Temporini (ed.) (1972–) *Aufstieg und Niedergang der römischen Welt* II.6: Berlin and New York: De Gruyter 732–66.

Williamson, C. (1987) "Monuments of Bronze: Roman Legal Documents on Bronze Tablets," *Classical Antiquity* 6: 160–83.

—— (1995) "The Display of Law and Archival Practice in Rome," in Solin–Salomies–Liertz 1995: 239–52.

Wilmanns, J. C. (1995) *Der Sanitätsdienst im römischen Reich. Eine sozialhistorische Studie zum römischen Militärsanitätswesen nebst einer Prosopographie des Sanitätspersonals* (Medizin der Antike 2), Hildesheim: Olms and Weidemann.

Winnett, F. V. (1957) *Safaitic Inscriptions from Jordan* (Near and Middle East Series 2), Toronto: University of Toronto Press.

Wistrand, E. (1976) *The So-called Laudatio Turiae* (Studia Graeca et Latina Gothoburgensia 34), Göteborg: Acta Universitatis Gothoburgensis.

—— (1981) " 'Popular Politics' in an Italian Municipality (*CIL* V 5049 = CE 417)," *Eranos* 79: 105–16.

Woodard, R. D. (1997) *Greek Writing from Knossos to Homer*, New York: Oxford University Press.

Woodhead, A. G. (1981, 1992) *The Study of Greek Inscriptions*, 2nd ed., Cambridge, 1981; reprinted with a new preface, Norman and London: University of Oklahoma Press, 1992.

Woolf, G. (1996) "Monumental Writing and the Expansion of Roman Society in the Early Empire," *Journal of Roman Studies* 86: 22–39.

—— (1998) *Becoming Roman. The Origins of Provincial Civilization in Gaul*, Cambridge: Cambridge University Press.

Wörrle, M. (1988) *Stadt und Fest im kaiserzeitlichen Kleinasien. Studien zu einer agonistischen Stiftung aus Oinoanda* (Vestigia 39), Munich: C. H. Beck.

Wünsch, R. (1898) *Sethianische Verfluchungstafeln aus Rom*, Leipzig: B. G. Teubner.

Zabehlicky-Scheffenegger, S. (1985) "TK- Zur kommerziellen Verbindung des Magdalensberges mit Aquileia," in *Lebendige Altertumswissenschaft: Festgabe zur Vollendung des 70. Lebensjahres von Hermann Vetters dargebracht von Freunden, Schulern und Kollegen*, Vienna: Adolf Holzausen: 252–4.

Zaccaria, C. (ed.) (1993) *I laterizi di età romana nell'area nordadriatica*, Rome: "L'Erma" di Bretschneider.

Index of sources

Inscriptions

For full titles of the works cited, see the List of abbreviations and the Bibliography.

AE
1953, 73: 86
1957, 250: 86
1958, 78: 136
1964, 255: 47
1965, 209: 136
1967, 113: 26
1968, 25: 90
1971, 62: 87
1971, 88: 9, 111
1972, 174–5: 10
1972, 212: 88
1974, 251: 31, 32 (Figure 1.6)
1983, 517: 88
1984, 508: 9
1987, 163: 86
1988, 1051: 86
1989, 247: 16
1991, 20–2: 45

Audollent 1904
155: 22 (Figure 1.3), 176 n. 8

Bull. ép.
1972, 166–7: 181 n. 5
1984, 190: 28 (Figure 1.4), 29 (Figure 1.5)

Calabi-Limentani 1974
no. 128: 53 (Figure 1.7), 54

CEG
454: 4, 19

Chelotti et al. 1985
35: 122, 123 (Figure 5.2)

CIG
II
2214c: 129

CIL
I²
3: 49
366: 129
581: 43
594: 120 (Figure 5.1), 182 Ch. 5 n. 1
698: 9, 53 (Figure 1.7), 54
756: 129
857: 23
861: 23
1210: 18
1221: 105, 106 (Figure 4.2)
2662: 55
2832a: 4, 181 n. 6

II
1963: 182 Ch. 5 n. 1
1964: 182 Ch. 5 n. 1
3783: 92
3788: 92
5439: 120 (Figure 5.1), 182 Ch. 5 n. 1
6013: 92

II²/5
1115: 4

XIV
385: 25
2112: 116, 134
4123: 49
4725: 92

XV
290: 148
354: 148 (Figure 6.2)
7172: 18

XVI
47: 90
48: 90

CLE
53: 18
120: 18
301: 26
417: 41
513: 18
514: 26
959: 105, 106 (Figure 4.2)
1097: 18
1212: 18
1552: 39
1988: 40

Courtney 1995
108: 41
199A–B: 39

D'Arms 1973
156–7: 32 (Figure 1.6)

EphEp
6.52–78: 23

Fasti Ostienses (= Vidman 1982a)
45 (a. 100): 90

FIRA
I², 21: 120 (Figure 5.1), 182 Ch. 5 n. 1
I², 23: 182 Ch. 5 n. 1
I², 24: 182 Ch. 5 n. 1
III, 35: 116

GHI
2: 11
11: 42–3

Gonzalez 1986
182 Ch. 5 n. 1

Gordon 1983
1: 49
8: 43
14: 55
19: 129
28: 103
35: 47
42: 44
52: 30
65: 40

Guarducci 1967–78
1.139–40: 42
3.482: 18

GVI
68: 25
662: 26
1210: 16
1831–87: 18
1842: 18

Hiller von Gaertringen 1906
208: 136

IEphesos
810: 88
2061: 88
3046: 88

IG
I²
516: 142
761: 42
976: 99
982: 99
984: 99
1014: 25

I³
104: 11
256 *bis* [addenda]: 28 (Figure 1.4), 29
   (Figure 1.5)
1194 *bis*: 99
1200: 99
1277: 99

7472: 105, 106 (Figure 4.2)
7776: 90
8394: 104
8561: 49
8726–33: 18
8727: 18
8973: 90

ILTun
699: 90

IMagn
98: 129

IPhilae
1.34: 62

IRT
99: 125
319: 124, 125
321–3: 124, 125
347: 125
599: 125

neo-Punic
12: 124
27: 124, 125
30: 125
32: 125

Jameson–Jordan–Kotansky
1993: 44, 128

Lang 1974
18: 179 n. 11

LSAG
239 no. 1: 4, 19
260 no. 4: 18
315 no. 1a: 11
446 no. 3a: 61

LSAM
17: 129
25: 130
32: 129
50: 133
74: 129

LSCG
18: 183 n. 10
20: 183 n. 10

51: 134
65: 130
100: 129
116: 129
151: 128

MAMA
8.411: 86

Marichal 1988 (La Graufesenque)
132 no. 12: 69 (Figure 2.3)

Marichal 1992 (Bu Njem)
77: 71
95.2–3: 70

Meiggs–Lewis *see GHI*

Meritt–Traill 1974
293: 127 (Figure 5.3)

OGIS
487: 86
737: 62

Pfohl 1966
18: 101

Pfohl 1967
152: 19

Pugliese Carratelli–Garbini 1964
4

RIB
2041.9: 4

RMD
2.97: 4

RS
25: 120 (Figure 5.1), 182 Ch. 5 n. 1
37: 45

SCPP
169: 45
170–1: 9
170–2: 45

SEG
8.464: 26
8.802: 18

General index

Ancient authors and other well-known persons are listed by their familiar "short" names (e.g. Cicero, Marcus Aurelius), other Romans by gentile name (e.g. L. Antonius).